D1613513

GLASGOW

THE PHOTOGRAPHIC ATLAS

getmapping® + HarperCollinsPublishers

First published in 2002 by
HarperCollinsPublishers,
77–85 Fulham Palace Road
London W6 8JB

The HarperCollins website address is
www.**fire**and**water**.com

Photography © 2002 Getmapping.com plc
Cartography © 2002 HarperCollinsPublishers Ltd

Getmapping.com plc hereby asserts its moral right to be identified as the author of this work.

Getmapping can produce an individual print of any area shown in this book, or of any area
within the United Kingdom. The image can be centred wherever you choose, printed at any size
from A6 to 7.5 metres square, and at any scale up to 1:1,000. For further information, please
contact Getmapping on +44 (0) 1530 835685 , or log on to www.getmapping.com

All cartography in this book is generated from the Bartholomew digital databases, and is also
available for purchase, in digital format. For further information, please contact Bartholomew
Data Sales on +44 (0) 141 306 3752/3162, or email bartholomew@harpercollins.co.uk

All rights reserved. No part of this publication may be reproduced, stored in a retrieval
system, or transmitted in any form or by any means, mechanical, photocopying, recording
or otherwise, without the prior written permission of the copyright owners.

The publisher regrets that it can accept no responsibility for any errors or omissions within
this publication, or for any expense or loss thereby caused.

The representation of a road, track or footpath is no evidence of a right of way.

A CIP catalogue record for this book is available from the British Library.

ISBN: 0 00 714414 8

Photographic image processing by Getmapping.com plc

Atlas prepared for HarperCollinsPublishers by Cosmographics, Watford, England
Colour origination by Colourscan, Singapore
Printed and bound in Great Britain by Bath Press Colourbooks

contents

The key to photography on page 10 indicates complete area of coverage
The corresponding cartography page reference is located at the bottom left of each spread
The photography and the cartography share the same standard grid system
The grid interval is 500 metres for the photography (pages 12-103) and for the cartography (pages 104-111)

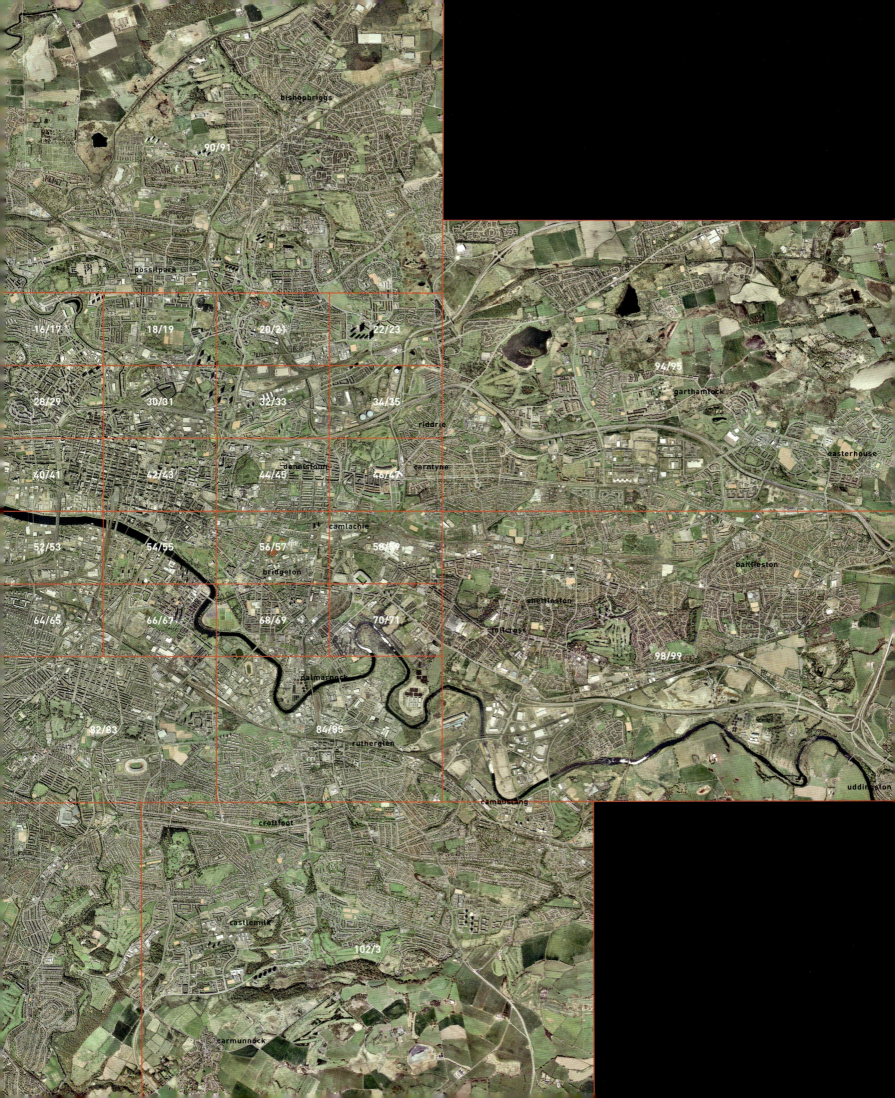

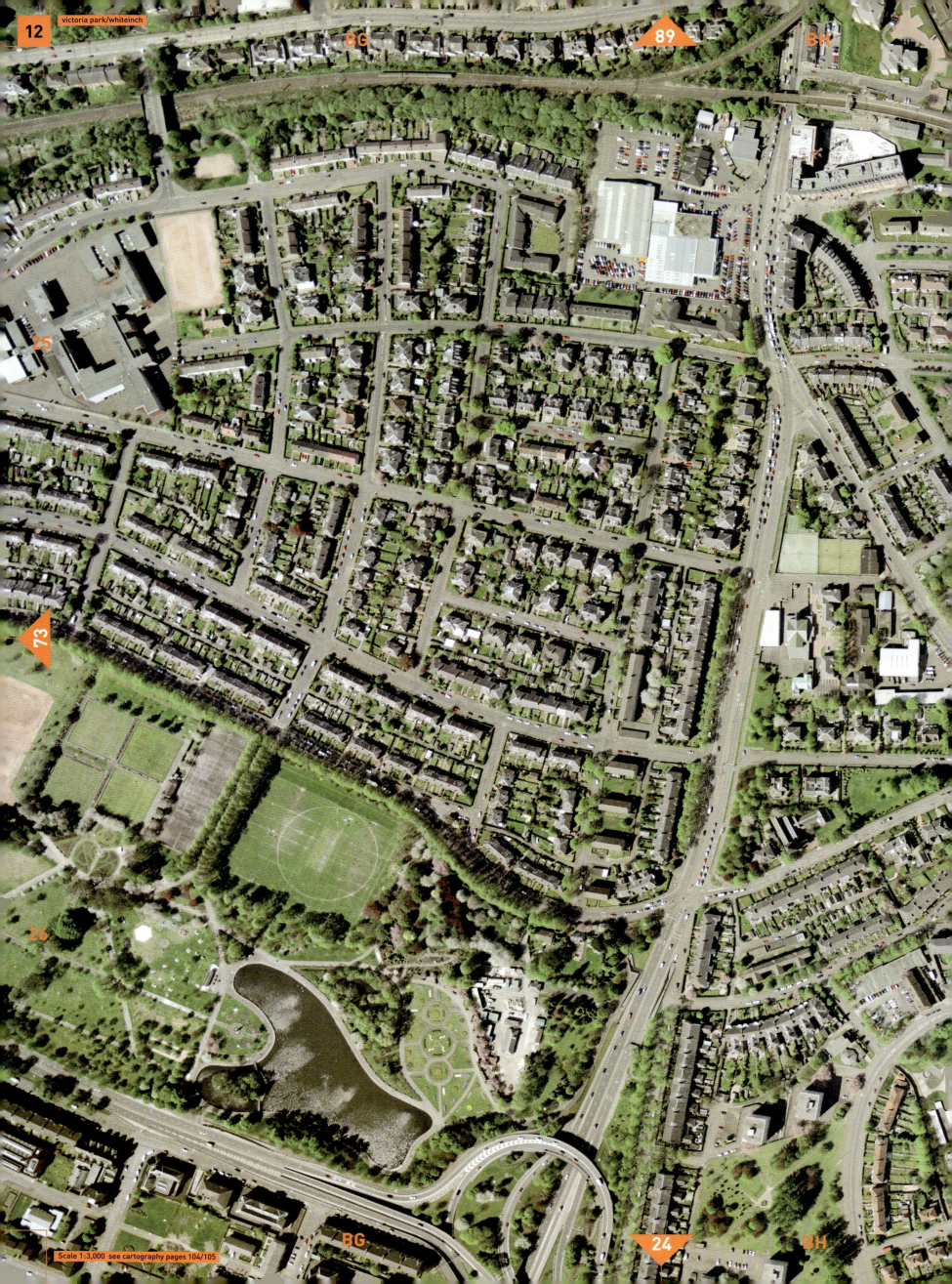

BG

89

BH

25

73

26

BG

24

BH

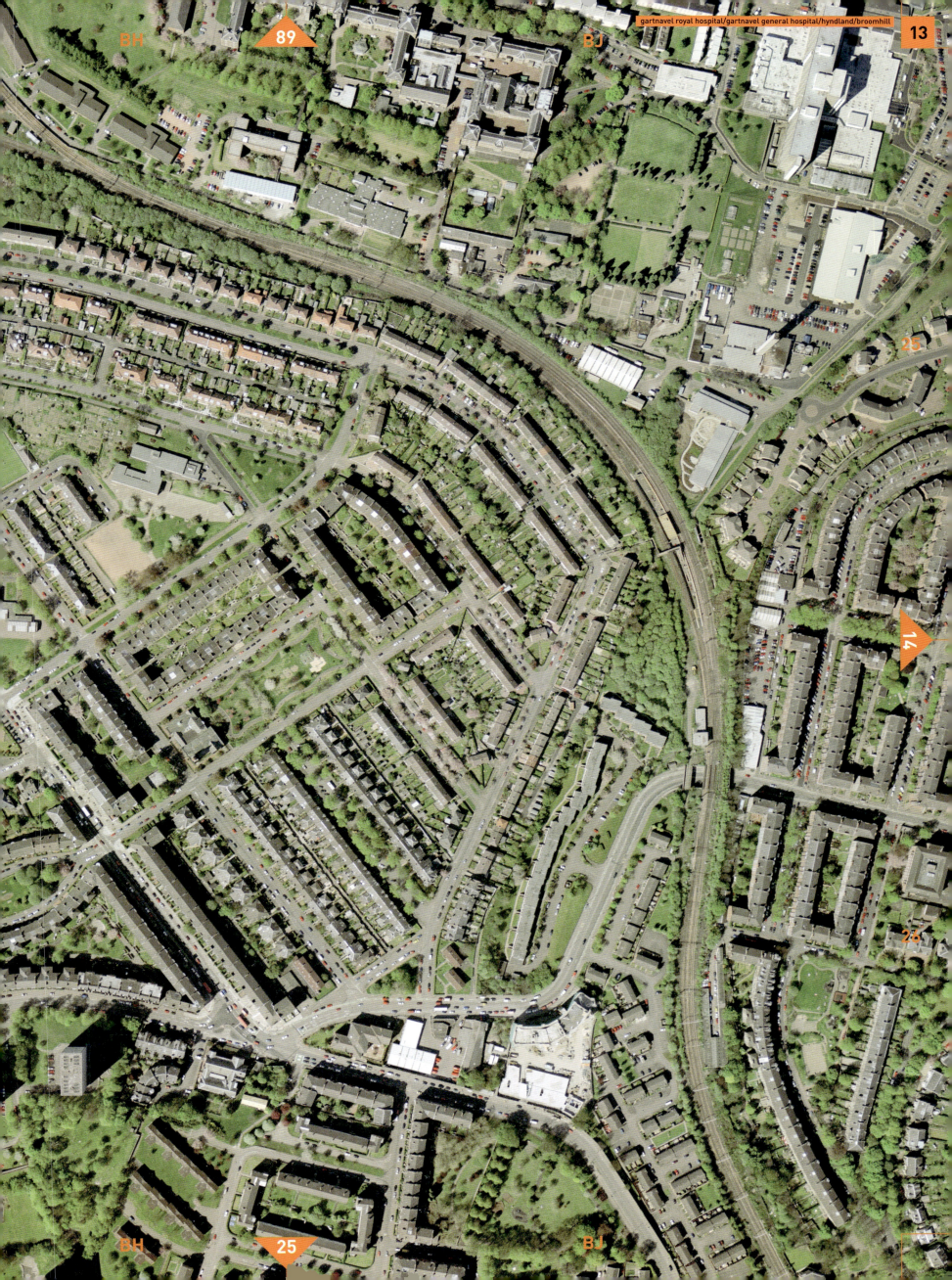

25

14

26

BK

89

BL

25

13

26

BK

26

BL

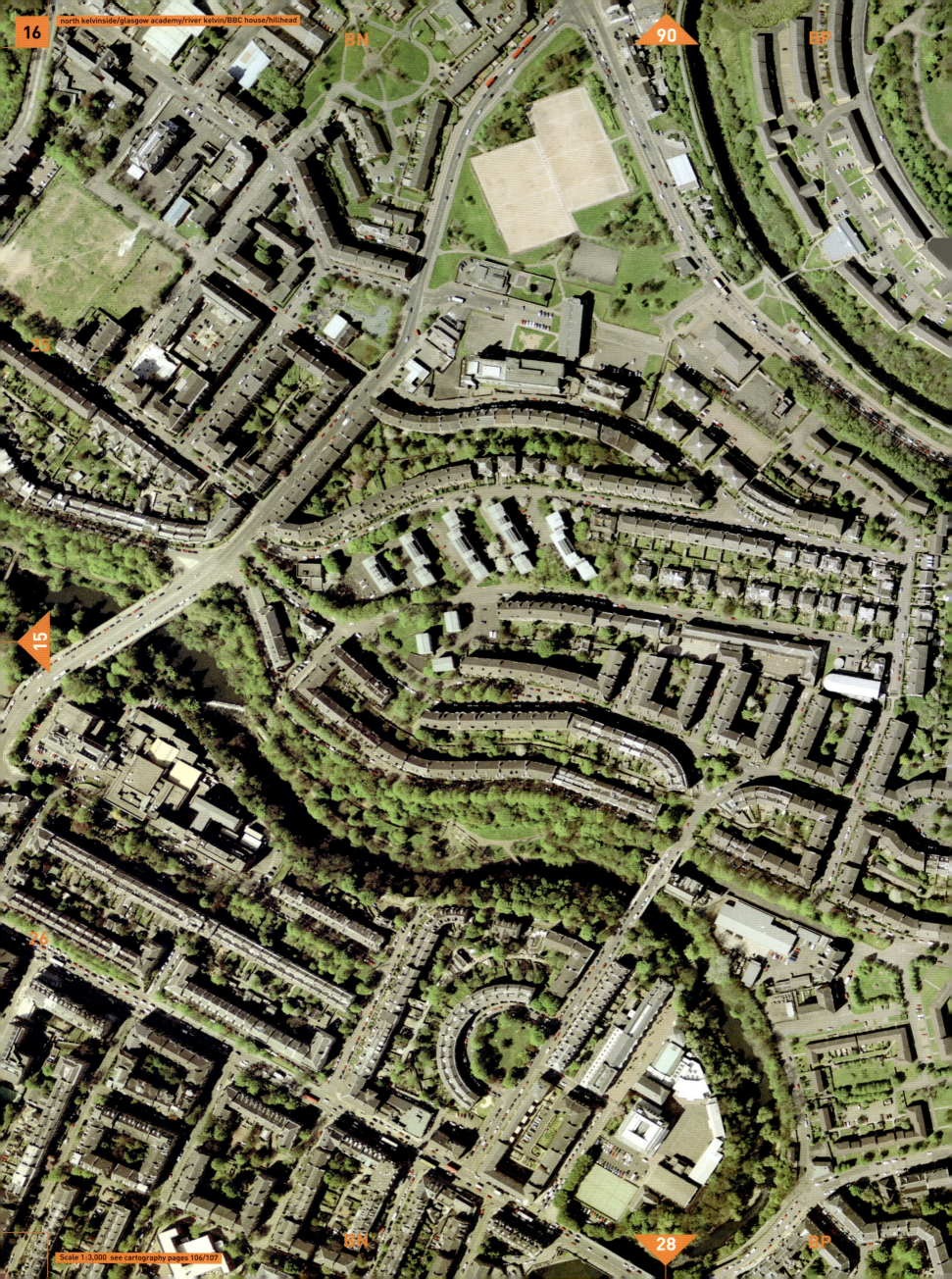

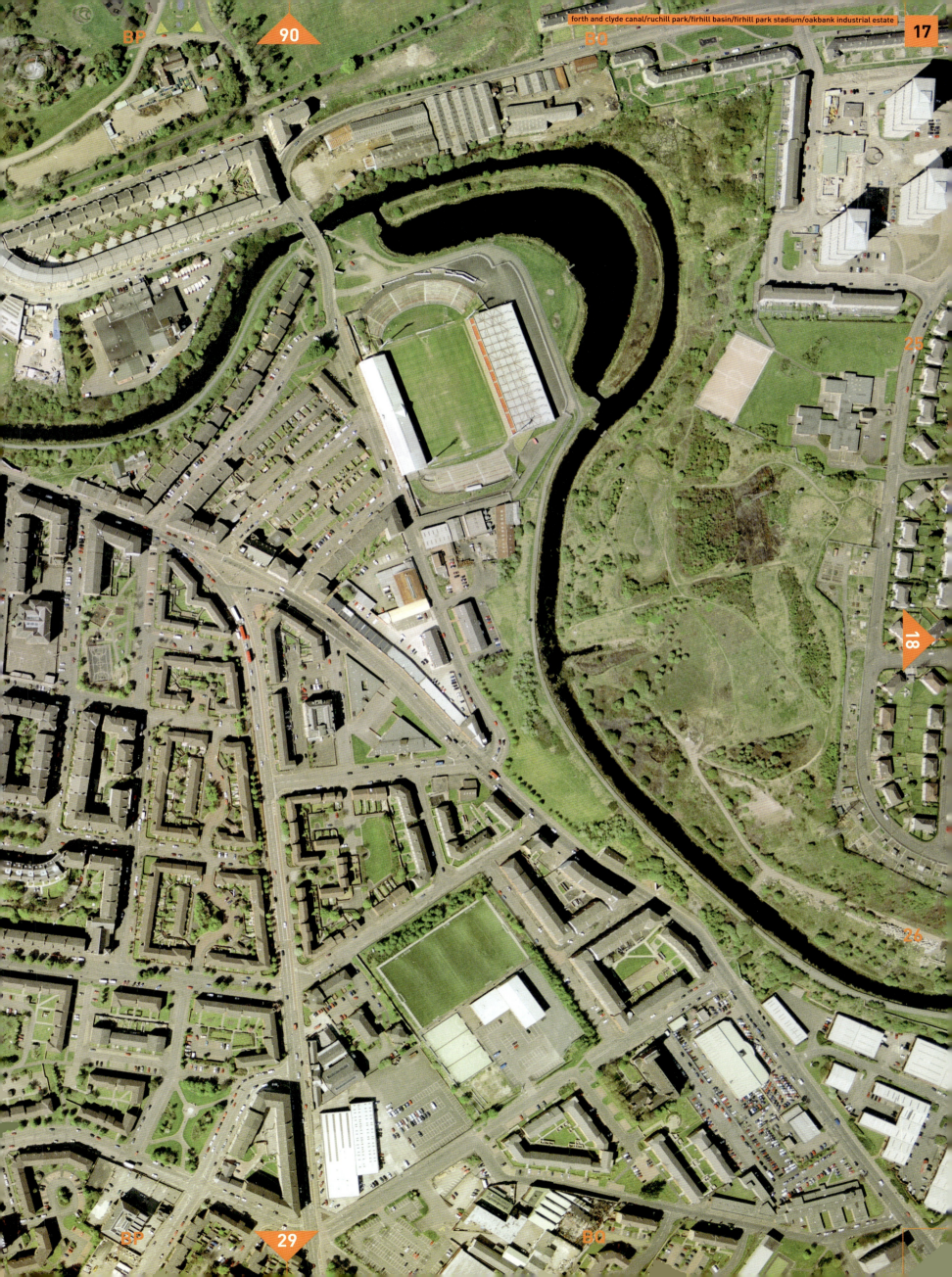

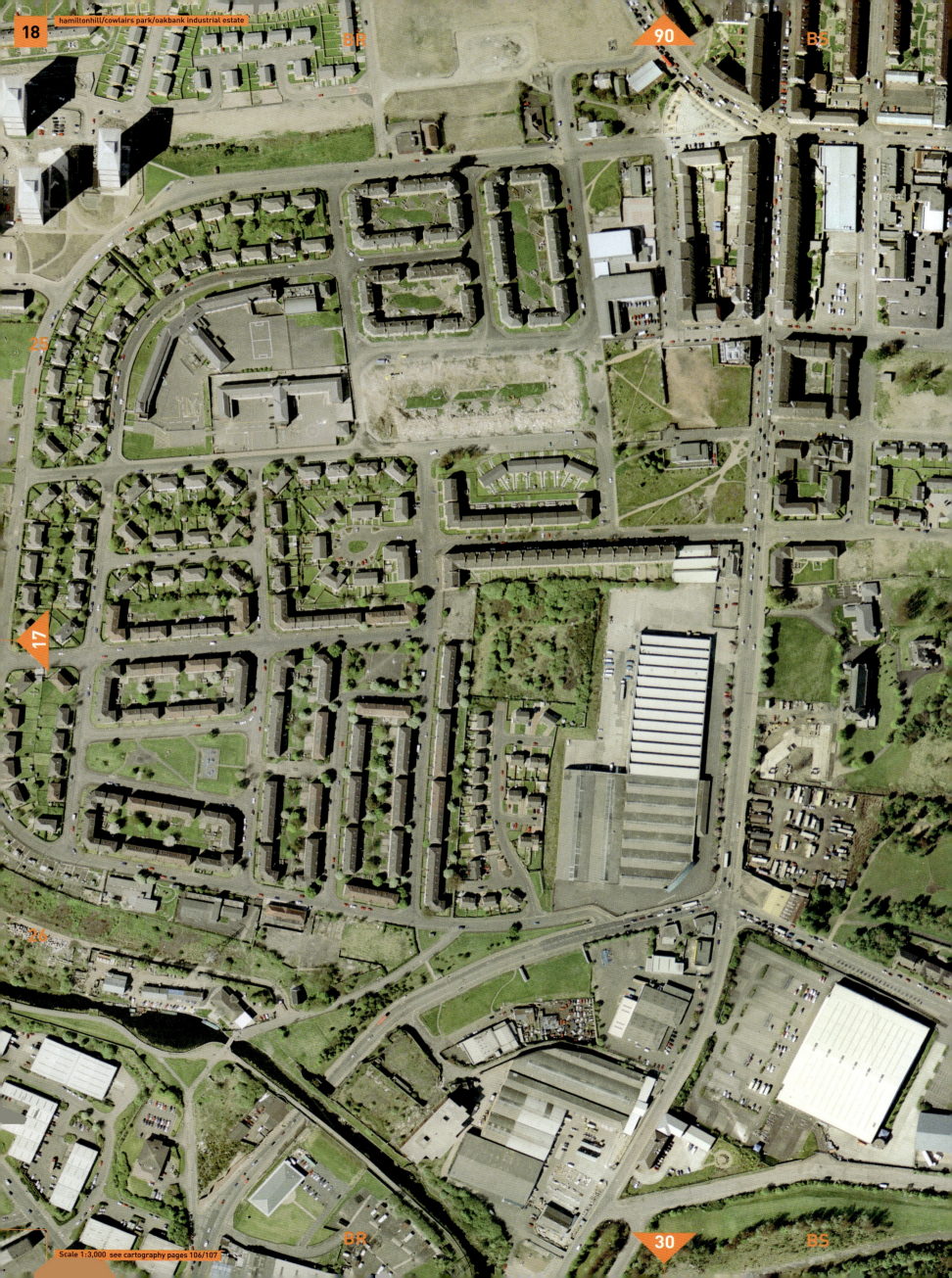

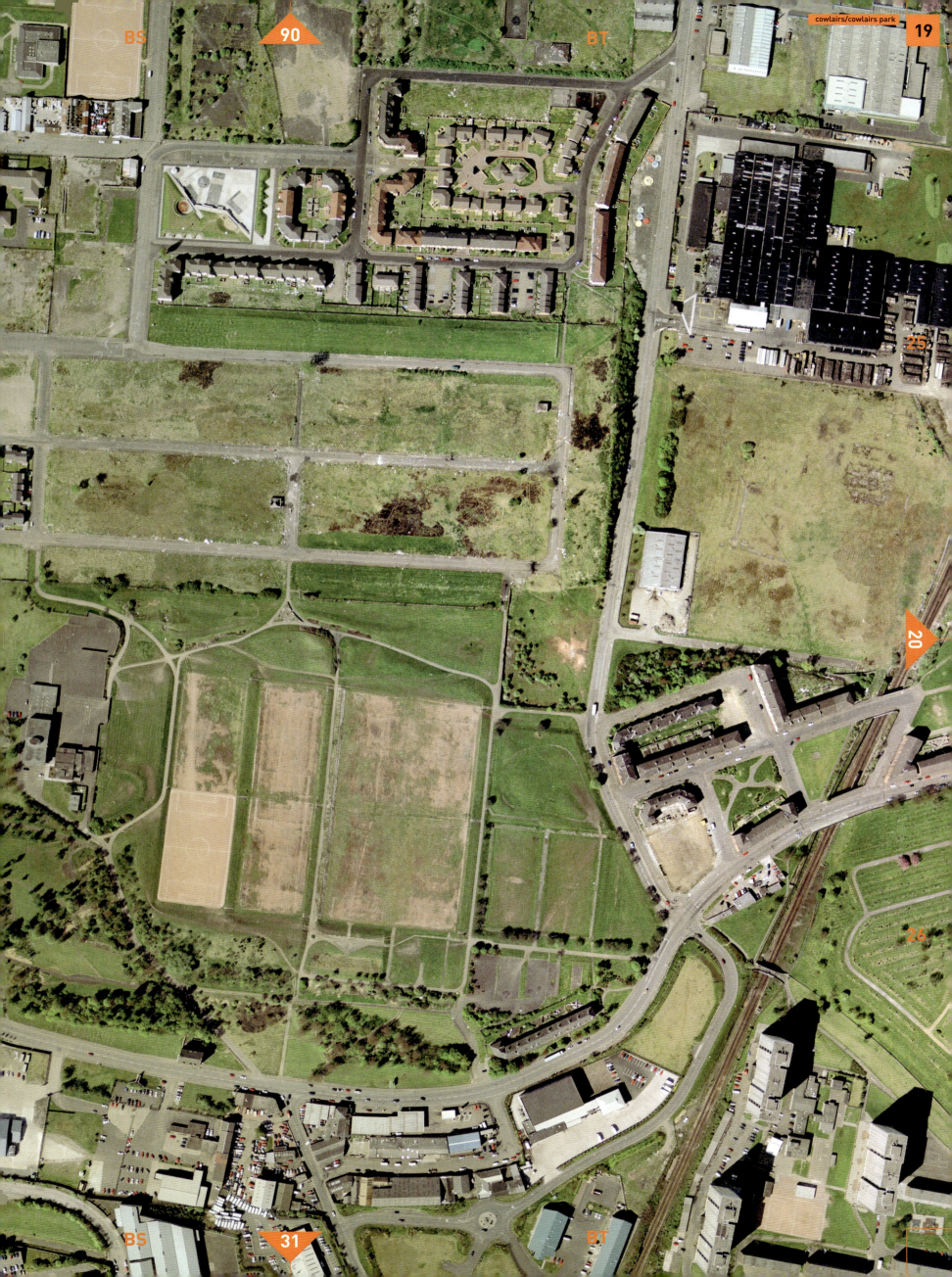

BS

90

BT

25

20

26

77

BS

31

BT

23

19

26

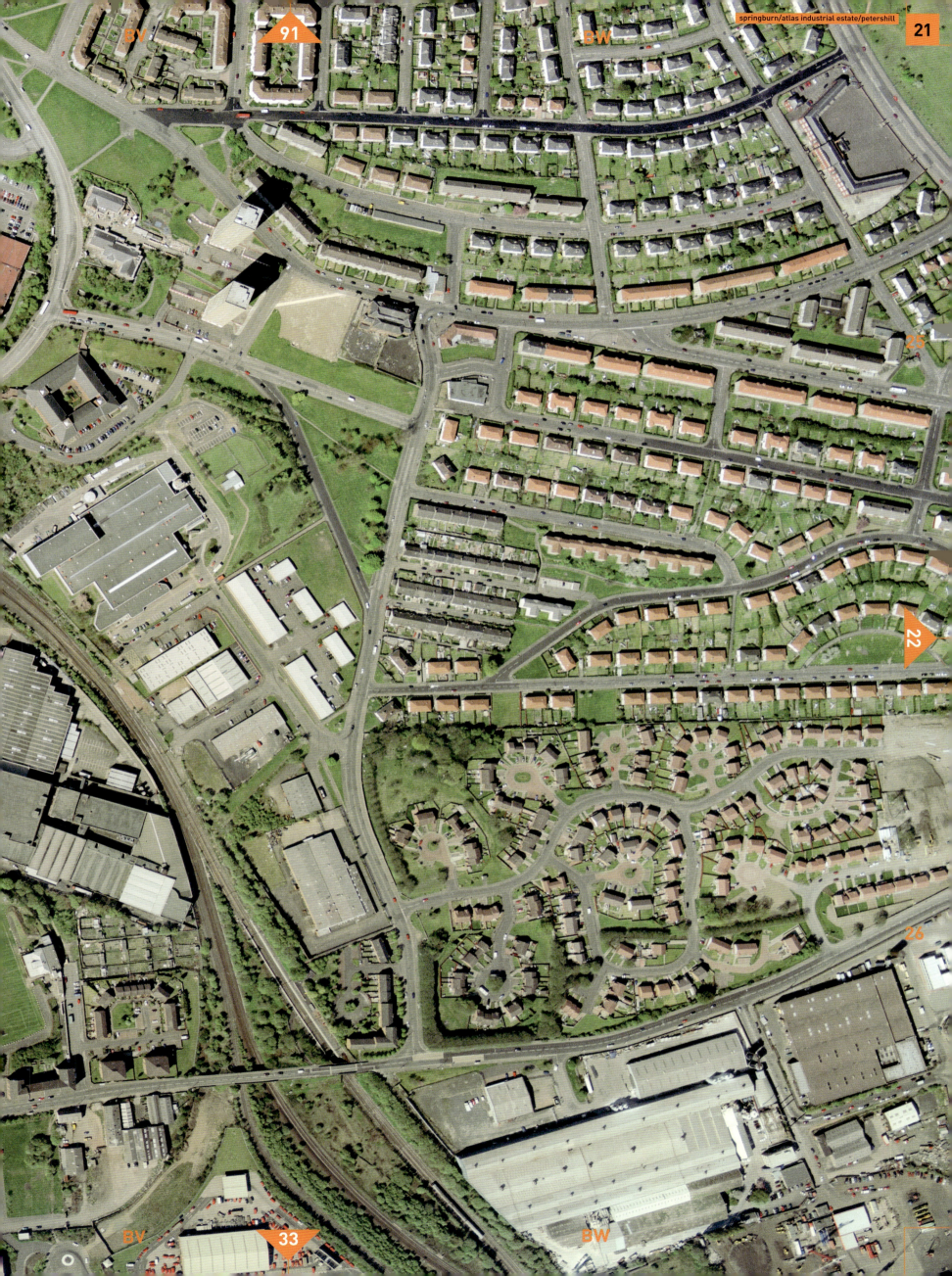

BV

91

BW

25

22

26

BV

33

BW

BX

91

BY

25

21

26

BX

34

BY

BY

91

BZ

25

94

26

indoor bowling centre/meadowside quay/river clyde

27

73

28

Scale 1:3,000 see cartography pages 104/105

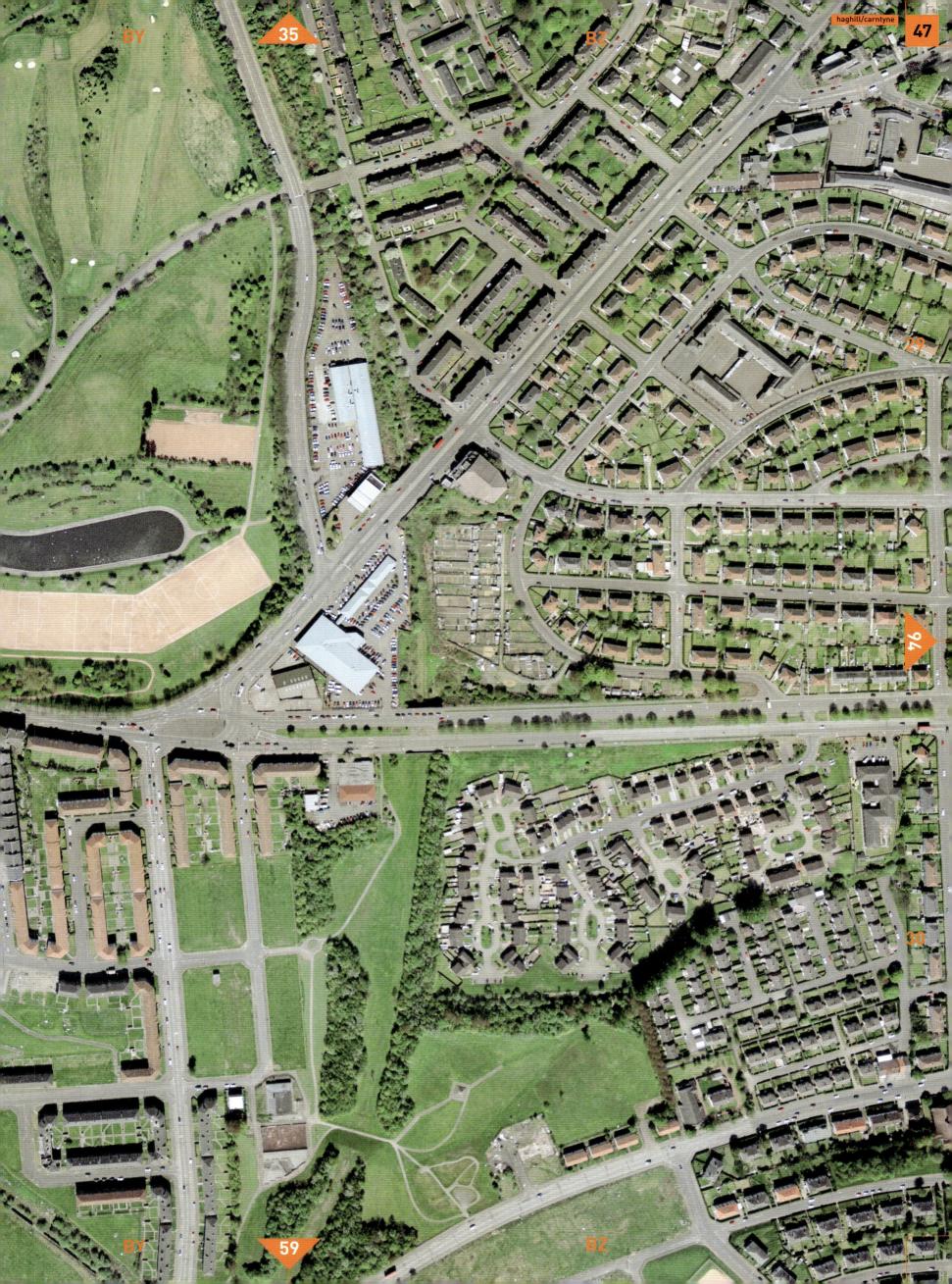

BG

36

BH

31

75

32

RG

60

BH

ibrox stadium/ibrox industrial estate

BK

38

BL

31

67

32

BK

62

BL

Scale 1:3,000 see cartography pages 108/109

31

51

32

BN

64

BN

BP

BD

31

54

32

BR

BS

31

53

32

BR

BS

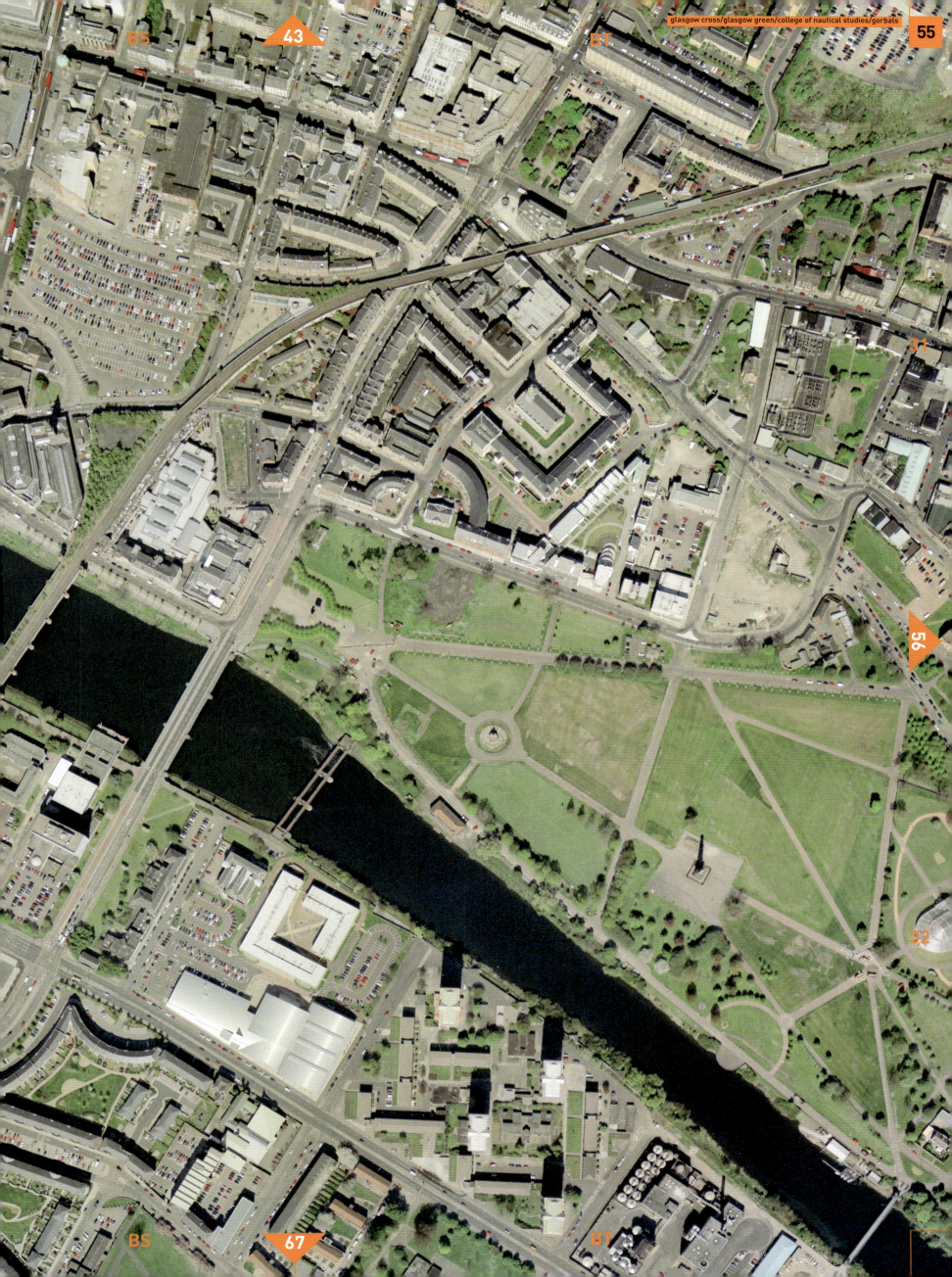

BU

44

BV

31

55

32

BV

45

BW

57

31

58

32

BV

69

BW

BX

46

BY

31

57

32

70

BX

BY

31

98

32

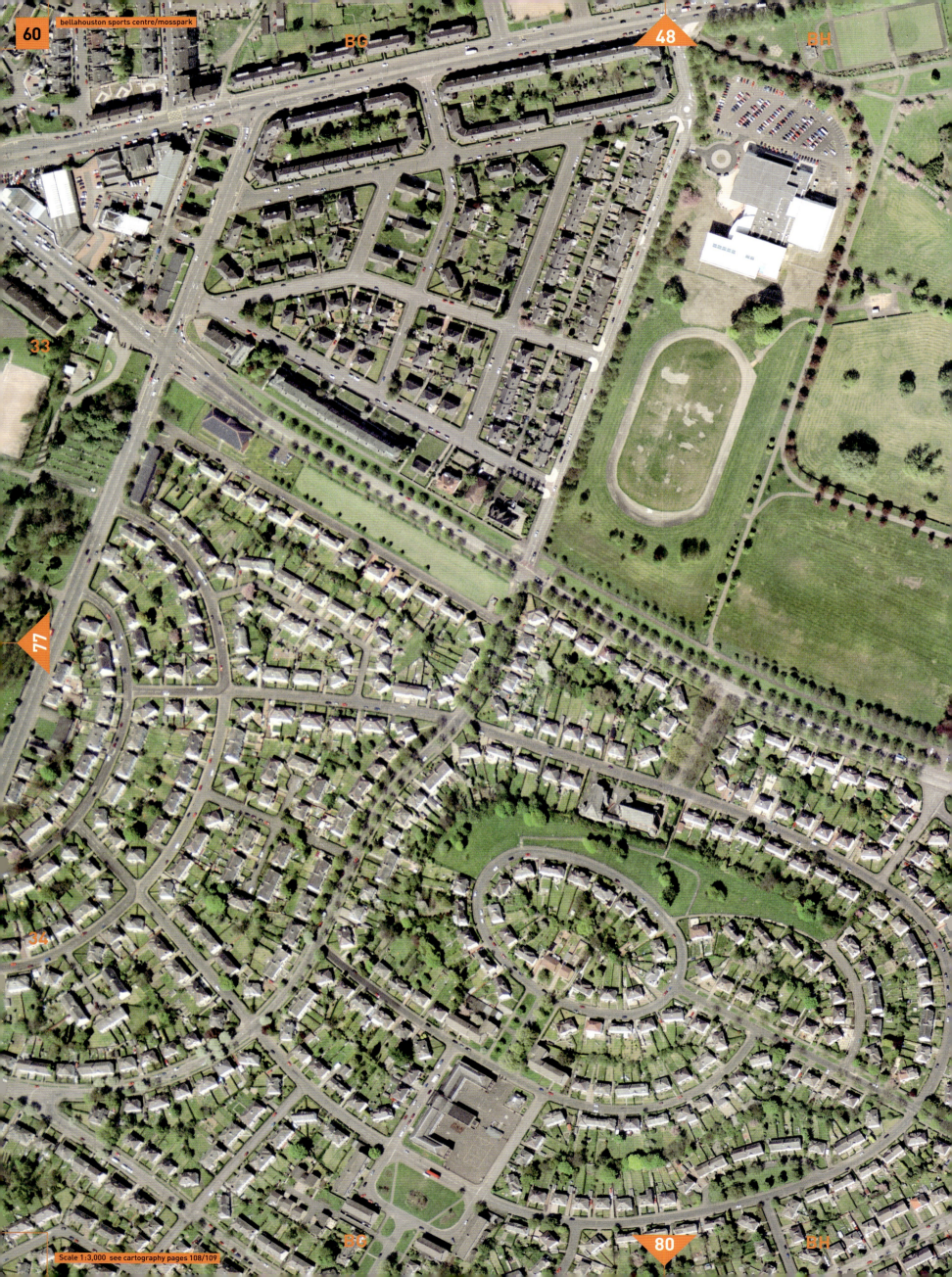

BG

48

BH

33

77

34

80

BG

BH

BH
49
BJ
33
62
32
BH 80 BJ

BK

50

BL

33

61

34

BK

81

BL

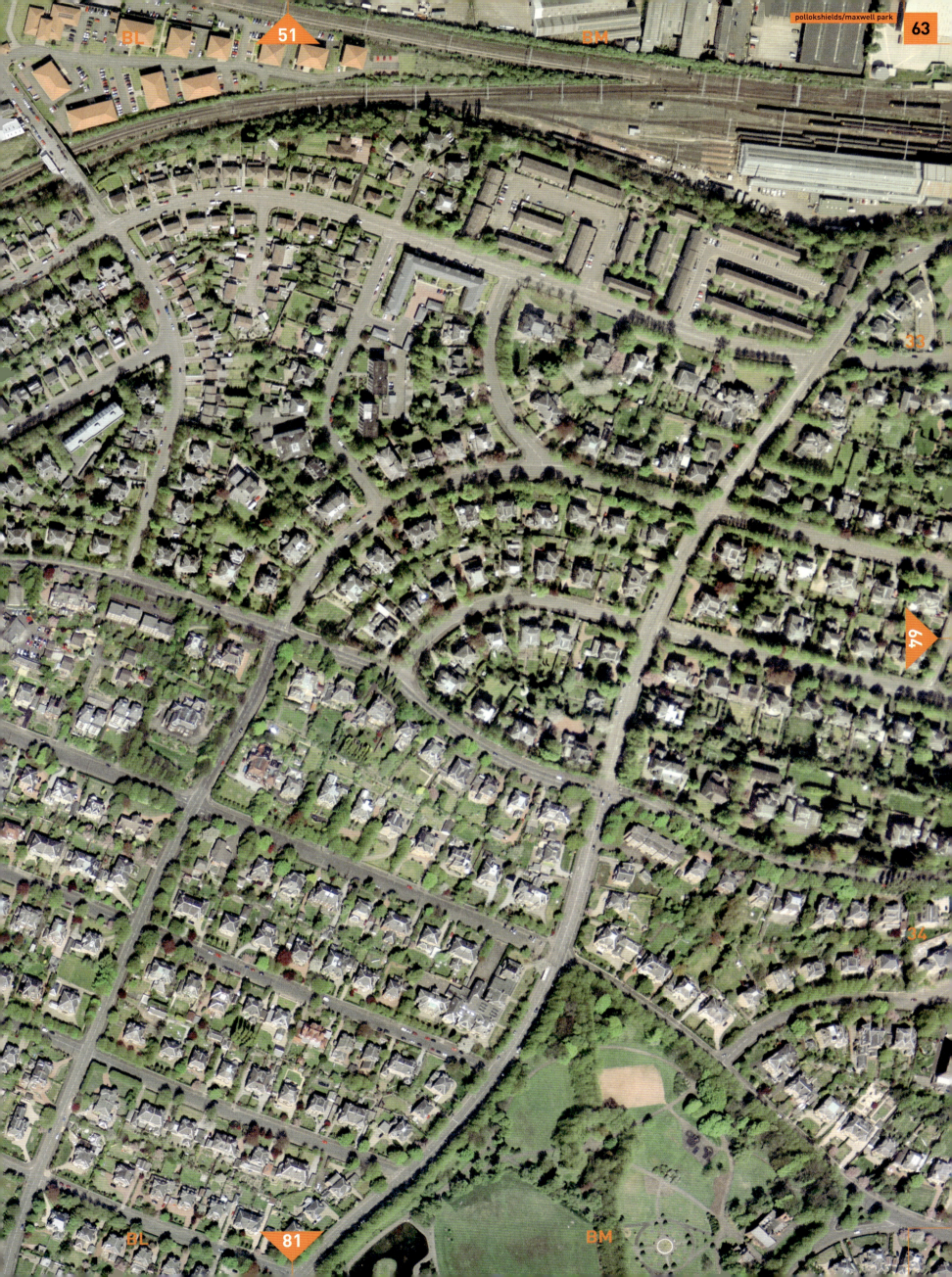

BL

51

BM

63

33

64

34

BL

81

BM

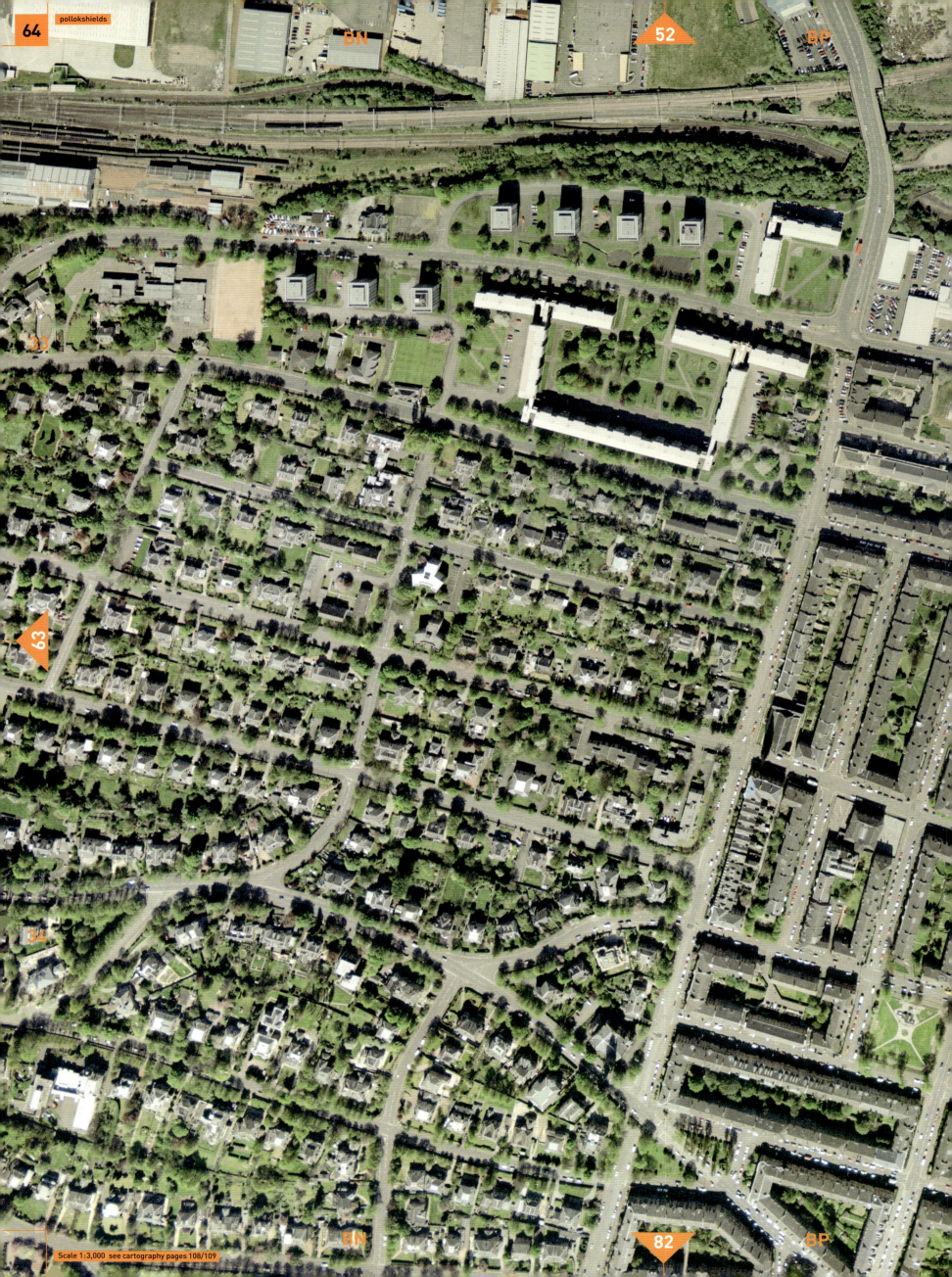

BN

52

BP

33

63

34

BN

82

BP

BR

54

BS

23

65

34

BR

83

BS

BS

55

BT

33

89

34

BU

56

BV

33

67

34

BU

84

BV

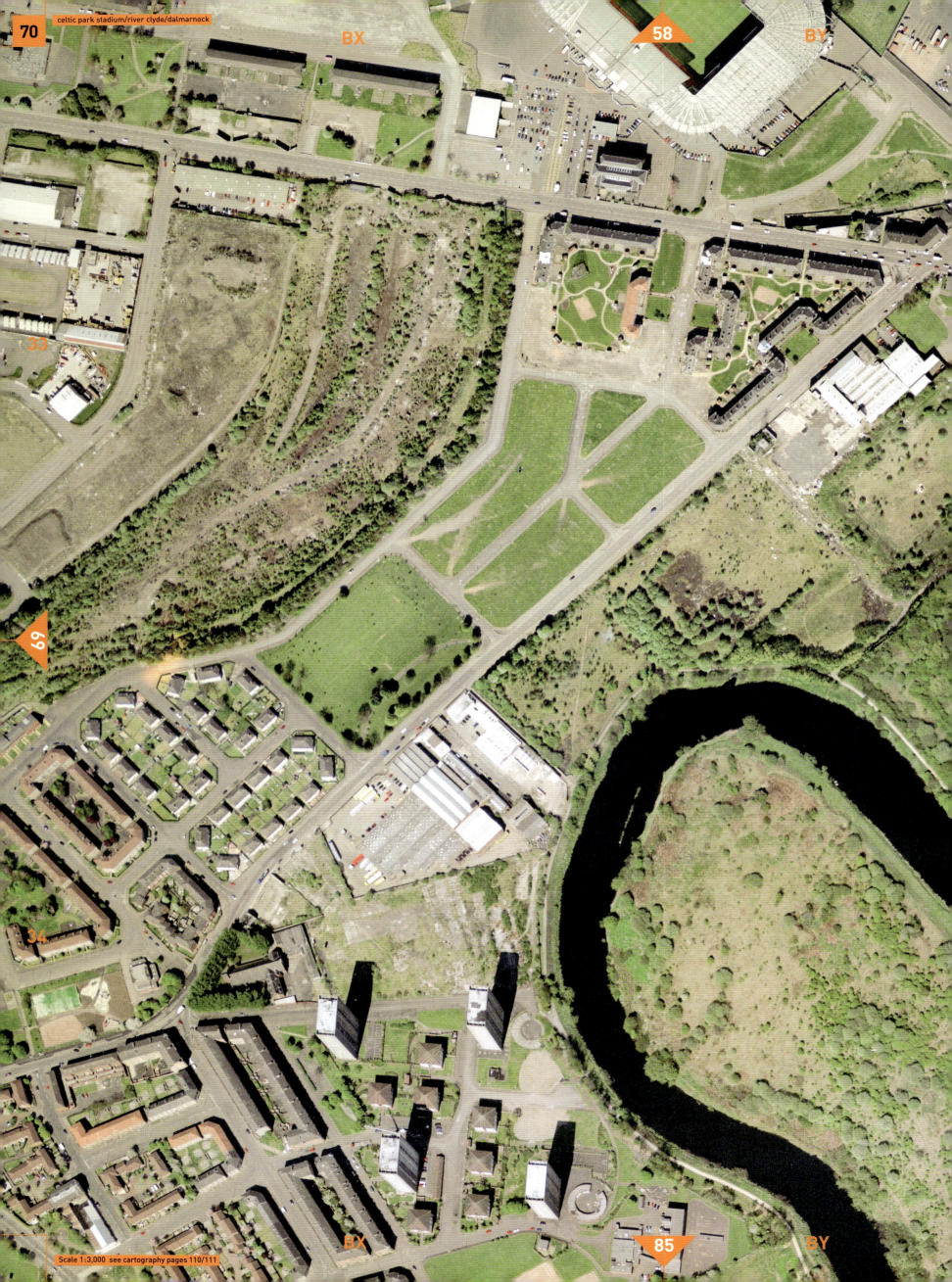

32

69

34

AY   AZ   BA   BB   74/5   BC   BD

31

75

32

33

34

77

35

36

37

79

38

CA   CB   CC   CD   94   CE   CF

31

59

32

33

71

34

35

36

85

37

38

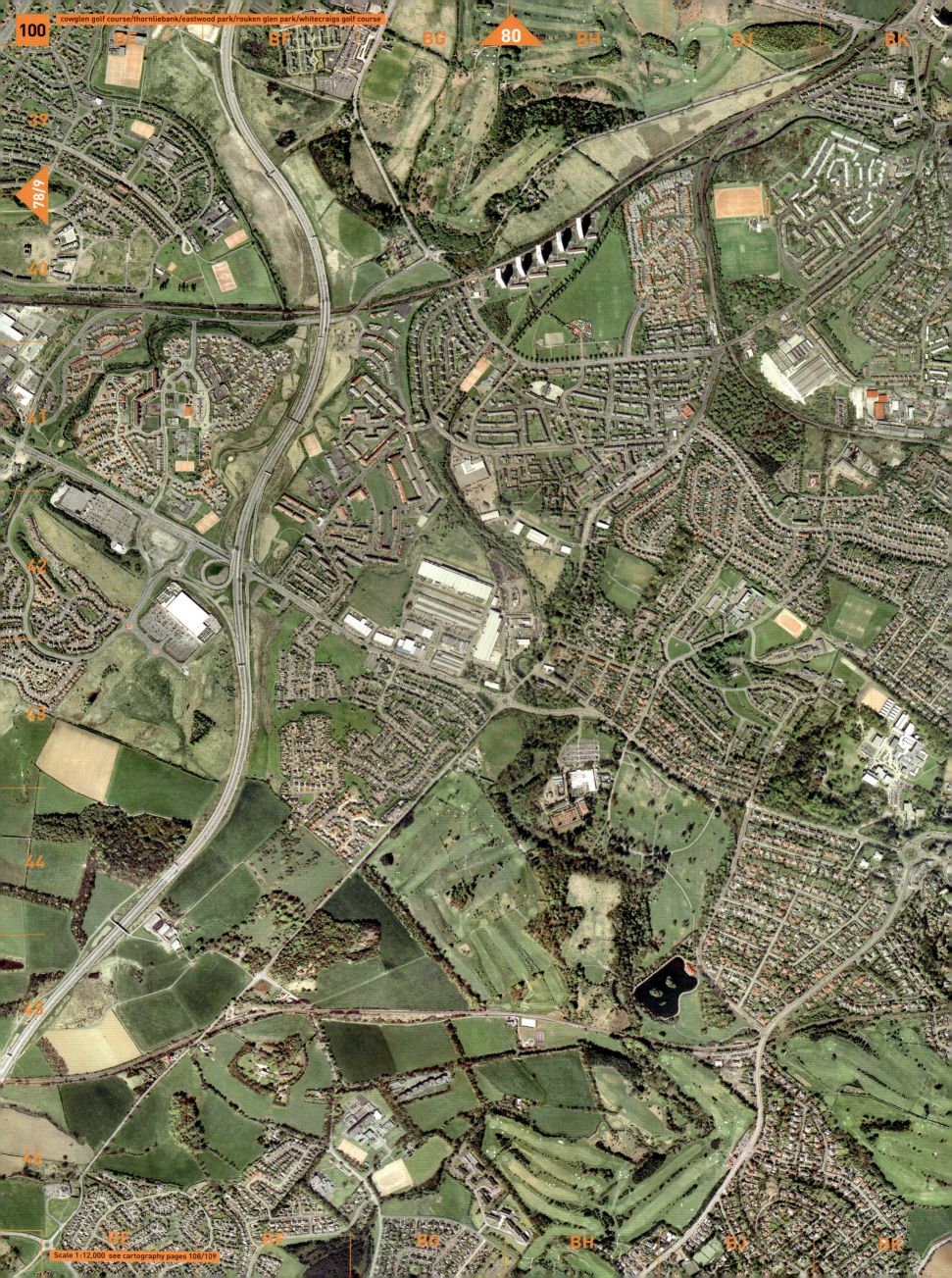

39

78/9

40

41

42

43

44

45

46

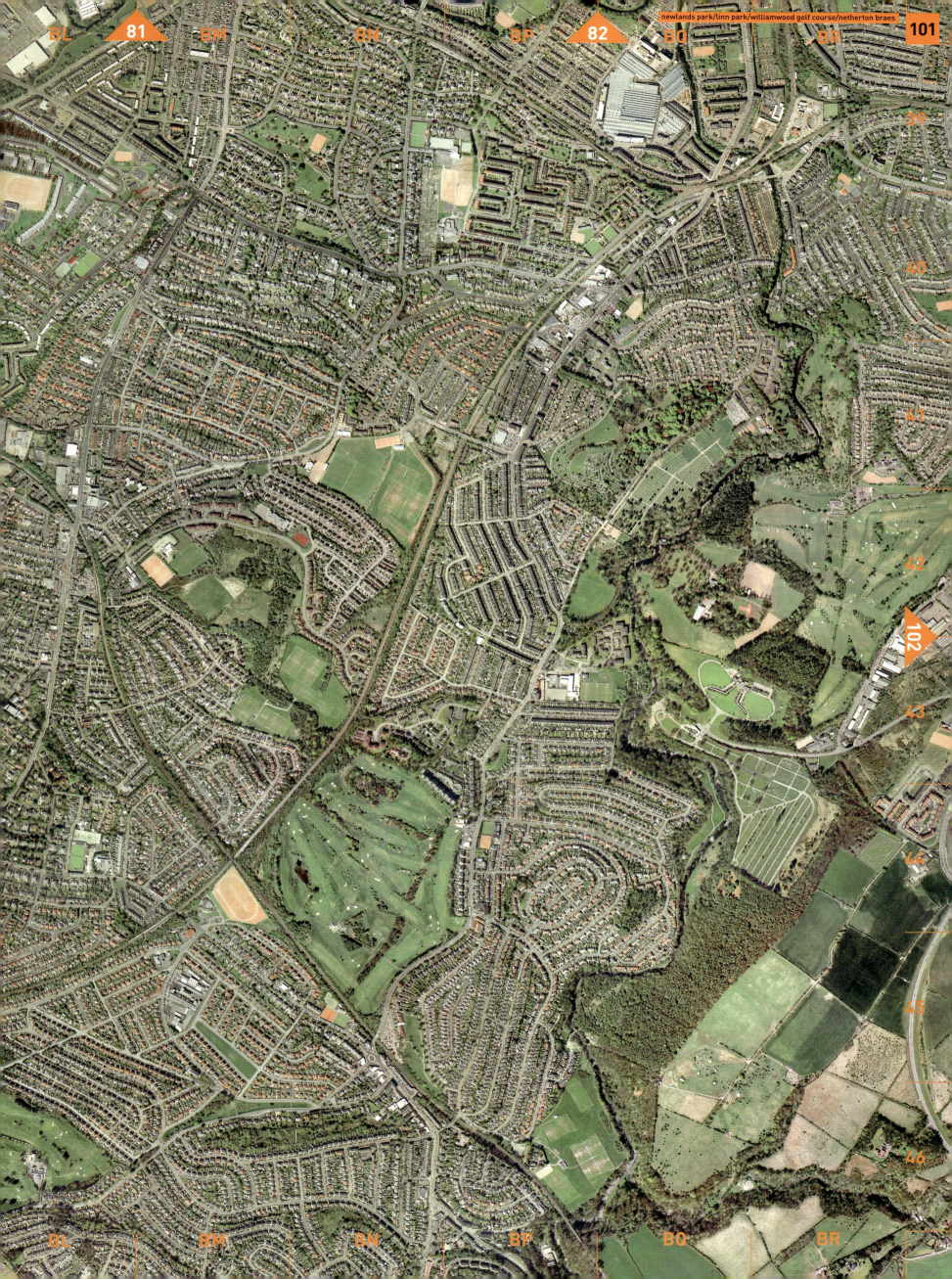

BL
81
BM
BM
BP
82
BQ
BR

39

40

41

42

102

43

44

45

46

BS   BT   BU   84   BV   BW   BX

39

40

41

42

101

43

44

45

46

BS   BT   BU   BV   BW   BX

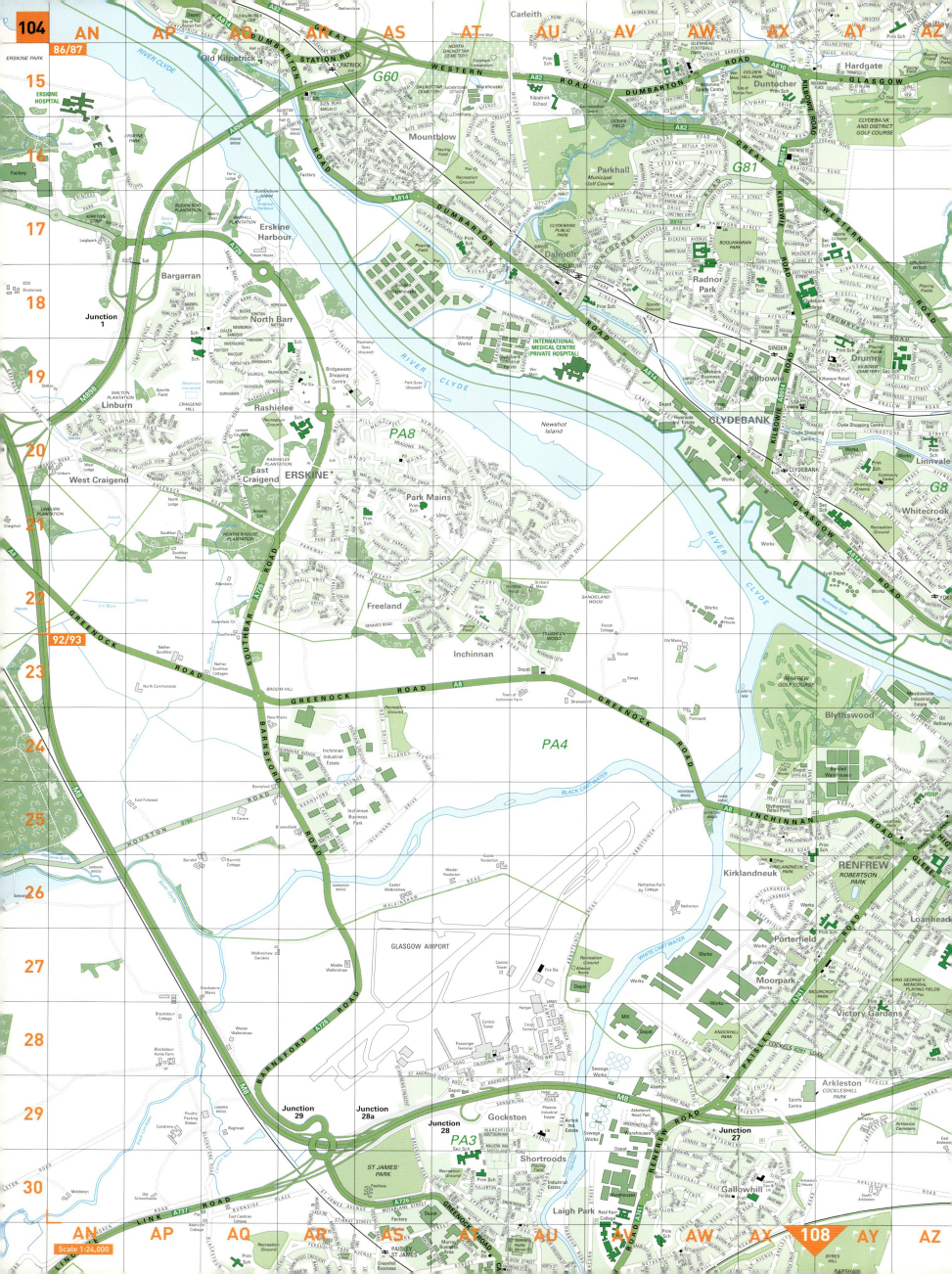

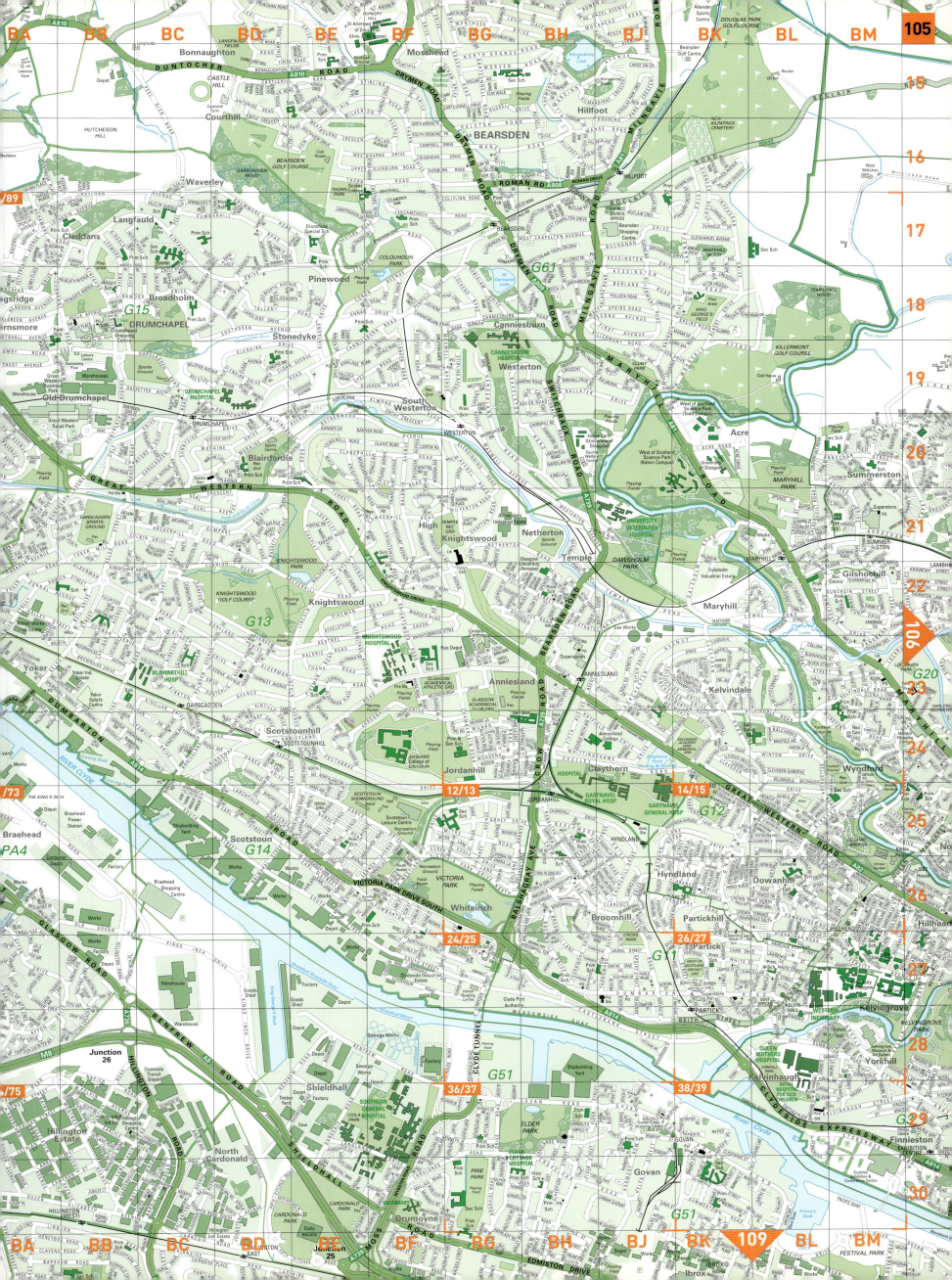

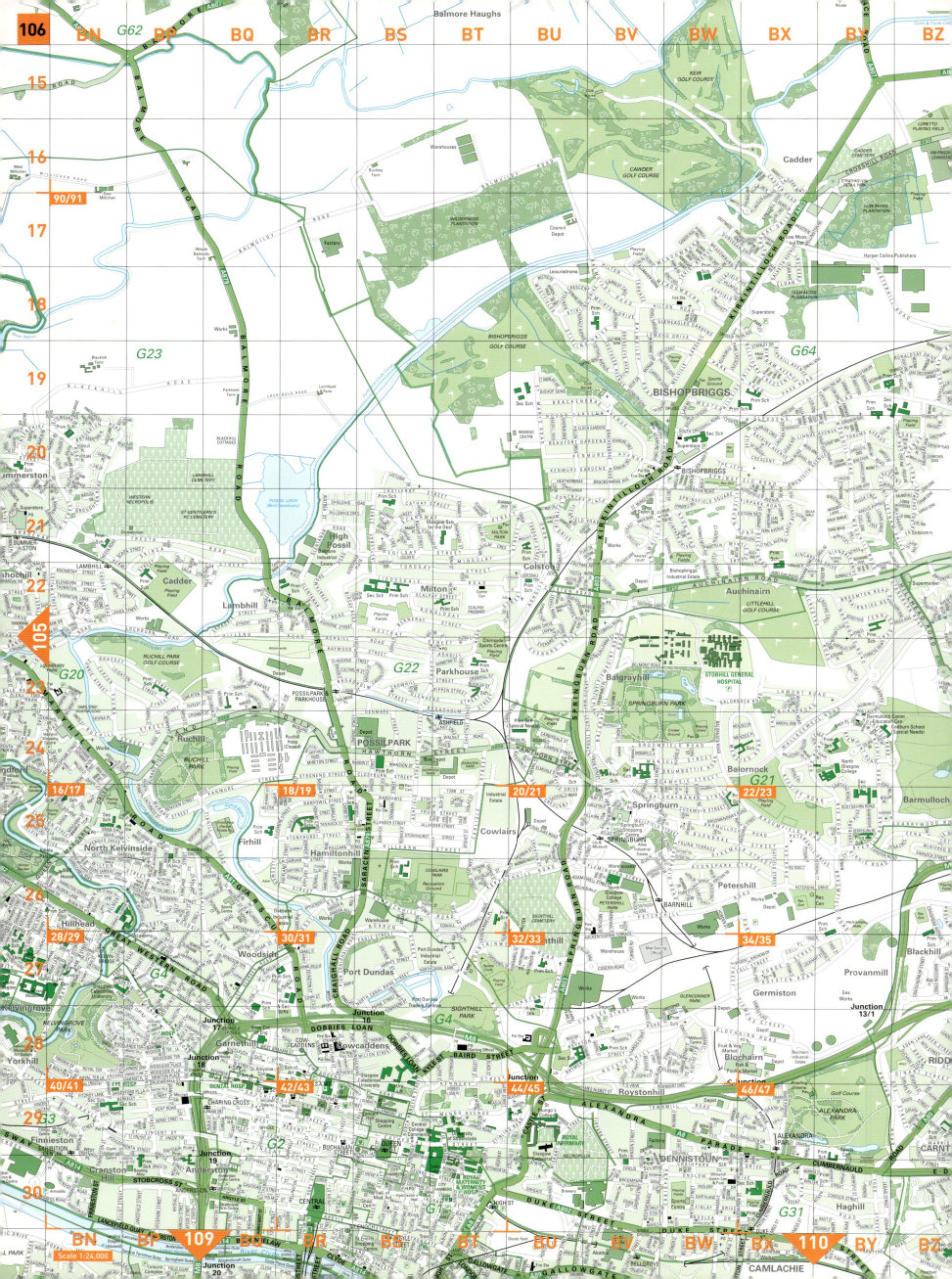

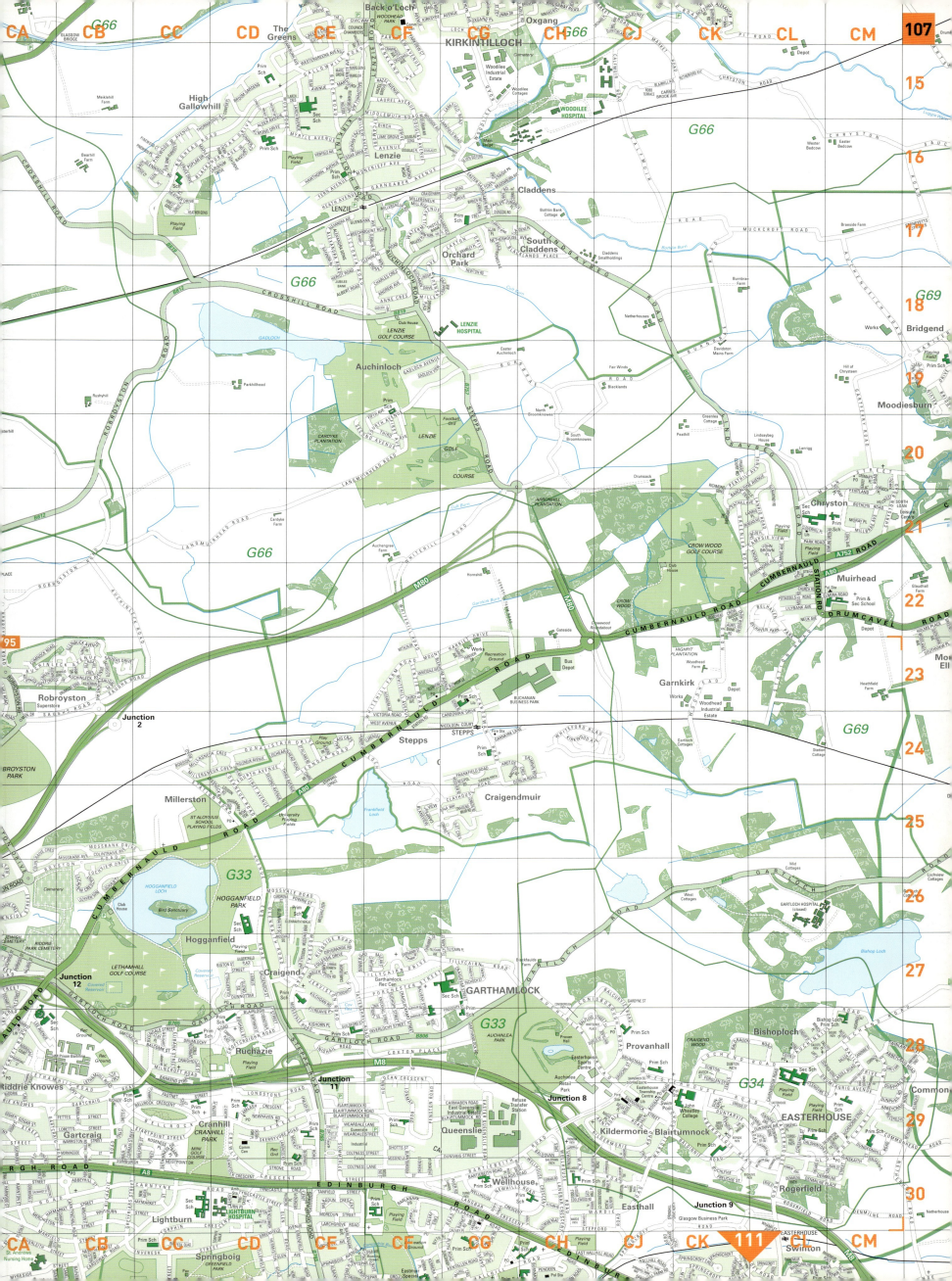

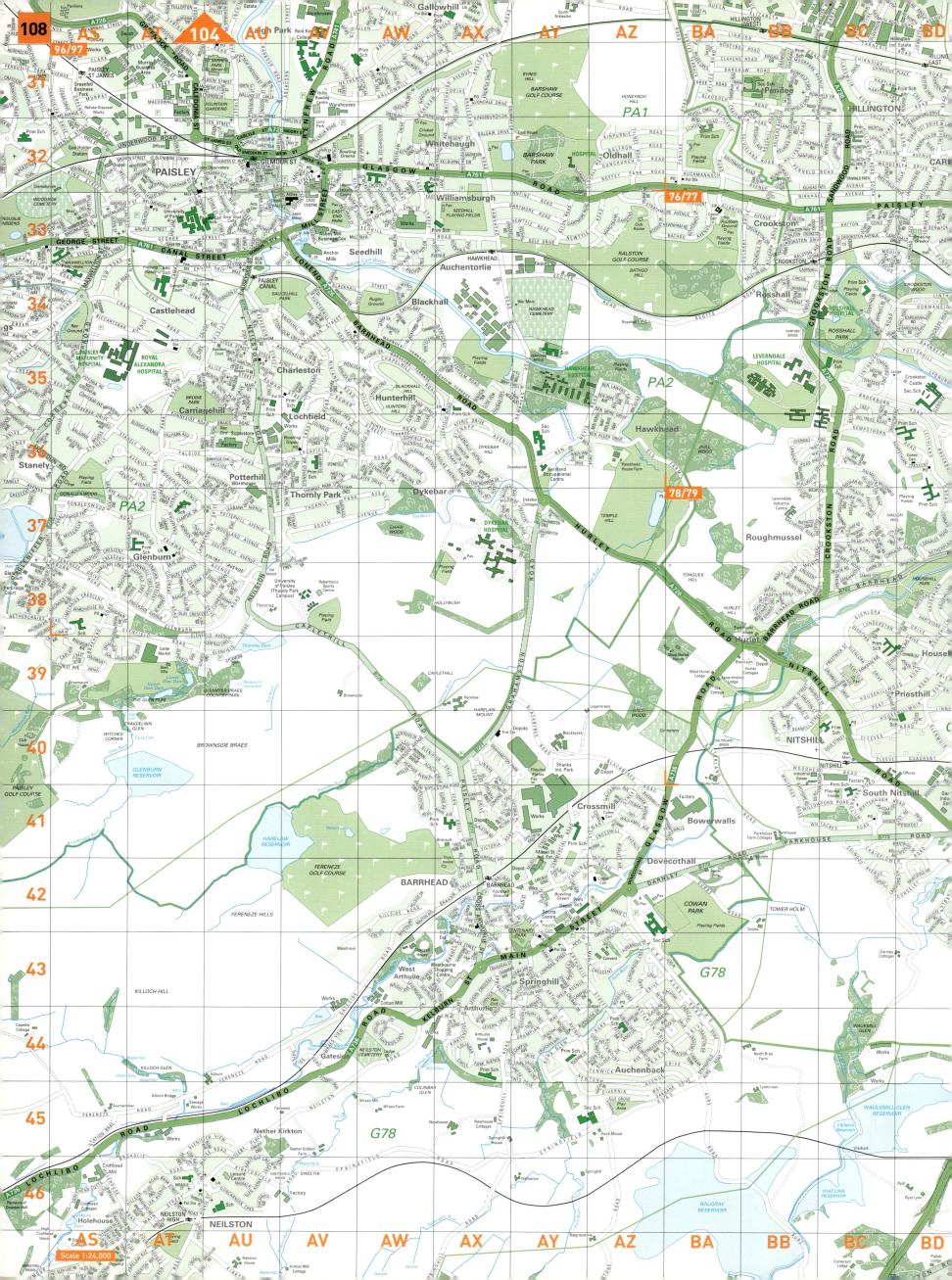

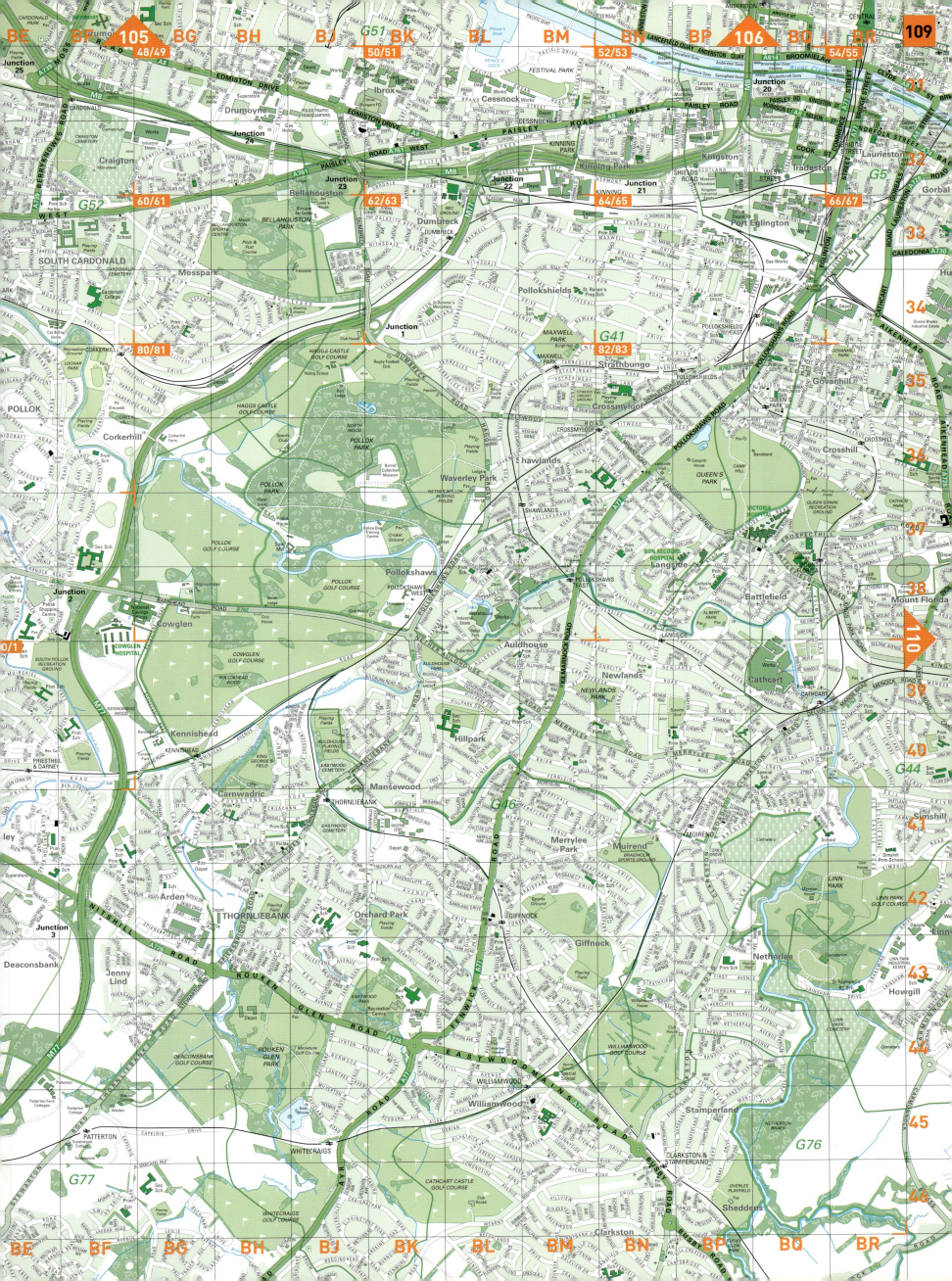

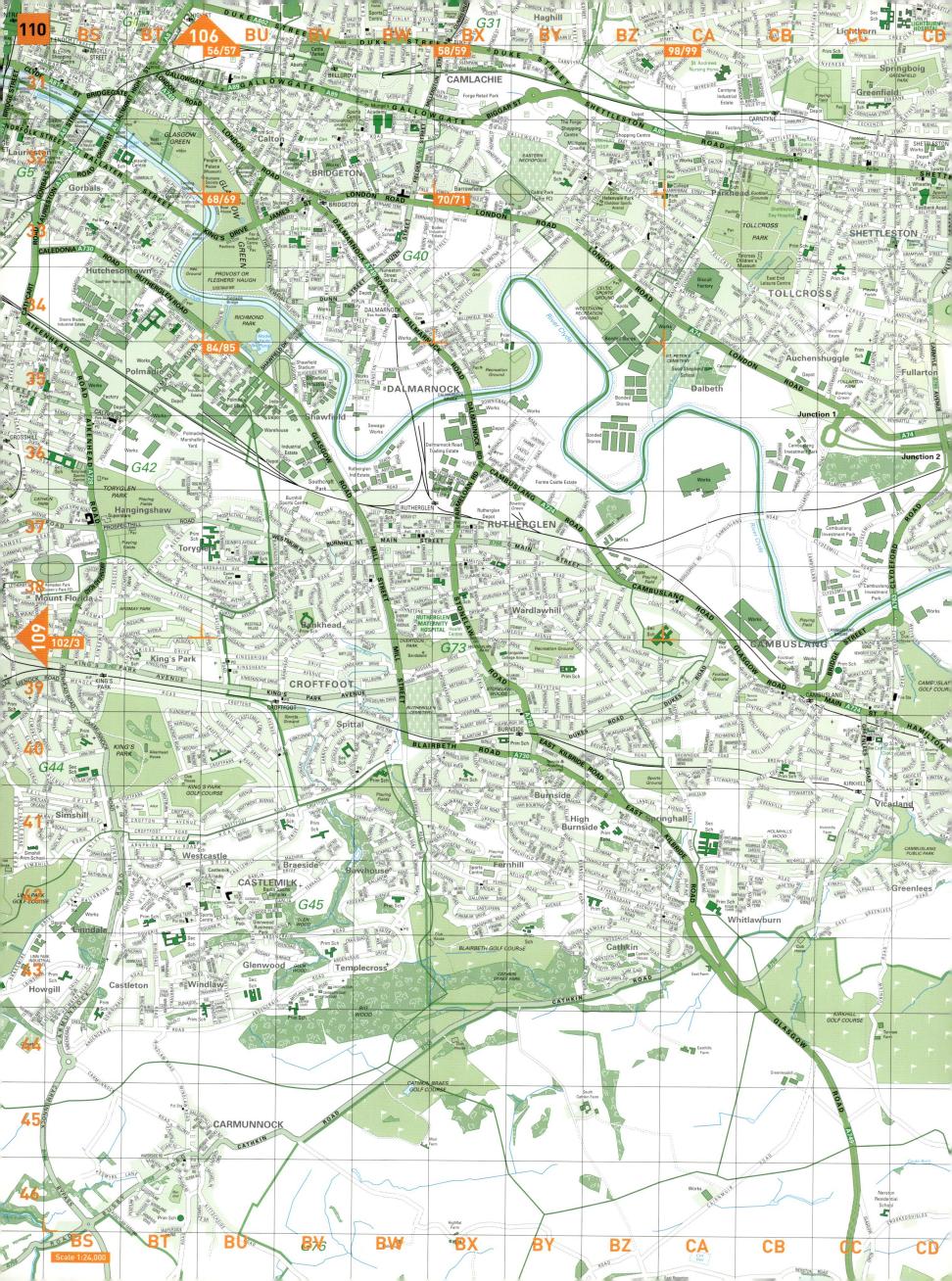

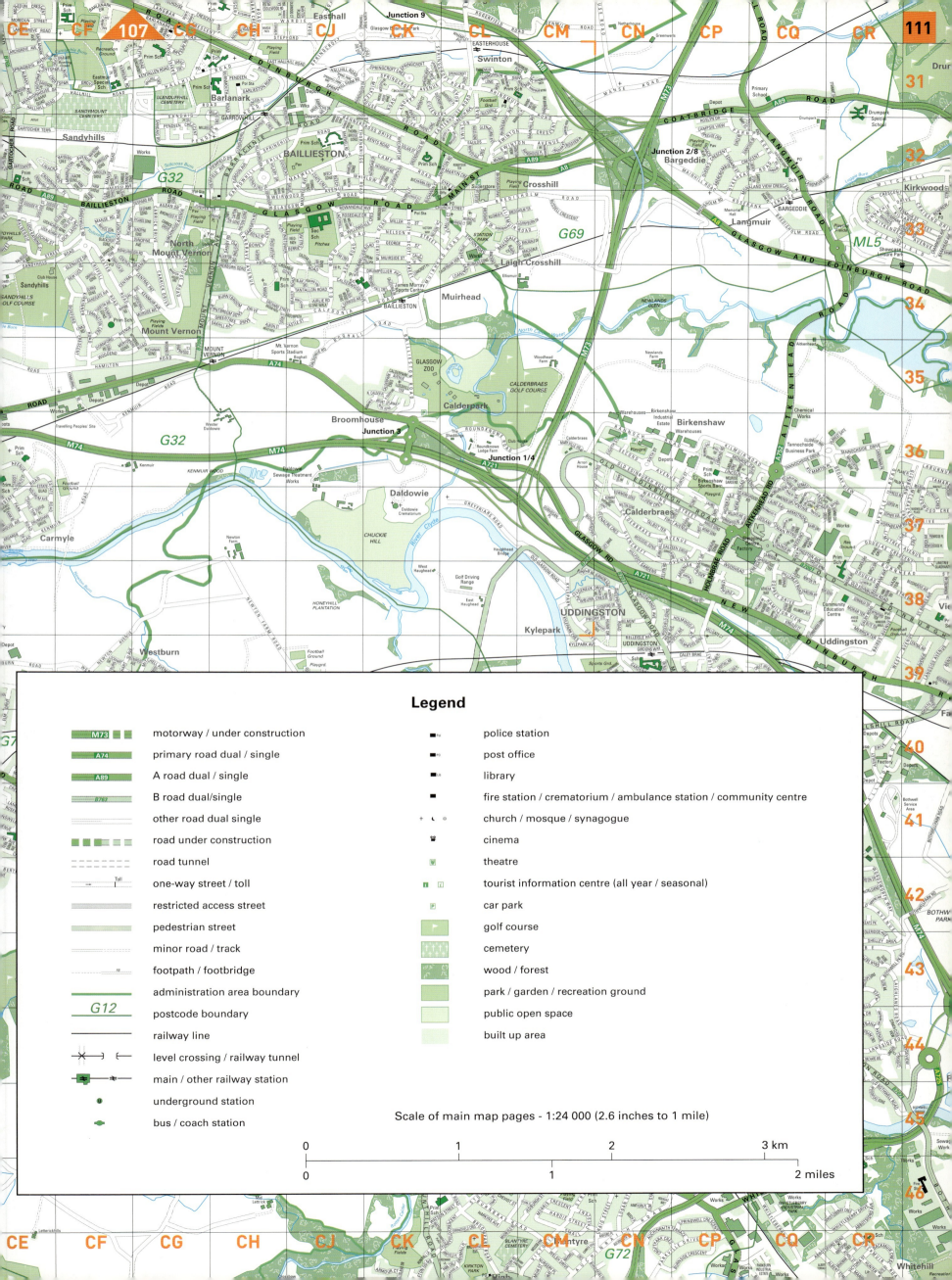

Legend

M73	motorway / under construction
A74	primary road dual / single
A89	A road dual / single
B763	B road dual/single
	other road dual single
	road under construction
	road tunnel
Toll	one-way street / toll
	restricted access street
	pedestrian street
	minor road / track
	footpath / footbridge
	administration area boundary
G12	postcode boundary
	railway line
	level crossing / railway tunnel
	main / other railway station
	underground station
	bus / coach station

Pol	police station
PO	post office
Lb	library
	fire station / crematorium / ambulance station / community centre
	church / mosque / synagogue
	cinema
	theatre
i	tourist information centre (all year / seasonal)
P	car park
	golf course
	cemetery
	wood / forest
	park / garden / recreation ground
	public open space
	built up area

Scale of main map pages - 1:24 000 (2.6 inches to 1 mile)

```
0               1               2            3 km
0                       1                2 miles
```

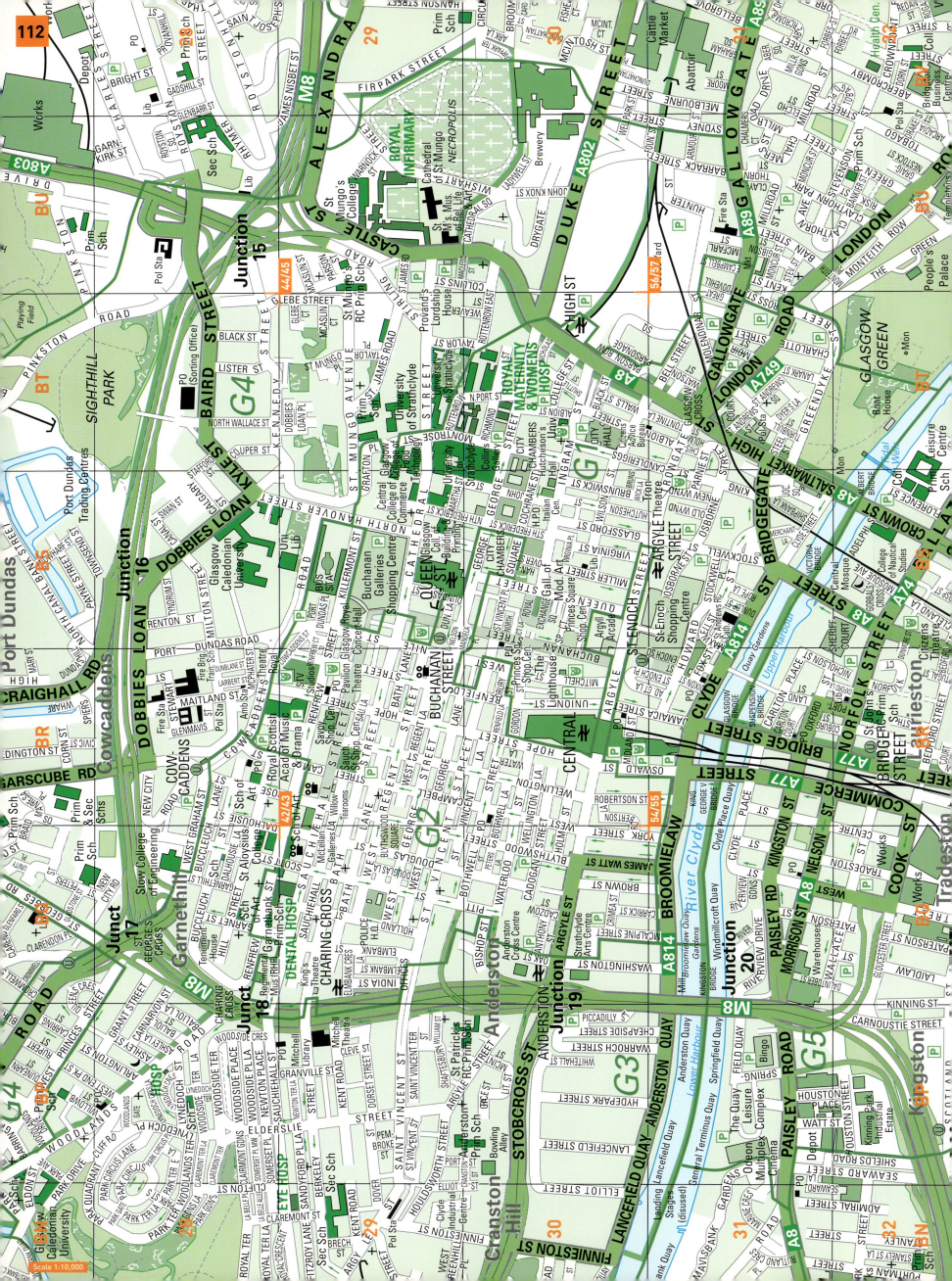

Index

The index reads in this sequence : street name/postal district or post town/photography page number/cartography page number/grid reference.

The index also contains some roads for which there is insufficient space to name within the cartography. These are printed in light type.

General abbreviations used within the cartography and index

All	Alley	Circ	Circus	
Allot	Allotments	Cl	Close	
Amb	Ambulance	Co	County	
App	Approach	Coll	College	
Arc	Arcade	Comm	Community	
Av	Avenue	Conv	Convent	
Bdy	Broadway	Cor	Corner	
Bk	Bank	Coron	Coroners	
Bldgs	Buildings	Cors	Corners	
Boul	Boulevard	Cotts	Cottages	
Bowl	Bowling	Cov	Covered	
Br	Bridge	Crem	Crematorium	
Cath	Cathedral	Cres	Crescent	
Cem	Cemetery	Ct	Court	
Cen	Central, Centre	Cts	Courts	
Cft	Croft	Ctyd	Courtyard	
Cfts	Crofts	Dep	Depot	
Ch	Church	Dev	Development	
Chyd	Churchyard	Dr	Drive	
Cin	Cinema	Dws	Dwellings	

E	East
Ed	Education
Elec	Electricity
Embk	Embankment
Est	Estate
Ex	Exchange
Exhib	Exhibition
FB	Footbridge
FC	Football Club
Fld	Field
Flds	Fields
Fm	Farm
Gall	Gallery
Gar	Garage
Gdn	Garden
Gdns	Gardens
Govt	Government
Gra	Grange
Grd	Ground
Grds	Grounds
Grn	Green
Grns	Greens
Gro	Grove
Gros	Groves
Gt	Great
Ho	House
Hos	Houses
Hosp	Hospital
Hts	Heights
Ind	Industrial
Int	International
Junct	Junction
La	Lane
Las	Lanes
Lib	Library
Lo	Lodge
Ln	Loan
Lwr	Lower
Mag	Magistrates
Mans	Mansions
Mem	Memorial
Mkt	Market
Mkts	Markets
Ms	Mews
Mt	Mount
Mus	Museum
N	North
NTS	National Trust for Scotland
Nat	National
PH	Public House
PO	Post Office

Par	Parade
Pas	Passage
Pav	Pavilion
Pk	Park
Pl	Place
Pol	Police
Prec	Precinct
Prim	Primary
Prom	Promenade
Pt	Point
Quad	Quadrant
RC	Roman Catholic
Rd	Road
Rds	Roads
Rec	Recreation
Res	Reservoir
Ri	Rise
S	South
Sch	School
Sec	Secondary
Shop	Shopping
Sq	Square
St.	Saint
St	Street
Sta	Station
Sts	Streets
Sub	Subway
Swim	Swimming
TA	Territorial Army
TH	Town Hall
Tenn	Tennis
Ter	Terrace
Thea	Theatre
Trd	Trading
Twr	Tower
Twrs	Towers
Uni	University
Vil	Villas
Vil	Villa
Vw	View
W	West
Wd	Wood
Wds	Woods
Wf	Wharf
Wk	Walk
Wks	Works
Yd	Yard

Post town abbreviations used within the index

Bell.	Bellshill
Bish.	Bishopton
Clyde.	Clydebank
Coat.	Coatbridge
Ersk.	Erskine
Ham.	Hamilton
Pais.	Paisley
Renf.	Renfrew

District abbreviations used within the index

Abbots.	Abbotsinch
Baill.	Baillieston
Barr.	Barrhead
Bears.	Bearsden
Bishop.	Bishopbriggs
Blan.	Blantyre
Both.	Bothwell
Camb.	Cambuslang
Carm.	Carmunnock
Chry.	Chryston
Clark.	Clarkston
Deac.	Deaconsbank
Dunt.	Duntocher
E.Kil.	East Kilbride
Gart.	Gartcosh
Giff.	Giffnock
Inch.	Inchinnan
Kirk.	Kirkintilloch
Lenz.	Lenzie
Miln.	Milngavie
Mood.	Moodiesburn
Muir.	Muirhead
Neil.	Neilston
Newt. M.	Newton Mearns
Old Kil.	Old Kilpatrick
Ruther.	Rutherglen
Thornlie.	Thornliebank
Udd.	Uddingston

College St G1	43	106	BT30
Collessie Dr G33	94	107	CE27
Collina St G20	89	105	BL23
Collins St G4	44	106	BU30
Coll Pl G21	34	106	BX27
Coll St G21	34	106	BX27
Collylinn Rd (Bears.) G61	89	105	BG17
Colmonell Av G13	88	105	BB22
Colonsay Av, Renf. PA4	93	104	AY28
Colonsay Rd G52	48	109	BG32
Colonsay Rd, Pais. PA2	96	108	AT38
Colquhoun Av G52	74	105	BC30
Colston Av (Bishop.) G64	91	106	BV22
Colston Dr (Bishop.) G64	91	106	BV22
Colston Gdns (Bishop.) G64	91	106	BU22
Colston Path (Bishop.) G64	91	106	BU22
Colston Pl (Bishop.) G64	91	106	BU22
Colston Rd (Bishop.) G64	91	106	BU22
Coltmuir Av (Bishop.) G64	91	106	BU21
Coltmuir Cres (Bishop.) G64	91	106	BU21
Coltmuir Dr (Bishop.) G64	91	106	BU21
Coltmuir Gdns (Bishop.) G64	91	106	BU21
Coltmuir St G22	90	106	BR23
Coltness La G33	94	107	CE30
Coltness St G33	94	107	CE29
Coltpark Av (Bishop.) G64	91	106	BU21
Coltpark La (Bishop.) G64	91	106	BU21
Columba, Clyde. G81	87	104	AZ19
Columba St G51	38	105	BK30
Colvend Dr (Ruther.) G73	102	110	BX42
Colvend La G40	69	110	BV34
Colvend St G40	69	110	BV34
Colville Dr (Ruther.) G73	103	110	BZ39
Comedie Rd G33	95	107	CG25
Comelypark Pl G31	57	110	BW31
Comelypark St G31	57	110	BV31
Commerce St G5	54	109	BR32
Commercial Ct G5	55	110	BT32
Commercial Rd G5	67	110	BS33
Commonhead Rd G34	95	107	CM29
Commore Dr G13	88	105	BC22
Comrie Rd G33	94	107	CE24
Comrie St G32	98	110	CD34
Cona St (Thornlie.) G46	100	109	BG41
Congress Rd G3	39	105	BM30
Congress Way G3	40	106	BN30
Conisborough Path G34	95	107	CH27
Conisborough Rd G34	95	107	CH27
Conistone Cres (Baill.) G69	99	111	CH33
Connal St G40	70	110	BX34
Conniston St G32	94	107	CA30
Connollys Land, Clyde. G81	87	104	AW15
Conon Av (Bears.) G61	88	105	BE18
Consett La G33	94	107	CE29
Consett St G33	94	107	CE29
Contin Pl G12	89	105	BM24
Convair Way, Renf. PA4	93	104	AZ28
Conval Way, Pais. PA3	92	104	AT29
Cook St G5	53	109	BQ32
Cooperage Ct G14	93	104	AZ23
Coopers Well La G11	26/7	105	BL28
Coopers Well St G11	26	105	BL28
Copland Pl G51	38	105	BK30
Copland Quad G51	50	109	BK31
Copland Rd G51	50	109	BK31
Coplaw St G42	65	109	BQ34
Coppice, The, Ersk. PA8	86	104	AT21
Corbett Ct G32	98	110	CB34
Corbett St G32	98	110	CB34
Cordiner St G44	83	109	BR38
Corkerhill Gdns G52	60	109	BG33
Corkerhill Pl G52	77	109	BF35
Corkerhill Rd G52	77	109	BF35
Corlaich Av G42	84	110	BU38
Corlaich Dr G42	84	110	BU38
Cornaig Rd G53	79	108	BD37
Cornalee Gdns G53	78	108	BC37
Cornalee Pl G53	79	108	BD38
Cornalee Rd G53	79	108	BD37
Cornhill St G21	91	106	BW24
Cornock Cres, Clyde. G81	87	104	AX18
Cornock St, Clyde. G81	87	104	AX18
Corn St G4	30	106	BR27
Cornwall Av (Ruther.) G73	103	110	BZ40
Cornwall St G41	51	109	BM32
Cornwall St S G41	63	109	BM33
Coronation Way (Bears.) G61	89	105	BH19
Corpach Pl G34	95	107	CM28
Corran St G33	94	107	CB29
Corrie Dr, Pais. PA1	76	108	BA33
Corrie Gro G44	101	109	BP41
Corrour Rd G43	81	109	BM38
Corsebar Av, Pais. PA2	96	108	AS35
Corsebar Cres, Pais. PA2	96	108	AS36
Corsebar Dr, Pais. PA2	96	108	AS35
Corsebar Way, Pais. PA2	96	108	AS34
Corsehill Path G34	95	107	CL29
Corsehill Pl G34	95	107	CL29
Corsehill St G34	95	107	CL29
Corse Rd G52	74	108	BA31
Corsewall Av G32	99	111	CG34
Corsford Dr G53	79	109	BE39
Corsock St G31	46	106	BY30
Corston St G33	47	106	BZ29
Cortachy Pl (Bishop.) G64	91	106	BZ20
Coruisk Dr (Clark.) G76	101	109	BM45
Corunna St G3	40	106	BN29
Coshneuk Rd G33	94	107	CD24
Cottar St G20	90	106	BN22
Cotton St G40	84	110	BW35
Cotton St, Pais. PA1	96	108	AV33
Coulin Gdns G22	19	106	BT25
County Av (Camb.) G72	85	110	BZ38
County Pl, Pais. PA1	96	108	AU32
County Sq, Pais. PA1	96	108	AU32
Couper St G4	31	106	BT28
Courthill Av G44	101	109	BR40
Coustonhill St G43	81	109	BL38
Coustonholm Rd G43	81	109	BM37
Coventry Dr G31	46	106	BX29
Cowal Rd G20	89	105	BK22
Cowal St G20	89	105	BL22
Cowan La G12	28	106	BN27
Cowan St G12	28	106	BN27
Cowcaddens Rd G4	30	106	BR28
Cowden Dr (Bishop.) G64	91	106	BW18
Cowdenhill Circ G13	88	105	BF21
Cowdenhill Pl G13	88	105	BF21
Cowdenhill Rd G13	88	105	BF21
Cowden St G51	75	105	BF30
Cowdray Cres, Renf. PA4	93	104	AZ26
Cowell Vw, Clyde. G81	87	104	AX18
Cowglen Rd G53	79	109	BE38
Cowlairs Rd G21	20	106	BU25
Coxhill St G21	19	106	BT26
Coxton Pl G33	94	107	CF28
Coylton Rd G43	101	109	BN40
Craggan Dr G14	88	105	BB23
Crags Av, Pais. PA2	96	108	AV36
Crags Cres, Pais. PA2	96	108	AV35
Crags Rd, Pais. PA2	96	108	AV36
Cragwell Pk (Clark.) G76	102	110	BU46
Craiganour La G43	101	109	BL39
Craiganour Pl G43	101	109	BL39
Craigard Pl (Ruther.) G73	103	110	BZ42
Craigbank Dr G53	78	108	BC39
Craigbarnet Cres G33	94	107	CD25
Craigbo Av G23	89	105	BM21
Craigbo Ct G23	89	105	BM21
Craigbo Dr G23	89	105	BM21
Craigbo Pl G23	89	105	BM21
Craigbo Rd G23	89	105	BM20
Craigbo St G23	89	105	BM20
Craigellan Rd G43	101	109	BM39
Craigenbay St G21	22	106	BX25
Craigencart Ct, Clyde. G81	87	104	AV15
Craigendmuir Rd G33	95	107	CG25
Craigendmuir St G33	35	106	BZ27
Craigendon Rd, Pais. PA2	96	108	AS38
Craigend Pl G13	89	105	BG23
Craigend St G13	89	105	BG23
Craighall Rd G4	30	106	BR27
Craighead Av G33	23	106	BZ26
Craighouse St G33	94	107	CC28
Craigiebar Dr, Pais. PA2	96	108	AS37
Craigieburn Gdns G20	89	105	BK21
Craigiehall Av, Ersk. PA8	86	104	AQ22
Craigiehall Cres, Ersk. PA8	86	104	AQ22
Craigiehall Pl G51	51	109	BM31
Craigiehall St G51	51	109	BM31
Craigiehall Way, Ersk. PA8	86	104	AQ22
Craigielea Ct, Renf. PA4	93	104	AY25
Craigielea Pk, Renf. PA4	93	104	AY26
Craigielea Rd, Renf. PA4	93	104	AY26
Craigielea St G31	45	106	BW29
Craigie St G42	82	109	BQ35
Craigievar St G33	95	107	CG27
Craigleith St G32	98	110	CA31
Craiglockhart St G33	94	107	CF27
Craigmaddie Ter La G3	28	106	BN28
Craigmillar Rd G42	82	109	BQ38
Craigmont Dr G20	90	106	BN24
Craigmont St G20	90	106	BN23
Craigmore St G31	58	110	BY31
Craigmuir Cres G52	74	108	BB31
Craigmuir Pl G52	74	108	BA31
Craigmuir Rd G52	74	108	BA31
Craigneil St G33	95	107	CG27
Craignethan Gdns G11	26	105	BK27
Craignethan Rd (Giff.) G46	100	109	BJ46
Craignure Rd (Ruther.) G73	102	110	BX42
Craigpark G31	45	106	BW30
Craigpark Dr G31	45	106	BW30
Craigpark Ter G31	45	106	BW30
Craig Rd G44	101	109	BQ40
Craigs Av, Clyde. G81	87	104	AV15
Craigsheen Av (Carm.) G76	102	110	BT46
Craigton Dr G51	48	109	BH31
Craigton Pl G51	48	109	BH30
Craigvicar Gdns G32	98	111	CF33
Craigwell Av (Ruther.) G73	103	110	BZ39
Crail St G31	59	110	BZ32
Cramond Av, Renf. PA4	72	105	BA27
Cramond St G5	83	110	BT35
Cramond Ter G32	98	110	CD32
Cranborne Rd G12	89	105	BJ24
Cranbrooke Dr G20	89	105	BM22
Cranston St G3	40	106	BP29
Cranworth La G12	15	105	BM26
Cranworth St G12	15	105	BM26
Crarae Av (Bears.) G61	89	105	BG19
Crathes Ct G44	101	109	BN41
Crathie Dr G11	25	105	BJ27
Crathie La G11	25	105	BJ27
Crawford Dr G15	88	105	BB20
Crawford La G11	25	105	BJ27
Crawford Path G11	25	105	BJ27
Crawford St G11	25	105	BJ27
Crawfurd Gdns (Ruther.) G73	103	110	BY41
Crawfurd Rd (Ruther.) G73	103	110	BX41
Craw Rd, Pais. PA2	96	108	AS34
Crebar St (Thornlie.) G46	100	109	BG41
Credon Gdns (Ruther.) G73	103	110	BY41
Cree Av (Bishop.) G64	91	106	BZ20
Cree Gdns G32	98	110	CB32
Creran Dr, Renf. PA4	93	104	AX25
Crescent Ct, Clyde. G81	87	104	AU18
Crescent Rd G13	88	105	BD24
Crescent Rd G14	88	105	BD24
Crescent, The, Clyde. G81	87	104	AU18
Cresswell La G12	15	105	BM26
Cresswell St G12	15	105	BM26
Cressy St G51	36	105	BG29
Crest Av G13	88	105	BD21
Crestlea Av, Pais. PA2	96	108	AU37
Crichton Ct G45	102	110	BV43
Crichton Pl G21	20	106	BU25
Crichton St G21	20	106	BU25
Crieff Ct G3	40/1	106	BP29
Criffell Gdns G32	98	111	CF34
Criffell Rd G32	98	111	CF33
Crimea St G2	41	106	BQ30
Crinan Gdns (Bishop.) G64	91	106	BY20
Crinan Rd (Bishop.) G64	91	106	BY20
Crinan St G31	46	106	BX29
Cripps Av, Clyde. G81	87	104	AZ20
Croftbank St G21	21	106	BV25
Croftburn Dr G44	102	110	BT41
Croftcroighn Rd G33	94	107	CD28
Croftend Av G44	102	110	BU39
Croftfoot Cres G45	102	110	BW41
Croftfoot Dr G45	102	110	BV41
Croftfoot Quad G45	102	110	BU41
Croftfoot Rd G44	102	110	BT41
Croftfoot Rd G45	102	110	BT41
Croftfoot St G45	102	110	BW41
Croftfoot Ter G45	102	110	BV41
Crofthill Rd G44	102	110	BU40
Crofthouse Dr G44	102	110	BU41
Croftmont Av G44	102	110	BU41
Crofton Av G44	102	110	BT41
Croftpark Av G44	102	110	BS41
Croft Rd (Camb.) G72	103	110	CD40
Croftside Av G44	102	110	BU41
Croftspar Av G32	98	111	CE31
Croftspar Ct G32	98	111	CF31
Croftspar Dr G32	98	111	CE31
Croftspar Gate G32	98	111	CF31
Croftspar Gro G32	98	111	CE31
Croftspar Pl G32	98	111	CE31
Croft Way, Renf. PA4	93	104	AZ28
Croftwood (Bishop.) G64	91	106	BW17
Croftwood Av G44	102	110	BT41
Cromarty Av G43	101	109	BP39
Cromarty Av (Bishop.) G64	91	106	BZ19
Cromarty Gdns (Clark.) G76	101	109	BQ44
Crombie Gdns (Baill.) G69	99	111	CJ34
Cromdale St G51	48	109	BG31
Cromer La, Pais. PA3	92	104	AT29
Cromer St G20	90	106	BP24
Cromer Way, Pais. PA3	92	104	AT30
Crompton Av G44	101	109	BR40
Cromwell La G20	29	106	BQ27
Cromwell St G20	29	106	BQ27
Cronberry Quad G52	76	108	BB34
Cronberry Ter G52	76	108	BB34
Crookedshields Rd (Camb.) G72	103	110	CC46
Crookedshields Rd (E.Kil.) G74	103	110	CC46
Crookston Av G52	76	108	BC33
Crookston Ct G52	76	108	BC33
Crookston Dr G52	76	108	BB33
Crookston Dr, Pais. PA1	76	108	BB33
Crookston Gdns G52	76	108	BB33
Crookston Gro G52	76	108	BC33
Crookstonhill Path G52	76	108	BB33
Crookston Path G52	76	108	BB33
Crookston Pl G52	76	108	BB33
Crookston Quad G52	76	108	BB33
Crookston Rd G52	76	108	BB34
Crookston Rd G53	78	108	BC37
Crosbie La G20	89	105	BL21
Crosbie St G20	89	105	BL21
Crossbank Av G42	84	110	BU36
Crossbank Dr G42	83	110	BT36
Crossbank Rd G42	83	110	BT36
Crossbank Ter G42	83	110	BT36
Cross Ct (Bishop.) G64	91	106	BV20
Crossflat Cres, Pais. PA1	96	108	AW32
Crossford Dr G23	90	106	BN20
Crosshill Av G42	83	109	BR36
Crosshill Dr (Ruther.) G73	102	110	BX39
Crosshill Sq (Baill.) G69	99	111	CL33
Crosslees Ct (Thornlie.) G46	100	109	BJ41
Crosslees Dr (Thornlie.) G46	100	109	BH42
Crosslees Pk (Thornlie.) G46	100	109	BH42
Crosslees Rd (Thornlie.) G46	100	109	BH43
Crosslee St G52	75	109	BF32
Crossloan Rd G51	36	105	BH30
Crossloan Ter G51	37	105	BJ30
Crossmyloof Gdns G41	81	109	BM36
Crosspoint Dr G23	90	106	BN20
Cross St G32	98	111	CE36
Cross St, Pais. PA1	96	108	AS33
Cross, The, Pais. PA1	96	108	AU32
Crosstobs Rd G53	78	108	BC36
Crossview Av (Baill.) G69	99	111	CM32
Crossview Pl (Baill.) G69	99	111	CM32
Crovie Rd G53	78	108	BC38
Crowhill Rd (Bishop.) G64	91	106	BV21
Crowhill St G22	90	106	BS23
Crow La G13	89	105	BH24
Crowlin Cres G33	94	107	CD29
Crown Av, Clyde. G81	87	104	AW18
Crown Circ G12	14	105	BL26
Crown Ct G1	42/3	106	BS30
Crown Gdns G12	14	105	BL26
Crownhall Pl G32	98	111	CE32
Crownhall Rd G32	98	111	CE32
Crown Mans G11	14	105	BK26
Crownpoint Rd G40	57	110	BV32
Crown Rd N G12	14	105	BK26
Crown Rd S G12	14	105	BK26
Crown St G5	55	110	BS32
Crown St (Baill.) G69	99	111	CH34
Crown Ter G12	14	105	BK26
Crow Rd G11	12	105	BH25
Crow Rd G13	89	105	BH24
Croy Pl G21	91	106	BY24
Croy Rd G21	91	106	BY24
Cruachan Av, Pais. PA2	96	108	AU37
Cruachan Av, Renf. PA4	93	104	AY28
Cruachan Rd (Ruther.) G73	103	110	BZ42
Cruachan St (Thornlie.) G46	100	109	BH41
Cruden St G51	48	109	BH31
Crum Av (Thornlie.) G46	100	109	BJ42
Crusader Av G13	88	105	BF20
Cubie St G40	57	110	BV32
Cuillins Rd (Ruther.) G73	103	110	BZ42
Culbin Dr G13	88	105	BB21
Cullen, Ersk. PA8	86	104	AQ18
Cullen St G32	98	110	CC33
Culloden St G31	46	106	BX29
Culrain Gdns G32	98	110	CC32
Culrain St G32	98	110	CC32
Culross La G32	98	111	CE33
Culross St G32	98	111	CE33
Cults St G51	49	109	BH31
Culzean Cres (Baill.) G69	99	111	CJ33
Culzean Dr G32	98	111	CF33
Cumberland Arc G5	66/7	110	BS33
Cumberland Pl G5	67	110	BS33
Cumberland St G5	54	109	BR32
Cumbernauld Rd G31	46	106	BX30
Cumbernauld Rd G33	35	106	BZ28
Cumbrae Ct, Clyde. G81	87	104	AX19
Cumbrae Rd, Pais. PA2	96	108	AU38
Cumbrae Rd, Renf. PA4	93	104	AZ28
Cumbrae St G33	94	107	CC29
Cumlodden Dr G20	89	105	BM22
Cumming Dr G42	83	109	BR37
Cumnock Rd G33	94	107	CA23
Cunard Ct, Clyde. G81	87	104	AX21
Cunard St, Clyde. G81	87	104	AX21
Cunningham Dr (Giff.) G46	101	109	BN42
Cunningham Dr, Clyde. G81	87	104	AV15
Cunningham Rd G52	74	105	BB29
Cunninghame Rd (Ruther.) G73	85	110	BY36
Curfew Rd G13	88	105	BF20
Curle St G14	73	105	BF27
Curling Cres G44	83	110	BS38
Currie St G20	90	106	BN23
Curtis Av G44	84	110	BU38
Curtis Av (Ruther.) G73	83	110	BS37
Curzon St G20	90	106	BN23
Custom Ho Quay G1	54/5	110	BS31
Cuthbertson St G42	82	109	BQ35
Cuthelton Dr G31	98	110	CA33
Cuthelton St G31	71	110	BZ33
Cuthelton Ter G31	71	110	BZ33
Cypress St G22	90	106	BT24
Cyril St, Pais. PA1	96	108	AW33
Daer Av, Renf. PA4	72	105	BA28
Dairsie Ct G44	101	109	BP41
Dairsie Gdns (Bishop.) G64	91	106	BZ21
Dairsie St G44	101	109	BP41
Daisy St G42	83	109	BR35
Dakota Way, Renf. PA4	93	104	AZ28
Dalbeth Pl G32	98	110	CB35
Dalbeth Rd G32	98	110	CB35
Dalcharn Path G34	95	107	CJ29
Dalcharn Pl G34	95	107	CJ29
Dalcross La G11	26/7	105	BL27
Dalcross St G11	26	105	BL27
Daldowie Av G32	99	111	CG34
Daldowie Rd (Udd.) G71	99	111	CJ35
Dale Path G40	68	110	BV33
Dale St G40	69	110	BV33
Daleview Av G12	89	105	BK23
Dale Way (Ruther.) G73	102	110	BX41
Dalfoil Ct, Pais. PA1	76	108	BB33
Dalgarroch Av, Clyde. G81	88	105	BA21
Dalgleish Av, Clyde. G81	87	104	AU15
Dalhousie Gdns (Bishop.) G64	91	106	BV19
Dalhousie La G3	29	106	BQ28
Dalhousie St G3	29	106	BQ28
Dalilea Dr G34	95	107	CM28
Dalilea Pl G34	95	107	CM28
Dalintober St G5	53	109	BQ32
Dalkeith Av G41	62	109	BK33
Dalkeith Av (Bishop.) G64	91	106	BX18
Dalkeith Rd (Bishop.) G64	91	106	BX17
Dalmahoy St G32	94	107	CA30
Dalmally St G20	17	106	BP26
Dalmarnock Br G40	85	110	BX35
Dalmarnock Br (Ruther.) G73	85	110	BX35
Dalmarnock Ct G40	70	110	BX34
Dalmarnock Rd G40	69	110	BV33
Dalmarnock Rd (Ruther.) G73	85	110	BX35
Dalmarnock Rd Trd Est G73	85	110	BX36
Dalmary Dr, Pais. PA1	96	108	AX31
Dalmellington Dr G53	78	108	BC37
Dalmellington Rd G53	78	108	BC37
Dalmeny Av (Giff.) G46	101	109	BL42
Dalmeny St G5	84	110	BU35
Dalmuir Ct, Clyde. G81	87	104	AU18
Dalnair St G3	27	105	BL28
Dalness Pas G32	98	110	CC33
Dalness St G32	98	110	CC34
Dalnottar Dr (Old Kil.) G60	86	104	AR16
Dalnottar Gdns (Old Kil.) G60	86	104	AR15
Dalnottar Hill Rd (Old Kil.) G60	86	104	AR15
Dalnottar Ter (Old Kil.) G60	86	104	AR15
Dalreoch Av (Baill.) G69	99	111	CL32
Dalreoch Path (Baill.) G69	99	111	CL31
Dalriada St G40	70	110	BY33
Dalry St G32	98	110	CD33
Dalserf Cres (Giff.) G46	100	109	BK44
Dalserf St G31	58	110	BX32
Dalsetter Av G15	88	105	BB19
Dalsetter Pl G15	88	105	BC19
Dalsholm Av G20	89	105	BK21
Dalsholm Ind Est G20	89	105	BK22
Dalsholm Rd G20	89	105	BK22
Dalswinton Path G34	95	107	CM29
Dalswinton Pl G34	95	107	CL29
Dalswinton St G34	95	107	CL29
Dalton Av, Clyde. G81	88	105	BA20
Dalton St G31	98	110	CA32
Dalveen St G32	98	110	CB32
Dalveen Way (Ruther.) G73	103	110	BY42
Dalziel Dr G41	63	109	BL34
Dalziel Quad G41	63	109	BL34
Dalziel Rd G52	74	105	BB29
Damshot Cres G53	77	109	BF36
Damshot Rd G53	79	109	BF38
Danby Rd (Baill.) G69	99	111	CH33
Danes Av G14	73	105	BE25
Danes Cres G14	88	105	BD24
Danes Dr G14	88	105	BD24
Danes La N G14	73	105	BE25
Danes La S G14	73	105	BE25
Dargarvel Av G41	62	109	BK33
Dargarvel Path G41	61	109	BJ34
Darleith St G32	98	110	CB32
Darnaway Av G33	94	107	CF27
Darnaway Dr G33	94	107	CF27
Darnaway St G33	94	107	CF27
Darnick St G21	22	106	BX26
Darnley Cres (Bishop.) G64	91	106	BV18
Darnley Gdns G41	82	109	BN35
Darnley Mains Rd G53	100	109	BE42
Darnley Path (Thornlie.) G46	100	109	BG40
Darnley Pl G41	82	109	BN35
Darnley Rd G41	82	109	BN35
Darnley St G41	82	109	BP35
Darroch Dr, Ersk. PA8	86	104	AP18
Dartford St G22	18	106	BR26
Darvel Cres, Pais. PA1	97	108	AZ32
Darvel St G53	78	108	BB39
Darwin Pl, Clyde. G81	86	104	AT17
Davaar Dr, Pais. PA2	96	108	AU38
Davaar Rd, Renf. PA4	93	104	AZ28
Davaar St G40	70	110	BX33
Dava St G51	37	105	BJ30
Daventry Dr G12	89	105	BJ24
David Pl (Baill.) G69	99	111	CH33
David Pl, Pais. PA3	93	104	AX30
Davidson Gdns G14	72	105	BG25
Davidson Pl G32	98	111	CE31
Davidson St G40	84	110	BW35
Davidson St, Clyde. G81	88	105	BA21
David St G40	57	110	BW32
David Way, Pais. PA3	93	104	AX30
Davieland Rd (Giff.) G46	100	109	BJ44
Davies Sq, Clyde. G81	87	104	AW15
Daviot St G51	75	109	BF31
Dawson Pl G4	18	106	BR26
Dawson Rd G4	18	106	BR26
Deaconsbank Av (Thornlie.) G46	100	109	BF44
Deaconsbank Cres (Thornlie.) G46	100	109	BF44
Deaconsbank Gdns (Thornlie.) G46	100	109	BG44
Deaconsbank Gro (Thornlie.) G46	100	109	BG44
Deaconsbank Pl (Thornlie.) G46	100	109	BF44
Deanfield Quad G52	74	108	BB31
Dean Pk Rd, Renf. PA4	72	105	BA27
Deanside La G4	43	106	BT30
Deanside Rd G52	74	105	BC29
Deanston Dr G41	81	109	BM37
Dean St, Clyde. G81	87	104	AY20
Deanwood Av G44	101	109	BP42
Deanwood Rd G44	101	109	BP42
Dechmont St G31	59	110	BY32
Dee Av, Renf. PA4	72	105	BA26
Deepdene Rd (Bears.) G61	88	105	BF18
Dee St G33	35	106	BZ28
Delhi Av, Clyde. G81	86	104	AS17
Delny Pl G33	95	107	CG30
Delvin Rd G44	101	109	BQ39
Denbeck St G32	98	110	CB32
Denbrae St G32	98	110	CB32
Dene Wk (Bishop.) G64	91	106	BY21
Denewood Av, Pais. PA2	96	108	AT37
Denham St G22	18	106	BR26
Denholm Dr (Giff.) G46	101	109	BL44
Denmark St G22	18	106	BS25
Denmilne Gdns G34	95	107	CL30
Denmilne Path G34	95	107	CL30
Denmilne Pl G34	95	107	CL30
Denmilne Rd (Baill.) G69	95	107	CM30
Denmilne St G34	95	107	CL30
Deramore Av (Giff.) G46	100	109	BJ46
Derby St G3	40	106	BN29
Derby Ter La G3	28	106	BN28
Derwent St G22	18	106	BR25
Despard Av G32	98	111	CF33
Despard Gdns G32	99	111	CG33
Deveron Av (Giff.) G46	101	109	BM43
Deveron Rd (Bears.) G61	88	105	BE19
Deveron St G33	35	106	BZ28
Devol Cres G53	79	108	BD37
Devon Gdns (Bishop.) G64	91	106	BV18
Devon Pl G41	66	109	BR33
Devonshire Gdns G12	14	105	BK25
Devonshire Gdns La G12	14	105	BK25
Devonshire Ter G12	14	105	BK25
Devonshire Ter La G12	14	105	BK25
Devon St G5	66	109	BR33
Diana Av G13	88	105	BD21
Dickens Av, Clyde. G81	87	104	AV17
Dick St G20	17	106	BP26
Dilwara Av G14	24	105	BG27
Dinard Dr (Giff.) G46	101	109	BL41
Dinart St G33	35	106	BZ28
Dinduff St G34	95	107	CL28
Dinmont Pl G41	82	109	BN36
Dinmont Rd G41	81	109	BM36
Dinwiddie St G21	34	106	BY27

Evanton Pl (Thornlie.) G46	100	109	BG42
Everard Ct G21	91	106	BU22
Everard Dr G21	91	106	BU23
Everard Pl G21	91	106	BU22
Everard Quad G21	91	106	BU23
Eversley St G32	98	110	CC34
Everton Rd G53	77	109	BE35
Ewing Pl G31	59	110	BY32
Ewing St (Ruther.) G73	84	110	BW38
Exchange Pl G1	42/3	106	BS30
Exeter Dr G11	25	105	BJ27
Exeter La G11	25	105	BJ27
Eynort St G22	90	106	BQ22
Eyrepoint Ct G33	94	107	CC29
Faifley Rd, Clyde. G81	87	104	AX15
Fairbairn Cres (Thornlie.) G46	100	109	BJ43
Fairbairn Path G40	69	110	BW33
Fairbairn St G40	69	110	BW33
Fairburn St G32	98	110	CB33
Fairfax Av G44	102	110	BS40
Fairfield Dr, Renf. PA4	93	104	AZ28
Fairfield Gdns G51	37	105	BH29
Fairfield Pl G51	37	105	BH29
Fairfield St G51	37	105	BH29
Fairhaven Rd G23	90	106	BN21
Fairhill Av G53	79	109	BE38
Fairholm St G32	98	110	CB33
Fairley St G51	50	109	BK31
Fairlie Pk Dr G11	25	105	BJ27
Fair Oaks (Clark.) G76	102	110	BU45
Fairway Av, Pais. PA2	96	108	AT37
Fairways Vw, Clyde. G81	87	104	AZ15
Falcon Ter G20	89	105	BL21
Falcon Ter La G20	89	105	BL21
Falfield St G5	65	109	BQ33
Falkland Cres (Bishop.) G64	91	106	BZ21
Falkland La G12	14	105	BK26
Falkland St G12	14	105	BK26
Falloch Rd G42	82	109	BQ38
Falloch Rd (Bears.) G61	88	105	BE19
Falside Av, Pais. PA2	96	108	AU36
Falside Rd G32	98	110	CD35
Falside Rd, Pais. PA2	96	108	AT36
Fara St G23	90	106	BP21
Farie St (Ruther.) G73	84	110	BV37
Farme Castle Ct (Ruther.) G73	85	110	BY36
Farme Castle Est G73	85	110	BY36
Farme Cross (Ruther.) G73	85	110	BX36
Farmeloan Ind Est G73	85	110	BX36
Farmeloan Rd (Ruther.) G73	85	110	BX37
Farmington Av G32	98	111	CF32
Farmington Gdns G32	98	111	CF32
Farmington Gate G32	98	111	CF33
Farmington Gro G32	98	111	CF32
Farm Rd G41	50	109	BK32
Farm Rd (Dalmuir), Clyde. G81	86	104	AT18
Farne Dr G44	101	109	BR41
Farnell St G4	30	106	BR27
Faskally Av (Bishop.) G64	91	106	BU18
Faskin Cres G53	78	108	BB38
Faskin Pl G53	78	108	BB38
Faskin Rd G53	78	108	BB38
Fasque Pl G15	88	105	BA17
Fastnet St G33	94	107	CC29
Fauldhouse St G5	67	110	BT34
Faulds (Baill.) G69	99	111	CL32
Faulds Gdns (Baill.) G69	99	111	CL32
Fauldshead Rd, Renf. PA4	93	104	AY26
Fauldspark Cres (Baill.) G69	99	111	CL31
Fearnmore Rd G20	89	105	BM22
Felton Pl G13	88	105	BB22
Fendoch St G32	98	110	CC33
Fenella St G32	98	110	CD32
Fennsbank Av (Ruther.) G73	103	110	BZ42
Fenwick Pl (Giff.) G46	100	109	BK44
Fenwick Rd (Giff.) G46	101	109	BL44
Fereneze Av (Clark.) G76	101	109	BL45
Fereneze Av, Renf. PA4	93	104	AW29
Fereneze Cres G13	88	105	BC22
Fereneze Dr, Pais. PA2	96	108	AS37
Fergus Ct G20	16	106	BN25
Fergus Dr G20	16	106	BN25
Fergus La G20	16	106	BP25
Ferguson Av, Renf. PA4	93	104	AZ26
Ferguson St, Renf. PA4	93	104	AZ25
Ferguston Rd (Bears.) G61	89	105	BF16
Fernan St G32	98	110	CB32
Fern Av (Bishop.) G64	91	106	BX21
Fern Av, Ersk. PA8	86	104	AR22
Fernbank St G21	91	106	BU24
Fernbank St G22	91	106	BU24
Fernbrae Av (Ruther.) G73	103	110	BY42
Fernbrae Way (Ruther.) G73	102	110	BX42
Fern Cotts G13	89	105	BH24
Ferncroft Dr G44	102	110	BT40
Ferndale Ct G23	89	105	BM21
Ferndale Dr G23	89	105	BM20
Ferndale Gdns G23	89	105	BM21
Ferndale Pl G23	89	105	BM21
Ferness Oval G21	91	106	BY22
Ferness Pl G21	91	106	BY22
Ferness Rd G21	91	106	BY23
Ferngrove Av G12	89	105	BJ24
Fernhill Rd (Ruther.) G73	102	110	BW41
Fernie Gdns G20	90	106	BN22
Fern La G13	89	105	BH24
Fernlea (Bears.) G61	89	105	BG18
Fernleigh Rd G43	101	109	BM40
Ferryden Ct G14	24	105	BG27
Ferryden St G14	24	105	BG28
Ferry Rd G3	26	105	BK28
Ferry Rd, Renf. PA4	93	104	AZ25
Fersit St G43	101	109	BL39
Fetlar Dr G44	102	110	BS40
Fettercairn Av G15	88	105	BA18
Fettercairn Gdns			
(Bishop.) G64	91	106	BY20
Fettes St G33	94	107	CB29
Fidra St G33	94	107	CB29
Fielden Pl G40	57	110	BW32
Fielden St G40	57	110	BW32
Fieldhead Dr G43	100	109	BJ40
Fieldhead Sq G43	100	109	BJ40
Fife Av G52	77	108	BD33
Fife Way (Bishop.) G64	91	106	BZ21
Fifth Av G12	89	105	BH25
Fifth Av (Stepps) G33	94	107	CD24
Fifth Av, Renf. PA4	93	104	AY27
Fifty Pitches Pl G51	75	105	BD30
Fifty Pitches Rd G51	75	105	BD30
Finart Dr, Pais. PA2	96	108	AX36
Finch Dr G13	88	105	BC21
Findhorn, Ersk. PA8	86	104	AQ19
Findhorn Av, Renf. PA4	72	105	BA26
Findhorn St G33	47	106	BZ29
Findochty, Ersk. PA8	86	104	AQ18
Findochty St G33	95	107	CG27
Fingal La G20	89	105	BL22
Fingal St G20	89	105	BM22
Fingask St G32	98	111	CE33
Finglas Av, Pais. PA2	96	108	AX36
Finhaven St G32	98	110	CA34
Finlarig St G34	95	107	CL30
Finlas St G22	19	106	BT25
Finlay Dr G31	45	106	BW30
Finnart Sq G40	69	110	BV34
Finnart St G40	69	110	BV34
Finnieston Quay G3	40	106	BN30
Finnieston Sq G3	40	106	BN29
Finnieston St G3	40	106	BN30
Finsbay St G51	75	109	BF31
Fintry Av, Pais. PA2	96	108	AU37
Fintry Cres (Bishop.) G64	91	106	BY21
Fintry Dr G44	83	110	BS38
Firdon Cres G15	88	105	BC20
Firhill Rd G20	17	106	BQ25
Firhill St G20	17	106	BQ25
Firpark Pl G31	44/5	106	BV29
Firpark Rd (Bishop.) G64	91	106	BX21
Firpark St G31	44	106	BV29
Firpark Ter G31	44	106	BV30
Fir Pl (Baill.) G69	99	111	CJ34
First Av (Millerston) G33	94	107	CD24
First Av G44	101	109	BP43
First Av (Bears.) G61	89	105	BJ18
First Av, Renf. PA4	93	104	AY27
First Gdns G41	61	109	BJ33
First Ter, Clyde. G81	87	104	AW18
Firwood Dr G44	102	110	BS39
Fisher Ct G31	45	106	BW30
Fisher Cres, Clyde. G81	87	104	AX15
Fishers Rd, Renf. PA4	93	104	AY23
Fishescoates Av (Ruther.) G73	103	110	BY40
Fishescoates Gdns			
(Ruther.) G73	103	110	BY40
Fitzalan Dr, Pais. PA3	96	108	AW31
Fitzalan Rd, Renf. PA4	93	104	AW28
Fitzroy La G3	40	106	BN29
Fitzroy Pl G3	28	106	BN28
Fleet Av, Renf. PA4	72	105	BA28
Fleet St G32	98	110	CD33
Fleming Av, Clyde. G81	87	104	AZ20
Fleming St G31	58	110	BX31
Fleming St, Pais. PA3	93	104	AU30
Flemington St G21	20	106	BV26
Fleurs Av G41	62	109	BK33
Fleurs Rd G41	62	109	BK33
Flora Gdns (Bishop.) G64	91	106	BY19
Florence Dr (Giff.) G46	101	109	BL43
Florence Gdns (Ruther.) G73	103	110	BY41
Florence St G5	55	110	BS32
Florida Av G42	83	109	BR37
Florida Cres G42	83	109	BR37
Florida Dr G42	82	109	BQ37
Florida Gdns (Baill.) G69	99	111	CJ32
Florida Sq G42	83	109	BR37
Florida St G42	83	109	BR37
Florish Rd, Ersk. PA8	86	104	AT21
Flures Av, Ersk. PA8	87	104	AU21
Flures Cres, Ersk. PA8	87	104	AU21
Flures Dr, Ersk. PA8	87	104	AU21
Flures Pl, Ersk. PA8	87	104	AU21
Fochabers Dr G52	75	109	BE31
Fogo Pl G20	89	105	BM23
Foinaven Dr (Thornlie.) G46	100	109	BH39
Foinaven Gdns (Thornlie.) G46	100	109	BJ39
Foinaven Way (Thornlie.) G46	100	109	BJ40
Forbes Dr G40	56	110	BV32
Forbes Pl, Pais. PA1	96	108	AU33
Forbes St G40	56	110	BV31
Fordneuk St G40	57	110	BW32
Fordoun St G34	95	107	CM29
Ford Rd G12	15	105	BM25
Fordyce St G11	26	105	BK27
Foremount Ter La G12	14	105	BK26
Foresthall Cres G21	21	106	BW26
Foresthall Dr G21	21	106	BW26
Forest Pl, Pais. PA2	96	108	AU35
Fore St G14	73	105	BE26
Forfar Av G52	77	108	BD33
Forfar Cres (Bishop.) G64	91	106	BY21
Forgan Gdns (Bishop.) G64	91	106	BZ21
Forge Pl G21	34	106	BX27
Forge Retail Pk G31	58	110	BX31
Forge Shop Cen, The G31	59	110	BY32
Forge St G21	34	106	BX27
Forge, The (Giff.) G46	101	109	BM42
Forglen St G34	95	107	CK28
Formby Dr G23	89	105	BM20
Forres Av (Giff.) G46	101	109	BL42
Forres Gate (Giff.) G46	101	109	BM43
Forres St G23	90	106	BN20
Forrester Ct (Bishop.) G64	91	106	BV21
Forrestfield St G21	33	106	BW28
Forrest St G40	57	110	BW32
Forteviot Av (Baill.) G69	99	111	CL32
Forteviot Pl (Baill.) G69	99	111	CL32
Forth Rd (Bears.) G61	88	105	BE19
Forth St G41	65	109	BP34
Forth St, Clyde. G81	87	104	AY20
Forties Ct (Thornlie.) G46	100	109	BJ40
Forties Cres (Thornlie.) G46	100	109	BJ40
Forties Gdns (Thornlie.) G46	100	109	BJ40
Forties Way (Thornlie.) G46	100	109	BJ40
Fortingall Av G12	89	105	BL23
Fortingall Pl G12	89	105	BL23
Fortrose St G11	26	105	BK27
Fotheringay La G41	81	109	BM35
Fotheringay Rd G41	81	109	BM35
Foulis La G13	89	105	BH23
Foulis St G13	89	105	BH23
Foundry St G21	21	106	BV25
Fountain Av (Inch.), Renf. PA4	92	104	AR25
Fountain Cres (Inch.),			
Renf. PA4	92	104	AR24
Fountain Dr (Inch.), Renf. PA4	92	104	AS24
Fountain St G31	56	110	BU31
Fountainwell Av G21	31	106	BT26
Fountainwell Dr G21	31	106	BT27
Fountainwell Pl G21	31	106	BT27
Fountainwell Rd G21	31	106	BT27
Fountainwell Sq G21	32	106	BU27
Fountainwell Ter G21	32	106	BU27
Fourth Av G33	94	107	CD24
Fourth Av, Renf. PA4	93	104	AY27
Fourth Gdns G41	61	109	BJ33
Foxbar Dr G13	88	105	BD23
Foxhills Pl G23	90	106	BN20
Foxley St G32	98	111	CE36
Fox St G1	54	109	BR31
Foyers Ter G21	21	106	BW25
Francis St G5	65	109	BQ33
Frankfield Rd G33	95	107	CG24
Frankfield St G33	35	106	BZ27
Frankfort St G41	82	109	BN36
Franklin St G40	68	110	BV34
Fraser Av (Ruther.) G73	85	110	BY38
Fraser St (Camb.) G72	103	110	CA39
Frazer St G40	57	110	BW32
Freeland Ct G53	79	109	BE39
Freeland Cres G53	79	108	BD39
Freeland Dr G53	79	108	BD39
Freeland Dr (Inch.), Renf. PA4	92	104	AS23
Freelands Ct (Old Kil.) G60	86	104	AS16
Freelands Cres (Old Kil.) G60	86	104	AS16
Freelands Pl (Old Kil.) G60	86	104	AS17
Freelands Rd (Old Kil.) G60	86	104	AS16
French St G40	68	110	BV34
French St, Clyde. G81	87	104	AU18
French St, Renf. PA4	93	104	AX27
Freuchie St G34	95	107	CK30
Friar Av (Bishop.) G64	91	106	BX17
Friarscourt Av G13	88	105	BE21
Friars Pl G13	88	105	BF21
Friarton Rd G43	101	109	BP39
Friendship Way, Renf. PA4	93	104	AZ28
Fruin Pl G22	19	106	BS25
Fruin Rd G15	88	105	BB20
Fruin St G22	19	106	BS25
Fulbar Av, Renf. PA4	93	104	AY25
Fulbar Ct, Renf. PA4	93	104	AZ25
Fulbar La, Renf. PA4	93	104	AZ25
Fulbar Rd G51	75	105	BE30
Fulbar St, Renf. PA4	93	104	AZ25
Fullarton Av G32	98	110	CC35
Fullarton Dr G32	98	110	CC36
Fullarton La G32	98	110	CC35
Fullarton Rd G32	98	110	CB37
Fullerton St, Pais. PA3	92	104	AT30
Fullerton Ter, Pais. PA3	93	104	AU30
Fulmar Ct (Bishop.) G64	91	106	BV21
Fulton St G13	88	105	BF22
Fulwood Av G13	88	105	BC22
Fulwood Pl G13	88	105	BB22
Fyvie Av G43	100	109	BK40
Gadie Av, Renf. PA4	72	105	BA27
Gadie St G33	47	106	BZ29
Gadloch St G22	90	106	BS23
Gadsburn Ct G21	91	106	BY23
Gadshill St G21	32	106	BV28
Gailes St G40	70	110	BX33
Gairbraid Av G20	89	105	BL23
Gairbraid Ct G20	89	105	BL23
Gairbraid Pl G20	89	105	BM23
Gala Av, Renf. PA4	72	105	BA27
Gala St G33	94	107	CA27
Galbraith Av G51	36	105	BG29
Galbraith Dr G51	75	105	BF29
Galbraith St G51	75	105	BF29
Galdenoch St G33	94	107	CD27
Gallan Av G23	90	106	BN20
Galloway Dr (Ruther.) G73	102	110	BX42
Galloway St G21	91	106	BV23
Gallowflat St (Ruther.) G73	85	110	BX37
Gallowgate G1	55	110	BT31
Gallowgate G4	56	110	BU31
Gallowgate G31	57	110	BW31
Gallowgate G40	56	110	BU31
Gallowhill Ct, Pais. PA3	93	104	AW29
Gallowhill Rd (Carm.) G76	102	110	BT45
Gallowhill Rd, Pais. PA3	96	108	AW31
Galston St G53	78	108	BB39
Gamrie Dr G53	78	108	BC38
Gamrie Gdns G53	78	108	BC38
Gamrie Rd G53	78	108	BC37
Gannochy Dr (Bishop.) G64	91	106	BY20
Gantock Cres G33	94	107	CD30
Gardenside Av G32	98	110	CD37
Gardenside Cres G32	98	110	CD37
Gardenside Gro G32	98	110	CD37
Gardenside Pl G32	98	110	CD37
Gardner St G11	26	105	BK27
Gardyne St G34	95	107	CJ27
Garfield St G31	57	110	BW31
Garforth Rd (Baill.) G69	99	111	CH33
Gargrave Av (Baill.) G69	99	111	CH33
Garion Dr G13	88	105	BD23
Garlieston Rd G33	99	111	CH31
Garmouth Ct G51	37	105	BJ29
Garmouth Gdns G51	37	105	BJ29
Garmouth St G51	37	105	BH29
Garnet Ct G4	29	106	BQ28
Garnethill St G3	29	106	BQ28
Garnet St G3	29	106	BQ28
Garnie Av, Ersk. PA8	86	104	AT20
Garnie Cres, Ersk. PA8	86	104	AT20
Garnieland Rd, Ersk. PA8	86	104	AT21
Garnie La, Ersk. PA8	86	104	AT21
Garnie Oval, Ersk. PA8	86	104	AT20
Garnie Pl, Ersk. PA8	86	104	AT20
Garnkirk La G33	95	107	CG24
Garnkirk St G21	32	106	BU28
Garnock St G21	33	106	BV27
Garrioch Cres G20	89	105	BM24
Garrioch Dr G20	89	105	BM24
Garrioch Gate G20	90	106	BN24
Garriochmill Rd G20	16	106	BN26
Garriochmill Way G20	16/7	106	BP26
Garrioch Quad G20	89	105	BM24
Garrioch Rd G20	15	105	BM25
Garrowhill Dr (Baill.) G69	99	111	CH33
Garry Av (Bears.) G61	89	105	BJ18
Garry St G44	82	109	BQ38
Garscadden Rd G15	88	105	BC20
Garscadden Rd S G13	88	105	BC21
Garscadden Vw, Clyde. G81	87	104	AZ18
Garscube Cross G4	30	106	BR27
Garscube Rd G4	17	106	BQ26
Garscube Rd G20	17	106	BQ26
Gartartan Rd, Pais. PA1	74	108	BB32
Gartcraig Path G33	94	107	CC28
Gartcraig Pl G33	94	107	CB28
Gartcraig Rd G33	94	107	CA29
Gartferry St G21	21	106	BV25
Garthamlock Rd G33	95	107	CG28
Garthland Dr G31	45	106	BW30
Garthland La, Pais. PA1	96	108	AV32
Garth St G1	43	106	BS30
Gartloch Cotts (Muir.) G69	95	107	CK24
Gartloch Rd G33	94	107	CB27
Gartloch Rd G34	94	107	CE28
Gartloch Rd (Gart.) G69	95	107	CL26
Gartly St G44	101	109	BP41
Gartmore Rd, Pais. PA1	96	108	AX33
Gartmore Ter (Camb.) G72	103	110	CA42
Gartness St G31	46	106	BX30
Gartocher Dr G32	98	111	CE32
Gartocher Rd G32	98	111	CE32
Gartocher Ter G32	98	111	CE32
Gartons Rd G21	91	106	BY24
Garturk St G42	83	109	BR35
Garvald Ct G40	84	110	BW35
Garvald St G40	70	110	BX34
Garve Av G44	101	109	BQ41
Garvel Cres G33	99	111	CG31
Garvel Rd G33	99	111	CG31
Garvock Dr G43	100	109	BJ40
Gaskin Path G33	95	107	CG24
Gask Pl G13	88	105	BB21
Gatehouse St G32	98	110	CD32
Gateside St G31	58	110	BX31
Gauldry Av G52	77	109	BE34
Gauze St, Pais. PA1	96	108	AU32
Gavins Rd, Clyde. G81	87	104	AX16
Gavinton St G44	101	109	BP40
Gear Ter G40	85	110	BX35
Geary St G23	89	105	BM20
Geddes Rd G21	91	106	BY22
Gelston St G32	98	110	CD33
General Terminus Quay G51	52	109	BP31
Gentle Row, Clyde. G81	87	104	AV15
George Av, Clyde. G81	87	104	AY18
George Ct, Pais. PA1	96	108	AT33
George Cres, Clyde. G81	87	104	AY18
George Gray St (Ruther.) G73	85	110	BY37
George La, Pais. PA1	96	108	AU33
George Mann Ter			
(Ruther.) G73	102	110	BW40
George Pl, Pais. PA1	96	108	AU33
George Reith Av G12	89	105	BH24
George Sq G2	42	106	BS30
George St G1	43	106	BS30
George St (Baill.) G69	99	111	CK33
George St, Pais. PA1	96	108	AT33
Gibson Rd, Renf. PA4	93	104	AX29
Gibson St G12	28	106	BN27
Gibson St G40	56	110	BU31
Giffnock Pk Av (Giff.) G46	101	109	BL41
Gifford Dr G52	74	108	BC32
Gilbertfield Path G33	94	107	CD27
Gilbertfield Pl G33	94	107	CD27
Gilbertfield St G33	94	107	CD27
Gilbert St G3	39	105	BL29
Gilhill St G20	89	105	BM22
Gilia St (Camb.) G72	103	110	CA39
Gillies La (Baill.) G69	99	111	CL33
Gilmerton St G32	98	110	CC33
Gilmour Av, Clyde. G81	87	104	AX16
Gilmour Cres (Ruther.) G73	84	110	BV37
Gilmour Pl G5	67	110	BS33
Gilmour St, Clyde. G81	87	104	AY17
Gilmour St, Pais. PA1	96	108	AU32
Girthon St G32	98	111	CE33
Girvan St G33	35	106	BZ28
Gladney Av G13	88	105	BA21
Gladsmuir Rd G52	75	108	BD31
Gladstone St G4	29	106	BQ27
Gladstone St, Clyde. G81	87	104	AV19
Glaive Rd G13	88	105	BF20
Glamis Gdns (Bishop.) G64	91	106	BX17
Glamis Rd G31	71	110	BZ33
Glanderston Ct G13	88	105	BC21
Glanderston Dr G13	88	105	BC22
Glasgow Airport (Abbots.),			
Pais. PA3	92	104	AS27
Glasgow Br G1	54	109	BR31
Glasgow Br G5	54	109	BR31
Glasgow Business Pk G69	95	107	CK30
Glasgow Cross G1	55	110	BT31
Glasgow Grn G1	55	110	BT32
Glasgow Grn G40	55	110	BT32
Glasgow Rd (Baill.) G69	99	111	CH33
Glasgow Rd (Camb.) G72	103	110	CA39
Glasgow Rd (Turnlaw) G72	103	110	CB44
Glasgow Rd (Ruther.) G73	84	110	BV35
Glasgow Rd (E.Kil.) G74	103	110	CC46
Glasgow Rd, Clyde. G81	87	104	AX21
Glasgow Rd (Hardgate),			
Clyde. G81	87	104	AY15
Glasgow Rd, Pais. PA1	96	108	AW32
Glasgow Rd, Renf. PA4	72	105	BA26
Glasgow St G12	16	106	BN26
Glassel Rd G34	95	107	CM28
Glasserton Pl G43	101	109	BP40
Glasserton Rd G43	101	109	BP40
Glassford St G1	43	106	BS30
Glebe Av (Carm.) G76	102	110	BT46
Glebe Ct G4	43	106	BT29
Glebe Pl (Camb.) G72	103	110	CD40
Glebe Pl (Ruther.) G73	84	110	BV37
Glebe St G4	31	106	BT28
Glebe St, Renf. PA4	93	104	AZ26
Gleddoch Rd G52	74	108	BA31
Glenacre Dr G45	102	110	BT42
Glenacre St G45	102	110	BT42
Glenacre Ter G45	102	110	BT42
Glen Alby Pl G53	100	109	BE41
Glenalmond Rd (Ruther.) G73	103	110	BZ42
Glenalmond St G32	98	110	CC33
Glenapp Av, Pais. PA2	96	108	AX36
Glenapp Rd, Pais. PA2	96	108	AX36
Glenapp St G41	65	109	BP34
Glenarklet Dr, Pais. PA2	96	108	AW36
Glenashdale Way, Pais. PA2	96	108	AW36
Glen Av G32	98	110	CD31
Glenavon Rd G20	89	105	BM22
Glenbank Ct (Thornlie.) G46	100	109	BH43
Glenbank Dr (Thornlie.) G46	100	109	BH43
Glenbarr St G21	32	106	BV28
Glenbervie Pl G23	90	106	BN20
Glenbrittle Dr, Pais. PA2	96	108	AW36
Glenbrittle Way, Pais. PA2	96	108	AW36
Glenbuck Av G33	94	107	CB23
Glenbuck Dr G33	94	107	CB23
Glenburn Av (Baill.) G69	99	111	CL32
Glenburn Av (Camb.) G72	103	110	BZ40
Glenburn Cres, Pais. PA2	96	108	AT37
Glenburn Gdns (Bishop.) G64	91	106	BV19
Glenburnie Pl G34	95	107	CJ30
Glenburn La G20	90	106	BN22
Glenburn Rd (Giff.) G46	100	109	BK44
Glenburn St G20	90	106	BN22
Glenburn Wk (Baill.) G69	99	111	CL32
Glencairn Ct, Pais. PA3	93	104	AX29
Glencairn Dr G41	81	109	BM35
Glencairn Dr (Ruther.) G73	84	110	BV37
Glencairn Gdns G41	82	109	BN35
Glencairn La G41	82	109	BP35
Glencairn Path G32	98	111	CE31
Glencairn Rd, Pais. PA3	93	104	AW29
Glencally Av, Pais. PA2	96	108	AX36
Glenclora Dr, Pais. PA2	96	108	AW36
Glencloy St G20	89	105	BL22
Glen Clunie Av G53	100	109	BE41
Glen Clunie Dr G53	100	109	BE41
Glen Clunie Pl G53	100	109	BE41
Glencoe Pl G13	89	105	BG22
Glencoe Rd (Ruther.) G73	103	110	BZ42
Glencoe St G13	89	105	BH22
Glen Cona Dr G53	79	109	BE40
Glencorse Rd, Pais. PA2	96	108	AS35
Glencorse St G32	94	107	CA30
Glen Cres G13	88	105	BA22
Glencroft Rd G44	102	110	BT40
Glendale Cres (Bishop.) G64	91	106	BY21
Glendale Dr (Bishop.) G64	91	106	BY21
Glendale Pl G31	58	110	BX31
Glendale Pl (Bishop.) G64	91	106	BY22
Glendale St G31	58	110	BX31
Glendaruel Av (Bears.) G61	89	105	BK17
Glendaruel Rd (Ruther.) G73	103	110	CA43
Glendarvel Gdns G22	19	106	BT25
Glendee Gdns, Renf. PA4	93	104	AZ27
Glendee Rd, Renf. PA4	93	104	AZ27
Glendevon Pl, Clyde. G81	87	104	AV18
Glendevon Sq G33	94	107	CD27
Glendinning Rd G13	88	105	BG20
Glendore St G14	24	105	BG27
Glenduffhill Rd (Baill.) G69	99	111	CH32
Gleneagles Dr (Bishop.) G64	91	106	BW18
Gleneagles Gdns			
(Bishop.) G64	91	106	BV18
Gleneagles La N G14	73	105	BE25
Gleneagles La S G14	73	105	BE25
Glenelg Quad G34	95	107	CM28
Glen Esk Cres G53	100	109	BE41
Glen Esk Dr G53	100	109	BE41
Glen Esk Pl G53	100	109	BE41
Glen Etive Pl (Ruther.) G73	103	110	CA43
Glenfarg Cres (Bears.) G61	89	105	BK17
Glenfarg Rd (Ruther.) G73	102	110	BX41
Glenfarg St G20	29	106	BQ27
Glenfield Av, Pais. PA2	96	108	AT38

Glenfield Rd, Pais. PA2 96 108 AS38
Glenfinnan Dr G20 89 105 BM23
Glenfinnan Dr (Bears.) G61 89 105 BK18
Glenfinnan Pl G20 89 105 BM23
Glenfinnan Rd G20 89 105 BM23
Glenfruin Cres, Pais. PA2 96 108 AX36
Glengarry Dr G52 75 109 BE32
Glengavel Cres G33 94 107 CB23
Glengyre St G34 95 107 CL28
Glenhead Cres G22 90 106 BS23
Glenhead Rd, Clyde. G81 87 104 AV16
Glenhead St G22 90 106 BS23
Gleniffer Av G13 88 105 BC23
Gleniffer Rd, Renf. PA4 93 104 AX29
Gleniffer Vw, Clyde. G81 87 104 AZ18
Glenisla St G31 71 110 BZ34
Glenkirk Dr G15 88 105 BD19
Glen La, Pais. PA3 96 108 AU32
Glenlee Cres G52 76 108 BB34
Glen Livet Pl G53 100 109 BE41
Glenlora Dr G53 78 108 BC38
Glenlora Ter G53 79 108 BD38
Glen Loy Pl G53 100 109 BE41
Glenluce Dr G32 98 111 CF34
Glenlui Av (Ruther.) G73 102 110 BX40
Glen Lyon Pl (Ruther.) G73 103 110 BY42
Glen Markie Dr G53 100 109 BE41
Glenmavis St G4 30 106 BR28
Glenmore Av G42 84 110 BU37
Glen Moriston Rd G53 100 109 BE41
Glenmoss Av, Ersk. PA8 86 104 AP20
Glenmuir Dr G53 79 108 BD40
Glen Nevis Pl (Ruther.) G73 103 110 BY43
Glen Ogle St G32 98 111 CF33
Glen Orchy Dr G53 100 109 BE41
Glen Orchy Pl G53 100 109 BF41
Glenpark Av (Thornlie.) G46 100 109 BJ43
Glenpark Gdns (Camb.) G72 98 110 CA38
Glenpark Rd G31 58 110 BX31
Glenpark St G31 58 110 BX31
Glenpark Ter (Camb.) G72 98 110 CA38
Glen Pl (Clark.) G76 101 109 BN46
Glenraith Path G33 94 107 CD26
Glenraith Rd G33 94 107 CD26
Glenraith Sq G33 94 107 CD26
Glenraith Wk G33 94 107 CD26
Glen Rd G32 94 107 CD30
Glen Rd (Old Kil.) G60 86 104 AR15
Glen Sax Dr, Renf. PA4 72 105 BA28
Glenshee Ct G31 71 110 BZ34
Glenshee Gdns G31 98 110 CA34
Glenshee St G31 71 110 BZ33
Glenshiel Av, Pais. PA2 96 108 AW36
Glenshira Av, Pais. PA2 96 108 AW36
Glenside Av G53 77 108 BD35
Glenside Dr (Ruther.) G73 103 110 BZ39
Glenspean Pl G43 81 109 BM38
Glenspean St G43 101 109 BL39
Glen St, Pais. PA3 96 108 AT32
Glentanar Pl G22 90 106 BS21
Glentanar Rd G22 90 106 BR21
Glentarbert Rd (Ruther.) G73 103 110 BZ42
Glentrool Gdns G22 19 106 BS25
Glenturret St G32 98 110 CC33
Glentyan Dr G53 78 108 BC38
Glentyan Ter G53 78 108 BC38
Glenville Av (Giff.) G46 100 109 BK42
Glenwood Business Pk G45 102 110 BU42
Glenwood Dr (Thornlie.) G46 100 109 BH43
Glenwood Path G45 102 110 BU42
Glenwood Pl G45 102 110 BU42
Gloucester Av (Ruther.) G73 103 110 BZ40
Gloucester Av (Clark.) G76 101 109 BM46
Gloucester St G5 53 109 BQ32
Gockston Rd, Pais. PA3 92 104 AT30
Gogar Pl G33 94 107 CA29
Gogar St G33 94 107 CA29
Goldberry Av G14 88 105 BD24
Golf Ct G44 101 109 BN43
Golf Dr G15 88 105 BB20
Golf Dr, Pais. PA1 97 108 AY33
Golfhill Dr G31 45 106 BW29
Golfhill Ter G31 44/5 106 BV29
Golf Rd (Ruther.) G73 102 110 BX41
Golf Rd (Clark.) G76 101 109 BM46
Golf Vw, Clyde. G81 87 104 AV17
Golspie St G51 37 105 BJ29
Goosedubbs G1 54/5 110 BS31
Gorbals Cross G5 54 110 BS32
Gorbals La G5 54 109 BR31
Gorbals St G5 66 109 BR33
Gordon Av G44 101 109 BN43
Gordon Av G52 74 105 BA29
Gordon Av (Baill.) G69 99 111 CH32
Gordon Dr G44 101 109 BN42
Gordon La G1 42 106 BR30
Gordon Rd G44 101 109 BN43
Gordon St G1 42 106 BR30
Gordon St, Pais. PA1 96 108 AU33
Gorebridge St G32 94 107 CA30
Gorget Av G13 88 105 BE20
Gorget Pl G13 88 105 BE20
Gorget Quad G13 88 105 BD20
Gorsewood (Bishop.) G64 91 106 BX20
Gorstan Pl G20 89 105 BL24
Gorstan St G23 89 105 BM21
Gosford La G14 72 105 BC25
Goudie St, Pais. PA3 92 104 AS30
Gough St G33 47 106 BZ29
Gourlay Path G21 19 106 BT26
Gourlay St G21 19 106 BT26
Gourock St G5 65 109 BQ33
Govan Cross G51 37 105 BJ29
Govan Cross Shop Cen G51 37 105 BJ29
Govanhill St G42 83 109 BR35
Govan Rd G51 51 109 BL31
Gowanlea Av G15 88 105 BC20
Gowanlea Dr (Giff.) G46 101 109 BM41
Gower La G51 51 109 BM32
Gower St G41 63 109 BL33
Gower St G51 63 109 BL33
Gower Ter G41 50 109 BL32
Goyle Av G15 88 105 BE18
Grace St G3 41 106 BP30
Graffham Av (Giff.) G46 101 109 BM42
Grafton Pl G1 43 106 BS29
Graham Av, Clyde. G81 87 104 AX18
Graham Sq G31 56 110 BV31
Grahamston Ct, Pais. PA2 97 108 AY37
Grahamston Cres, Pais. PA2 97 108 AY37
Grahamston Pl, Pais. PA2 97 108 AY37
Graham Ter (Bishop.) G64 91 106 BX22
Graignestock Pl G40 56 110 BU32
Graignestock St G40 56 110 BU32
Grainger Rd (Bishop.) G64 91 106 BZ20
Grampian Av, Pais. PA2 96 108 AT37
Grampian Cres G32 98 110 CD33
Grampian Pl G32 98 110 CD33
Grampian St G32 98 110 CD33
Granby La G12 15 105 BM26
Grandtully Dr G12 89 105 BL23
Grange Rd G42 81 109 BQ37
Gran St, Clyde. G81 88 105 BA21
Grantlea Gro G32 98 111 CF33
Grantlea Ter G32 98 111 CF33
Grantley Gdns G41 81 109 BM37
Grantley St G41 81 109 BM37
Granton St G5 84 110 BU35
Grants Av, Pais. PA2 96 108 AS36
Grant St G3 29 106 BP28
Grants Way, Pais. PA2 96 108 AS36
Granville St G3 41 106 BP29
Granville St, Clyde. G81 87 104 AX18
Gray Dr (Bears.) G61 89 105 BH18
Gray St G3 28 106 BN28
Great Dovehill G1 55 110 BT31
Great George St G12 15 105 BM26
Great Hamilton St, Pais. PA2 96 108 AU35
Great Kelvin La G12 28 106 BN27
Great Western Retail Pk G15 88 105 BB20
Great Western Rd G4 16 106 BN26
Great Western Rd G12 14 105 BK25
Great Western Rd G13 88 105 BB20
Great Western Rd G15 88 105 BB20
Great Western Ter G12 14 105 BL25
Great Western Ter La G12 14 105 BL25
Greenan Av G42 84 110 BU38
Greenbank Av (Giff.) G46 100 109 BJ46
Greenbank Dr, Pais. PA2 96 108 AT38
Greenbank St (Ruther.) G73 84 110 BW37
Greendyke St G1 55 110 BT31
Greenend Pl G32 94 107 CE30
Greenfield Av G32 94 107 CD30
Greenfield Pl G32 98 110 CD31
Greenfield Rd G32 94 107 CE30
Greenfield St G51 37 105 BH30
Greengairs Av G51 75 105 BF29
Greenhead Rd (Bears.) G61 89 105 BH17
Greenhead Rd (Inch.), Renf. PA4 86 104 AS22
Greenhead St G40 68 110 BU33
Greenhill (Bishop.) G64 91 106 BY21
Greenhill Av (Giff.) G46 100 109 BK44
Greenhill Business Pk, Pais. PA3 96 108 AS31
Greenhill Ct (Ruther.) G73 84 110 BW37
Greenhill Rd (Ruther.) G73 84 110 BW37
Greenhill Rd, Pais. PA3 96 108 AS31
Greenhill St (Ruther.) G73 84 110 BW38
Greenholm Av (Clark.) G76 101 109 BN46
Greenholme St G44 101 109 BQ39
Greenknowe Rd G43 100 109 BK39
Greenlaw Av, Pais. PA1 96 108 AW32
Greenlaw Cres, Pais. PA1 96 108 AW31
Greenlaw Dr, Pais. PA1 96 108 AW32
Greenlaw Rd G14 93 104 AZ23
Greenlea St G13 89 105 BG23
Greenlees Gdns (Camb.) G72 103 110 CB42
Greenlees Pk (Camb.) G72 103 110 CC42
Greenlees Rd (Camb.) G72 103 110 CC40
Greenloan Av G51 75 105 BF29
Greenlodge Ter G40 68 110 BU33
Greenmount G22 90 106 BQ22
Greenock Av G44 101 109 BR40
Greenock Rd, Pais. PA3 92 104 AS29
Greenock Rd (Inch.), Renf. PA4 92 104 AR23
Greenrig St G33 23 106 BZ26
Green Rd (Ruther.) G73 84 110 BW37
Greenshields Rd (Baill.) G69 99 111 CK32
Greenside (Clark.) G76 102 110 BT45
Greenside Cres G33 94 107 CA26
Greenside St G33 94 107 CA26
Green St G40 56 110 BU32
Green St, Clyde. G81 87 104 AW18
Green, The G40 56 110 BU32
Greentree Dr (Baill.) G69 99 111 CH34
Greenview St G43 81 109 BL37
Greenwood Dr (Bears.) G61 89 105 BJ17
Greenwood Quad, Clyde. G81 87 104 AZ20
Greenwood Rd (Clark.) G76 101 109 BM46
Greer Quad, Clyde. G81 87 104 AX17
Grenville Dr (Camb.) G72 103 110 CB41
Gretna St G40 70 110 BX33
Greyfriars Rd (Udd.) G71 99 111 CL37
Greyfriars St G32 94 107 CB30
Greystone Av (Ruther.) G73 103 110 BY39
Greywood St G13 89 105 BG22
Grier Path G31 59 110 BZ32
Grierson La G33 47 106 BZ29
Grierson St G33 47 106 BZ29
Grogarry Rd G15 88 105 BC17
Grosvenor Cres G12 15 105 BM26
Grosvenor Cres La G12 15 105 BM26
Grosvenor La G12 15 105 BM26
Grosvenor Ter G12 15 105 BM26
Groveburn Av (Thornlie.) G46 100 109 BJ41
Grovepark Ct G20 29 106 BQ27
Grovepark Gdns G20 29 106 BQ27
Grovepark Pl G20 17 106 BQ26
Grovepark St G20 17 106 BQ26
Grove, The (Giff.) G46 100 109 BK45
Grudie St G34 95 107 CJ29
Gryffe Av, Renf. PA4 93 104 AX24
Gryffe St G44 82 109 BQ38
Guildford St G33 94 107 CE28
Gullane St G11 26 105 BK27
Guthrie St G20 89 105 BM23

Haberlea Av G53 100 109 BE42
Haberlea Gdns G53 100 109 BE43
Haggs Rd G41 81 109 BL36
Haggswood Av G41 81 109 BL35
Haghill Rd G31 58 110 BY31
Haig Dr (Baill.) G69 99 111 CH33
Haig St G21 21 106 BW25
Hailes Av G32 98 111 CF32
Haining Rd, Renf. PA4 93 104 AY26
Haining, The, Renf. PA4 93 104 AZ27
Hairst St, Renf. PA4 93 104 AZ25
Halbeath Av G15 88 105 BB18
Halbert St G41 82 109 BN36
Haldane La G14 73 105 BF26
Haldane St G14 73 105 BF26
Halgreen Av G15 88 105 BA19
Halifax Way, Renf. PA4 93 104 AY28
Hallbrae St G33 94 107 CA27
Halley Dr G13 88 105 BA23
Halley Pl G13 88 105 BA23
Halley Sq G13 88 105 BA23
Halley St G13 88 105 BA22
Hallforest St G33 94 107 CD27
Hallhill Cres G33 99 111 CG31
Hallhill Rd G32 99 111 CE31
Hallhill Rd G33 99 111 CG31
Halliburton Cres G34 95 107 CJ30
Halliburton Rd G34 95 107 CH30
Halliburton Ter G34 95 107 CJ30
Hallidale Cres, Renf. PA4 72 105 BB27
Hallrule Dr G52 75 109 BE32
Hallside Pl G5 67 110 BS33
Hall St, Clyde. G81 87 104 AW20
Hallydown Dr G13 88 105 BE24
Halton Gdns (Baill.) G69 99 111 CH33
Hamilton Av G41 63 109 BM34
Hamilton Ct, Pais. PA2 96 108 AU35
Hamilton Cres, Renf. PA4 93 104 AZ24
Hamilton Dr G12 16 106 BN26
Hamilton Dr (Giff.) G46 101 109 BM43
Hamilton Dr (Camb.) G72 103 110 CB40
Hamilton Dr, Ersk. PA8 86 104 AP18
Hamiltonhill Cres G22 18 106 BR25
Hamiltonhill Rd G22 18 106 BR26
Hamilton Pk Av G12 16 106 BN26
Hamilton Rd G32 98 111 CF35
Hamilton Rd (Udd.) G71 99 111 CJ35
Hamilton Rd (Camb.) G72 103 110 CD40
Hamilton Rd (Ruther.) G73 85 110 BX37
Hamilton St G42 83 110 BS36
Hamilton St, Clyde. G81 87 104 AZ22
Hamilton St, Pais. PA3 96 108 AV31
Hamilton Ter, Clyde. G81 87 104 AZ22
Hampden Dr G42 83 109 BR38
Hampden La G42 83 109 BR37
Hampden Ter G42 83 109 BR37
Hampden Way, Renf. PA4 93 104 AZ28
Hangingshaw Pl G42 83 110 BS37
Hanover Cl G42 82 109 BQ37
Hanover Ct, Pais. PA1 96 108 AW32
Hanover Gdns, Pais. PA1 96 108 AS33
Hanover St G1 42 106 BS30
Hanson St G31 45 106 BV29
Hapland Av G53 77 109 BE35
Hapland Rd G53 77 109 BE35
Harbour La, Pais. PA3 96 108 AU32
Harbour Rd, Pais. PA3 96 108 AU31
Harburn Pl G23 90 106 BN19
Harbury Pl G14 88 105 BB23
Harcourt Dr G31 46 106 BX29
Hardgate Dr G51 75 105 BE29
Hardgate Gdns G51 75 105 BE29
Hardgate Path G51 75 105 BE29
Hardgate Pl G51 75 105 BE29
Hardgate Rd G51 75 105 BE29
Hardie Av (Ruther.) G73 85 110 BY37
Hardridge Pl G52 80 109 BG35
Hardridge Rd G52 77 109 BF35
Harefield Dr G14 88 105 BD24
Harelaw Av G44 101 109 BP41
Harelaw Cres, Pais. PA2 96 108 AS38
Harhill St G51 37 105 BH30
Harland Cotts G14 73 105 BE26
Harland St G14 73 105 BE26
Harlaw Gdns (Bishop.) G64 91 106 BZ19
Harley St G51 51 109 BL32
Harmetray St G22 90 106 BT23
Harmony Ct G52 37 105 BJ30
Harmony Pl G51 37 105 BJ30
Harmony Row G51 37 105 BJ30
Harmony Sq G51 37 105 BJ30
Harmsworth St G11 24 105 BG27
Harport St (Thornlie.) G46 100 109 BG40
Harriet Pl G43 100 109 BK39
Harriet St (Ruther.) G73 84 110 BW37
Harris Cres (Old Kil.) G60 86 104 AR16
Harris Dr (Old Kil.) G60 86 104 AR16
Harris Gdns (Old Kil.) G60 86 104 AS16
Harrison Dr G51 50 109 BK31
Harris Rd G23 89 105 BM20
Harris Rd (Old Kil.) G60 86 104 AR16
Harrow Ct G15 88 105 BB18
Harrow Pl G15 88 105 BB18
Hartfield Ter, Pais. PA2 96 108 AV35
Hartlaw Cres G52 74 108 BC31
Hartree Av G13 88 105 BA21
Hartstone Pl G53 79 108 BD38
Hartstone Rd G53 79 108 BD38
Hartstone Ter G53 79 108 BD38
Hart St G31 98 110 CA32
Harvey St G4 30 106 BS27
Harvie St G51 51 109 BM31
Harwood St G32 47 110 CA30
Hastie St G3 27 105 BM28
Hatfield Dr G12 89 105 BH24
Hathaway Dr (Giff.) G46 100 109 BK43
Hathaway La G20 90 106 BN24
Hathaway St G20 90 106 BN24
Hathersage Av (Baill.) G69 99 111 CK32
Hathersage Dr (Baill.) G69 99 111 CK32
Hathersage Gdns (Baill.) G69 99 111 CK32
Hatton Dr G52 76 108 BC33
Hatton Gdns G52 76 108 BC33
Hatton Path G52 76 108 BC33
Haughburn Pl G53 79 108 BD38
Haughburn Rd G53 79 108 BD38
Haughburn Ter G53 79 109 BE38
Haugh Rd G3 39 105 BM29
Havelock La G11 27 105 BL27
Havelock St G11 26 105 BL27
Hawick St G13 88 105 BA22
Hawkhead Av, Pais. PA2 96 108 AX35
Hawkhead Rd, Pais. PA1 96 108 AX33
Hawkhead Rd, Pais. PA2 97 108 AY36
Hawthorn Av (Bishop.) G64 91 106 BX21
Hawthorn Av, Ersk. PA8 87 104 AU21
Hawthorn Cres, Ersk. PA8 87 104 AU21
Hawthornden Gdns G23 90 106 BN19
Hawthorn Quad G22 90 106 BS24
Hawthorn Rd, Ersk. PA8 87 104 AU21
Hawthorn St G22 90 106 BS24
Hawthorn St, Clyde. G81 87 104 AW17
Hawthorn Wk (Camb.) G72 103 110 BZ40
Hawthorn Way, Ersk. PA8 87 104 AU21
Hayburn Ct G11 26 105 BK27
Hayburn Cres G11 13 105 BJ26
Hayburn Gate G11 26 105 BK27
Hayburn La G11 13 105 BJ26
Hayburn St G11 26 105 BK28
Hayfield St G5 67 110 BT33
Haylynn St G14 24 105 BG27
Haymarket St G32 94 107 CA30
Hayston Cres G22 90 106 BR24
Hayston St G22 90 106 BR24
Haywood St G22 90 106 BR23
Hazel Av G44 101 109 BP41
Hazel Av La G44 101 109 BP41
Hazel Dene (Bishop.) G64 91 106 BX20
Hazelden Gdns G44 101 109 BN41
Hazellea Dr (Giff.) G46 101 109 BM41
Hazelwood Gdns (Ruther.) G73 103 110 BY41
Hazelwood Rd G41 62 109 BL33
Hazlitt Gdns G20 90 106 BQ23
Hazlitt Pl G20 90 106 BR23
Hazlitt St G20 90 106 BR23
Heath Av (Bishop.) G64 91 106 BX21
Heathcot Av G15 88 105 BA19
Heathcot Pl G15 87 104 AZ19
Heatherbrae (Bishop.) G64 91 106 BU20
Heathfield St G33 94 107 CE29
Heathside Rd (Giff.) G46 101 109 BM42
Heathwood Dr (Thornlie.) G46 100 109 BJ42
Hecla Av G15 88 105 BB18
Hecla Pl G15 88 105 BB18
Hecla Sq G15 88 105 BB19
Hector Rd G41 81 109 BM37
Heddle Pl G2 41 106 BQ30
Helena Pl (Clark.) G76 101 109 BN45
Helena Ter, Clyde. G81 87 104 AW15
Helensburgh Dr G13 88 105 BF23
Helen St G51 37 105 BJ30
Helen St G52 49 109 BH32
Helenvale Ct G31 71 110 BZ33
Helenvale St G31 71 110 BY33
Hemlock St G13 89 105 BG22
Henderland Dr (Bears.) G61 89 105 BG19
Henderland Rd (Bears.) G61 89 105 BG19
Henderson St G20 17 106 BP26
Henderson St, Clyde. G81 88 105 BA21
Henderson St, Pais. PA1 96 108 AT32
Henrietta St G14 73 105 BE26
Hepburn Rd G52 75 105 BD30
Herald Av G13 88 105 BF20
Herald Way, Renf. PA4 93 104 AY28
Herbert St G20 17 106 BP26
Hercules Way, Renf. PA4 93 104 AZ28
Heriot Cres (Bishop.) G64 91 106 BW18
Herma St G23 90 106 BN21
Hermiston Av G32 98 110 CD31
Hermiston Pl G32 98 111 CE31
Hermiston Rd G32 94 107 CD30
Hermitage Av G13 88 105 BE22
Heron Ct, Clyde. G81 87 104 AX16
Heron St G40 69 110 BV33
Heron Way, Renf. PA4 93 104 AY28
Herries Rd G41 81 109 BL35
Herriet St G41 64 109 BP34
Hertford Av G12 89 105 BK23
Hexham Gdns G41 81 109 BM36
Hickman St G42 83 110 BS35
Hickman Ter G42 83 110 BS35
Hickory St G22 91 106 BU24
High Beeches (Carm.) G76 102 110 BU45
Highburgh Dr (Ruther.) G73 103 110 BX40
Highburgh Rd G12 14 105 BL26
High Calside, Pais. PA2 96 108 AT34
High Craighall Rd G4 30 106 BR27
Highcroft Av G44 102 110 BT40
Highfield Av, Pais. PA2 96 108 AS38
Highfield Cres, Pais. PA2 96 108 AT38
Highfield Dr G12 89 105 BK23
Highfield Dr (Ruther.) G73 103 110 BY42
Highfield Dr (Clark.) G76 101 109 BM46
Highfield Pl G12 89 105 BK23
Highland La G51 38 105 BL29
High Parksail, Ersk. PA8 86 104 AS21
High Rd (Castlehead), Pais. PA2 96 108 AS34
High St G1 55 110 BT31
High St G4 55 110 BT31
High St (Ruther.) G73 84 110 BW37
High St, Pais. PA1 96 108 AT33
High St, Renf. PA4 93 104 AZ25
Hilary Dr (Baill.) G69 99 111 CH32
Hilda Cres G33 94 107 CA25
Hillary Av (Ruther.) G73 103 110 BZ39
Hillcrest (Carm.) G76 102 110 BT45
Hillcrest Av G32 98 110 CD37
Hillcrest Av G44 101 109 BN41
Hillcrest Rd G32 98 111 CE36
Hillcrest Rd (Bears.) G61 89 105 BH17
Hillcroft Ter (Bishop.) G64 91 106 BV21
Hillend Cres, Clyde. G81 87 104 AV15
Hillend Rd G22 90 106 BQ22
Hillend Rd (Ruther.) G73 102 110 BX40
Hillfoot Av (Ruther.) G73 84 110 BW38
Hillfoot St G31 45 106 BW30
Hillhead Av (Ruther.) G73 102 110 BX41
Hillhead Pl G12 28 106 BN27
Hillhead Pl (Ruther.) G73 102 110 BX41
Hillhead Rd G21 91 106 BZ22
Hillhead St G12 27 105 BM27
Hillhouse St G21 21 106 BW25
Hillington Gdns G52 77 109 BE33
Hillington Ind Est G52 74 105 BB29
Hillington Pk Circ G52 75 109 BE32
Hillington Quad G52 74 108 BC32
Hillington Rd G52 72 105 BB27
Hillington Rd S G52 74 108 BC32
Hillington Shop Cen (Hillington Ind. Est.) G52 74 105 BB29
Hillington Ter G52 74 108 BC32
Hillkirk Pl G21 20 106 BU25
Hillkirk St G21 20 106 BV25
Hillkirk St La G21 20/1 106 BV25
Hillpark Av, Pais. PA2 96 108 AT36
Hillpark Dr G43 101 109 BL39
Hill Path G52 74 108 BC32
Hill Pl G52 74 108 BC32
Hillsborough Rd (Baill.) G69 99 111 CH32
Hillsborough Ter G12 16 106 BN26
Hillside Av (Clark.) G76 101 109 BM46
Hillside Ct (Thornlie.) G46 100 109 BH42
Hillside Dr (Bishop.) G64 91 106 BW19
Hillside Gdns La G11 14 105 BK26
Hillside Pk, Clyde. G81 87 104 AX15
Hillside Quad G43 100 109 BK40
Hillside Rd G43 100 109 BK40
Hillside Rd, Pais. PA2 96 108 AW35
Hillside Ter (Old Kil.) G60 86 104 AR15
Hill St G3 29 106 BQ28
Hill St G14 88 105 BC24
Hillswick Cres G22 90 106 BR21
Hillview Dr (Clark.) G76 101 109 BM46
Hillview Gdns (Bishop.) G64 91 106 BZ21
Hillview Pl (Clark.) G76 101 109 BN46
Hillview St G32 98 110 CB32
Hillview Ter (Old Kil.) G60 86 104 AR15
Hilton Gdns G13 89 105 BH22
Hilton Pk (Bishop.) G64 91 106 BV17
Hilton Rd (Bishop.) G64 91 106 BV18
Hilton Ter G13 89 105 BG22
Hilton Ter (Bishop.) G64 91 106 BV17
Hilton Ter (Camb.) G72 103 110 CA42
Hinshaw St G20 17 106 BQ26
Hinshelwood Dr G51 49 109 BJ31
Hobart Cres, Clyde. G81 86 104 AT16
Hobart St G22 18 106 BR25
Hobden St G21 21 106 BW26
Hoddam Av G45 102 110 BV42
Hoddam Ter G45 102 110 BW42
Hogan Ct, Clyde. G81 87 104 AV15
Hogarth Av G32 47 106 BZ30
Hogarth Cres G32 47 106 BZ30
Hogarth Dr G32 47 106 BZ30
Hogarth Gdns G32 47 106 BZ30
Hogganfield St G33 35 106 BZ27
Holeburn La G43 101 109 BL39
Holeburn Rd G43 101 109 BL39
Holehouse Dr G13 88 105 BC23
Holland St G2 41 106 BQ29
Hollinwell Rd G23 89 105 BM21
Hollowglen Rd G32 98 110 CD31
Hollows, The (Giff.) G46 100 109 BK44
Hollybank Pl (Camb.) G72 103 110 CD41
Hollybank St G21 33 106 BW28
Hollybrook Pl G42 83 110 BS35
Hollybrook St G42 83 110 BS35
Hollybush Rd G52 74 108 BB32
Holly Dr G21 21 106 BW26
Hollymount (Bears.) G61 89 105 BH19
Holly St, Clyde. G81 87 104 AW17
Holm Av, Pais. PA2 96 108 AV35
Holmbank Av G41 82 109 BN38
Holmbyre Ct G45 101 109 BR44
Holmbyre Rd G45 102 110 BS44
Holmbyre Ter G45 102 110 BS43
Holmes Av, Renf. PA4 93 104 AY28
Holmfauldhead Dr G51 36 105 BG29
Holmfauldhead Pl G51 24 105 BG28
Holmfauld Rd G51 24 105 BG28
Holmhead Cres G44 101 109 BQ39
Holmhead Pl G44 101 109 BQ39
Holmhead Rd G44 101 109 BQ40
Holmhill Av (Camb.) G72 103 110 CC41

Holmhills Dr (Camb.) G72 103 110 CB42
Holmhills Gdns (Camb.) G72 103 110 CB41
Holmhills Gro (Camb.) G72 103 110 CB41
Holmhills Pl (Camb.) G72 103 110 CB41
Holmhills Rd (Camb.) G72 103 110 CB42
Holmhills Ter (Camb.) G72 103 110 CB41
Holmlea Rd G44 82 109 BQ38
Holms Cres, Ersk. PA8 86 104 AP19
Holm St G2 41 106 BQ30
Holmwood Gro G44 101 109 BQ41
Holyrood Cres G20 28 106 BP27
Holyrood Quad G20 29 106 BP27
Holywell St G31 58 110 BX32
Honeybog Rd G52 74 105 BA30
Hood St, Clyde. G81 87 104 AY19
Hopefield Av G12 89 105 BL24
Hopehill Gdns G20 17 106 BQ26
Hopehill Rd G20 17 106 BQ26
Hopeman, Ersk. PA8 86 104 AQ18
Hopeman Av (Thornlie.) G46 100 109 BG41
Hopeman Dr (Thornlie.) G46 100 109 BG41
Hopeman Path (Thornlie.) G46 100 109 BG40
Hopeman Rd (Thornlie.) G46 100 109 BG41
Hopeman St (Thornlie.) G46 100 109 BG41
Hope St G2 42 106 BR30
Hopetoun Pl G23 90 106 BN19
Hopetoun Ter G21 21 106 BW26
Hornbeam Dr, Clyde. G81 87 104 AV17
Hornbean Ct (Bishop.) G64 91 106 BW17
Horndean Cres G33 94 107 CF29
Horne St G22 91 106 BU24
Hornshill St G21 21 106 BW25
Horsburgh St G33 94 107 CF27
Horselethill Rd G12 15 105 BL25
Horseshoe La (Bears.) G61 89 105 BG17
Hospital St G5 54 110 BS32
Hotspur St G20 90 106 BN24
Houldsworth La G3 40 106 BN29
Houldsworth St G3 40 106 BN29
Househillmuir Cres G53 79 109 BE39
Househillmuir La G53 79 109 BE38
Househillmuir Pl G53 79 109 BE38
Househillmuir Rd G53 79 108 BD39
Househillwood Cres G53 79 108 BD38
Househillwood Rd G53 79 108 BD39
Housel Av G13 88 105 BD23
Houston Pl G5 52 109 BP31
Houston Rd (Inch.), Renf. PA4 92 104 AP25
Houston St G5 52 109 BP32
Houston St, Renf. PA4 93 104 AZ25
Howard St G1 54 109 BR31
Howard St, Pais. PA1 96 108 AW32
Howat St G51 37 105 BJ29
Howcraigs Ct, Clyde. G81 87 104 AZ22
Howford Rd G52 77 108 BD33
Howgate Av G15 88 105 BB18
Howie Bldgs (Clark.) G76 101 109 BN45
Howieshill Av (Camb.) G72 103 110 CD40
Howth Dr G13 89 105 BH21
Howth Ter G13 89 105 BH21
Hoylake Pl G23 90 106 BN20
Hughenden Dr G12 14 105 BK25
Hughenden Gdns G12 13 105 BJ25
Hughenden La G12 14 105 BK25
Hughenden Rd G12 14 105 BK25
Hughenden Ter G12 14 105 BK25
Hugo St G20 90 106 BP24
Hume St, Clyde. G81 87 104 AX20
Hunterfield Dr (Camb.) G72 103 110 CA40
Hunterhill Av, Pais. PA2 96 108 AV34
Hunterhill Rd, Pais. PA2 96 108 AV34
Hunter Rd (Ruther.) G73 85 110 BY36
Hunters Hill Ct G21 91 106 BV23
Huntershill Rd (Bishop.) G64 91 106 BW21
Huntershill St G21 91 106 BV23
Huntershill Way (Bishop.) G64 91 106 BW21
Hunter St G4 56 110 BU31
Hunter St, Pais. PA1 96 108 AU32
Huntingdon Rd G21 32 106 BU27
Huntingdon Sq G21 32 106 BU27
Huntingtower Rd (Baill.) G69 99 111 CH33
Huntley Rd G52 74 105 BB29
Huntly Av (Giff.) G46 101 109 BM43
Huntly Ct (Bishop.) G64 91 106 BW21
Huntly Dr (Camb.) G72 103 110 CD41
Huntly Gdns G12 15 105 BL26
Huntly Rd G12 15 105 BL26
Huntly Ter, Pais. PA2 96 108 AW36
Hurlet Rd G53 97 108 AY37
Hurlet Rd, Pais. PA2 97 108 AY37
Hurlford Av G13 88 105 BB22
Hurly Hawkin (Bishop.) G64 91 106 BZ21
Hutcheson Rd (Thornlie.) G46 100 109 BJ43
Hutcheson St G1 43 106 BS30
Hutchinsontown Ct G5 67 110 BS33
Hutchison Ct (Giff.) G46 101 109 BL44
Hutchison Dr (Bears.) G61 89 105 BJ19
Hutton G12 89 105 BJ23
Hutton Dr G51 36 105 BG29
Huxley St G20 90 106 BP23
Hydepark St G3 40 106 BP30
Hyndal Av G53 77 108 BD36
Hyndland Av G11 26 105 BK27
Hyndland Rd G12 14 105 BK25
Hyndland St G11 26 105 BL27
Hyndlee Dr G52 75 109 BE32
Hyslop Pl, Clyde. G81 87 104 AW18

Ian Smith Ct, Clyde. G81 87 104 AZ21
Ibroxholm Av G51 50 109 BK32
Ibroxholm Oval G51 50 109 BK32
Ibroxholm Pl G51 50 109 BK32
Ibrox Ind Est G51 50 109 BL31
Ibrox St G51 50 109 BL31
Ibrox Ter G51 50 109 BK31
Ibrox Ter La G51 50 109 BK31
Ilay Av (Bears.) G61 89 105 BH21
Ilay Ct (Bears.) G61 89 105 BJ21
Ilay Rd (Bears.) G61 89 105 BJ21
Inchbrae Rd G52 77 109 BE33
Inchcruin Pl G15 88 105 BA17
Inchfad Dr G15 88 105 BA18
Inchfad Pl G15 88 105 BA18
Inchholm La G11 24 105 BG27
Inchholm St G11 24 105 BG27
Inchinnan Business Pk (Inch.), Renf. PA4 92 104 AS25
Inchinnan Dr (Inch.), Renf. PA4 92 104 AS25
Inchinnan Ind Est (Inch.), Renf. PA4 92 104 AR24
Inchinnan Rd, Pais. PA3 93 104 AU30
Inchinnan Rd, Renf. PA4 93 104 AX25
Inchkeith Pl G32 94 107 CD30
Inchlaggan Pl G15 88 105 BA17
Inchlee St G14 24 105 BG27
Inch Meadow, Ersk. PA8 86 104 AT21
Inchmoan Pl G15 88 105 BB17
Inchmurrin Dr (Ruther.) G73 103 110 BZ43
Inchmurrin Gdns (Ruther.) G73 103 110 BZ43
Inchmurrin Pl (Ruther.) G73 103 110 BZ43
Inchoch St G33 95 107 CG27
Inchrory Pl G15 88 105 BA17
Incle St, Pais. PA1 96 108 AV32
India Dr (Inch.), Renf. PA4 92 104 AS23
India St G2 41 106 BQ29
Inga St G20 90 106 BN22
Ingerbreck Av (Ruther.) G73 103 110 BZ41
Ingleby Dr G31 45 106 BW30
Inglefield St G42 66 109 BR34
Ingleneuk Av G33 94 107 CD24
Inglestone Av (Thornlie.) G46 100 109 BJ43
Inglis St G31 57 110 BW31
Ingram St G1 43 106 BS30
Inishail Rd G33 94 107 CE28
Inkerman Rd G52 74 108 BB32
Innerwick Dr G52 75 108 BD32
Inveraray Dr (Bishop.) G64 91 106 BX17
Inverbervie, Ersk. PA8 86 104 AQ19
Invercanny Dr G15 88 105 BC18
Invercanny Pl G15 88 105 BC17
Inverclyde Gdns (Ruther.) G73 103 110 BZ42
Inveresk Quad G32 98 110 CC31
Inveresk St G32 98 110 CC31
Inverewe Av (Thornlie.) G46 100 109 BF42
Inverewe Dr (Thornlie.) G46 100 109 BF43
Inverewe Gdns (Thornlie.) G46 100 109 BF43
Inverewe Pl (Thornlie.) G46 100 109 BF42
Invergarry Av (Thornlie.) G46 100 109 BF44
Invergarry Ct (Thornlie.) G46 100 109 BG44
Invergarry Dr (Thornlie.) G46 100 109 BF43
Invergarry Gdns (Thornlie.) G46 100 109 BF44
Invergarry Gro (Thornlie.) G46 100 109 BF43
Invergarry Pl (Thornlie.) G46 100 109 BG43
Invergarry Quad (Thornlie.) G46 100 109 BG43
Invergarry Vw (Thornlie.) G46 100 109 BG43
Inverglas Av, Renf. PA4 72 105 BB28
Invergordon Av G43 82 109 BP38
Invergyle Dr G52 75 108 BD32
Inverlair Av G43 101 109 BP39
Inverlair Av G44 101 109 BP39
Inverleith St G32 59 110 BZ31
Inverlochy St G33 94 107 CF28
Inverness St G51 75 109 BF31
Inveroran Dr (Bears.) G61 89 105 BK17
Inver Rd G33 95 107 CG30
Invershiel Rd G23 89 105 BM20
Invershin Dr G20 89 105 BM24
Inverurie St G21 19 106 BT26
Inzievar Ter G32 98 110 CD36
Iona Cres (Old Kil.) G60 86 104 AT16
Iona Dr (Old Kil.) G60 86 104 AS16
Iona Dr, Pais. PA2 96 108 AT38
Iona Gdns (Old Kil.) G60 86 104 AS16
Iona Pl (Old Kil.) G60 86 104 AS16
Iona Rd (Ruther.) G73 103 110 CA42
Iona Rd, Renf. PA4 93 104 AY28
Iona St G51 38 105 BK30
Iona Way (Stepps) G33 94 107 CF25
Iris Av G45 102 110 BW42
Irongray St G31 47 106 BY30
Irvine St G40 70 110 BX34
Irving Av, Clyde. G81 87 104 AX15
Irving Ct, Clyde. G81 87 104 AX15
Irving Quad, Clyde. G81 87 104 AX15
Iser La G41 82 109 BP37
Islay Av (Ruther.) G73 103 110 CA42
Islay Cres (Old Kil.) G60 86 104 AS16
Islay Cres, Pais. PA2 96 108 AT38
Islay Dr (Old Kil.) G60 86 104 AS16
Ivanhoe Rd G13 88 105 BF21

Jagger Gdns (Baill.) G69 99 111 CH33
Jamaica St G1 42 106 BR30
James Dunlop Gdns (Bishop.) G64 91 106 BX22
James Gray St G41 82 109 BN36
James Morrison St G1 55 110 BT31
James Nisbet St G21 44 106 BU29
James St G40 68 110 BU33
James Watt La G2 41 106 BQ30
James Watt St G2 41 106 BQ30
Jamieson Ct G42 83 109 BR35
Jamieson Path G42 83 109 BR35
Jamieson St G42 83 109 BR35
Janefield St G31 58 110 BX32
Jane Rae Gdns, Clyde. G81 87 104 AZ21
Janetta St, Clyde. G81 87 104 AW17
Jardine St G20 16 106 BP26
Jean Armour Dr, Clyde. G81 87 104 AY18
Jean Maclean Pl (Bishop.) G64 91 106 BX17
Jedburgh Av (Ruther.) G73 85 110 BX38
Jedburgh Gdns G20 16 106 BP26
Jedworth Av G15 88 105 BD18
Jedworth Pl G15 88 105 BE18
Jedworth Rd G15 88 105 BD18
Jellicoe St, Clyde. G81 87 104 AU18
Jenny's Well Ct, Pais. PA2 97 108 AY35
Jenny's Well Rd, Pais. PA2 96 108 AX35
Jerviston Rd G33 94 107 CE27
Jessie St G42 83 110 BT35
Jessiman Sq, Renf. PA4 93 104 AX28
Jocelyn Sq G1 55 110 BS31
John Knox La G4 44 106 BU30
John Knox St G4 44 106 BU30
John Knox St, Clyde. G81 87 104 AY21
John Marshall Dr (Bishop.) G64 91 106 BU22
Johnsburn Dr G53 79 108 BD39
Johnsburn Rd G53 79 108 BD39
Johnshaven, Ersk. PA8 86 104 AQ19
Johnshaven St G43 81 109 BL38
Johnson Dr (Camb.) G72 103 110 CC40
Johnston Av, Clyde. G81 87 104 AZ21
Johnstone Av G52 75 108 BD31
Johnstone Dr (Ruther.) G73 84 110 BW38
Johnston St, Pais. PA1 96 108 AU33
John St G1 43 106 BS30
John St, Pais. PA1 96 108 AS33
Joppa St G33 94 107 CA30
Jordanhill Cres G13 88 105 BF24
Jordanhill Dr G13 88 105 BE24
Jordanhill La G13 89 105 BG24
Jordan St G14 73 105 BF27
Jordanvale Av G14 73 105 BF27
Jowitt Av, Clyde. G81 87 104 AZ20
Jubilee Ct G52 74 105 BB30
Jubilee Gdns (Bears.) G61 89 105 BH17
Jubilee Path (Bears.) G61 89 105 BH17
Julian Av G12 14 105 BL25
Julian La G12 14 105 BL25
Juniper Pl G32 99 111 CH33
Juniper Ter G32 99 111 CG33
Jura Av, Renf. PA4 93 104 AZ28
Jura Ct G52 48 109 BG32
Jura Dr (Old Kil.) G60 86 104 AS16
Jura Gdns (Old Kil.) G60 86 104 AS16
Jura Pl (Old Kil.) G60 86 104 AS16
Jura Rd (Old Kil.) G60 86 104 AS16
Jura Rd, Pais. PA2 96 108 AT38
Jura St G52 48 109 BH32

Kaim Dr G53 79 109 BE39
Karol Path G4 29 106 BQ27
Katewell Av G15 88 105 BA17
Katewell Pl G15 88 105 BA17
Katrine Av (Bishop.) G64 91 106 BX20
Katrine Pl (Camb.) G72 103 110 CC39
Kaystone Rd G15 88 105 BC20
Kay St G21 20 106 BV25
Keal Av G15 88 105 BC21
Keal Cres G15 88 105 BC21
Keal Dr G15 88 105 BC21
Keal Pl G15 88 105 BC21
Kearn Av G15 88 105 BD20
Kearn Pl G15 88 105 BD20
Keir Dr (Bishop.) G64 91 106 BV19
Keir Hardie Ct (Bishop.) G64 91 106 BW20
Keir St G41 64 109 BP34
Keirs Wk (Camb.) G72 103 110 CC39
Keith Av (Giff.) G46 101 109 BM42
Keith Ct G11 26 105 BL28
Keith St G11 26 105 BL27
Kelbourne St G20 16 106 BN25
Kelburne Dr, Pais. PA1 96 108 AX32
Kelburne Gdns (Baill.) G69 99 111 CJ34
Kelburne Gdns, Pais. PA1 96 108 AW32
Kelburne Oval, Pais. PA1 96 108 AW32
Kelhead Av G52 74 108 BB32
Kelhead Dr G52 74 108 BB32
Kelhead Path G52 74 108 BB32
Kelhead Pl G52 74 108 BB32
Kellas St G51 37 105 BJ30
Kells Pl G15 88 105 BA17
Kelso Av (Ruther.) G73 85 110 BX38
Kelso Pl G14 88 105 BA23
Kelso St G13 88 105 BB21
Kelso St G14 88 105 BA23
Kelton St G32 98 110 CD33
Kelty Pl G5 54 109 BR32
Kelvin Av G52 74 105 BB29
Kelvin Ct G12 89 105 BH23
Kelvin Cres (Bears.) G61 89 105 BH19
Kelvindale Bldgs G12 89 105 BL24
Kelvindale Gdns G20 89 105 BL23
Kelvindale Pl G20 89 105 BM23
Kelvindale Rd G12 89 105 BK23
Kelvindale Rd G20 89 105 BM23
Kelvin Dr G20 89 105 BM25
Kelvin Dr (Bishop.) G64 91 106 BW19
Kelvingrove St G3 40 106 BN29
Kelvinhaugh Pl G3 39 105 BM29
Kelvinhaugh St G3 39 105 BL29
Kelvinside Av G20 16 106 BP25
Kelvinside Dr G20 16 106 BP25
Kelvinside Gdns G20 16 106 BN25
Kelvinside Gdns E G20 16 106 BP26
Kelvinside Gdns La G20 16 106 BN25
Kelvinside Ter S G20 16 106 BN26
Kelvinside Ter W G20 16 106 BN26
Kelvin Way G3 27 105 BM28
Kemp Av, Pais. PA3 93 104 AW28
Kempock St G31 70 110 BY33
Kempsthorn Cres G53 76 108 BC36
Kempsthorn Path G53 77 108 BD36
Kempsthorn Rd G53 76 108 BC36
Kemp St G21 20 106 BU25
Kendal Av G12 89 105 BJ23
Kendal Av (Giff.) G46 101 109 BL42
Kendal Dr G12 89 105 BJ23
Kendoon Av G15 88 105 BA18
Kenilworth Av G41 81 109 BM37
Kenmore St G32 98 110 CC32
Kenmuir Av G32 99 111 CG34
Kenmuirhill Rd G32 98 111 CF35
Kenmuir Rd G32 98 111 CE37
Kenmure Av (Bishop.) G64 91 106 BU20
Kenmure Cres (Bishop.) G64 91 106 BV20
Kenmure Dr (Bishop.) G64 91 106 BV20
Kenmure Gdns (Bishop.) G64 91 106 BU20
Kenmure La (Bishop.) G64 91 106 BV20
Kenmure Row G22 90 106 BR20
Kenmure St G41 82 109 BP35
Kenmure Way (Ruther.) G73 102 110 BX42
Kennedar Dr G51 36 105 BG29
Kennedy Ct (Giff.) G46 101 109 BL41
Kennedy Path G4 43 106 BT29
Kennedy St G4 31 106 BT28
Kennet St G21 33 106 BW28
Kennishead Av (Thornlie.) G46 100 109 BG40
Kennishead Path (Thornlie.) G46 100 109 BG40
Kennishead Pl (Thornlie.) G46 100 109 BG40
Kennishead Rd G43 100 109 BH40
Kennishead Rd (Thornlie.) G46 100 109 BG40
Kennisholm Av (Thornlie.) G46 100 109 BG40
Kennisholm Path (Thornlie.) G46 100 109 BG40
Kennisholm Pl (Thornlie.) G46 100 109 BG40
Kennoway Dr G11 25 105 BH27
Kennyhill Sq G31 46 106 BX29
Kensington Dr (Giff.) G46 101 109 BM44
Kensington Gate G12 14 105 BL25
Kensington Gate La G12 14 105 BL25
Kensington Rd G12 14 105 BL25
Kentallen Rd G33 99 111 CG31
Kent Dr (Ruther.) G73 103 110 BZ40
Kentigern Ter (Bishop.) G64 91 106 BW21
Kent Rd G3 40 106 BN29
Kent St G40 56 110 BU31
Keppel Dr G44 84 110 BU38
Keppochhill Dr G21 19 106 BT26
Keppochhill Pl G21 31 106 BT27
Keppochhill Rd G21 19 106 BT26
Keppochhill Rd G22 18 106 BS26
Keppochhill Way G21 31 106 BT27
Keppoch St G21 19 106 BT26
Kerfield La G15 88 105 BA17
Kerfield Pl G15 88 105 BA17
Kerr Dr G40 56 110 BV32
Kerrera Pl G33 98 111 CF31
Kerrera Rd G33 98 111 CF31
Kerr Pl G40 56 110 BV32
Kerr St G40 56 110 BV32
Kerr St, Pais. PA3 96 108 AT32
Kerrycroy Av G42 83 110 BT38
Kerrycroy Pl G42 83 110 BT37
Kerrycroy St G42 83 110 BT37
Kerrydale St G40 70 110 BX33
Kerrylamont Av G42 84 110 BU38
Kerry Pl G15 88 105 BA18
Kersland La G12 15 105 BM26
Kersland St G12 15 105 BM26
Kessington Dr (Bears.) G61 89 105 BJ17
Kessington Rd (Bears.) G61 89 105 BJ18
Kessock Dr G22 18 106 BR26
Kessock Pl G22 18 106 BR26
Kestrel Ct, Clyde. G81 87 104 AW16
Kestrel Rd G13 88 105 BE23
Kew Gdns G12 15 105 BM26
Kew La G12 15 105 BM26
Kew Ter G12 15 105 BM26
Kilbarchan St G5 54 109 BR32
Kilbeg Ter (Thornlie.) G46 100 109 BF42
Kilberry St G21 33 106 BW28
Kilbirnie Pl G5 65 109 BQ33
Kilbirnie St G5 65 109 BQ33
Kilbowie Ct, Clyde. G81 87 104 AX18
Kilbowie Retail Pk, Clyde. G81 87 104 AY19
Kilbowie Rd, Clyde. G81 87 104 AX15
Kilbride St G5 83 110 BT35
Kilburn Pl G13 88 105 BD23
Kilchattan Dr G44 83 110 BS38
Kilchoan Rd G33 94 107 CE27
Kilcloy Av G15 88 105 BC17
Kildale Way (Ruther.) G73 84 110 BV37
Kildary Av G44 101 109 BQ40
Kildary Rd G44 101 109 BQ40
Kildermorie Path G34 95 107 CJ29
Kildermorie Rd G34 95 107 CJ29
Kildonan Dr G11 25 105 BJ27
Kildrostan St G41 82 109 BP35
Kilearn Rd, Pais. PA3 93 104 AX30
Kilearn Sq, Pais. PA3 93 104 AX30
Kilearn Way, Pais. PA3 93 104 AX30
Kilfinan St G22 90 106 BR22
Kilkerran Dr G33 94 107 CB23
Killearn Dr, Pais. PA1 76 108 BB33
Killearn St G22 18 106 BR25
Killermont Av (Bears.) G61 89 105 BJ19
Killermont Ct (Bears.) G61 89 105 BK18
Killermont Rd (Bears.) G61 89 105 BJ18
Killermont St G2 42 106 BS29
Killermont Vw G20 89 105 BJ19
Killiegrew Rd G41 81 109 BM35
Killin St G32 98 110 CD34
Killoch Dr G13 88 105 BC22
Kilmailing Rd G44 101 109 BR40
Kilmair Pl G20 89 105 BM24
Kilmaluag Ter (Thornlie.) G46 100 109 BG42
Kilmany Dr G32 98 110 CB32
Kilmany Gdns G32 98 110 CB32
Kilmarnock Rd G41 101 109 BM39
Kilmarnock Rd G43 101 109 BM39
Kilmartin Pl (Thornlie.) G46 100 109 BG41
Kilmaurs Dr (Giff.) G46 101 109 BN42
Kilmaurs St G51 48 109 BH31
Kilmorie Dr (Ruther.) G73 84 110 BU38
Kilmuir Cres (Thornlie.) G46 100 109 BF41
Kilmuir Dr (Thornlie.) G46 100 109 BG41
Kilmuir Rd (Thornlie.) G46 100 109 BG41
Kilmun St G20 89 105 BM22
Kilncroft La, Pais. PA2 96 108 AU35
Kilnside Rd, Pais. PA1 96 108 AV32
Kiloran St (Thornlie.) G46 100 109 BH41
Kilpatrick Ct (Old Kil.) G60 86 104 AQ15
Kilpatrick Cres, Pais. PA2 96 108 AT36
Kilpatrick Dr, Ersk. PA8 86 104 AR18
Kilpatrick Dr, Renf. PA4 93 104 AX29
Kilpatrick Gdns (Clark.) G76 101 109 BL45
Kiltearn Rd G33 95 107 CH30
Kilvaxter Dr (Thornlie.) G46 100 109 BG41
Kilwynet Way, Pais. PA3 93 104 AW30
Kimberley St, Clyde. G81 86 104 AT16
Kinalty Rd G44 101 109 BQ40
Kinarvie Cres G53 78 108 BB38
Kinarvie Gdns G53 78 108 BB38
Kinarvie Pl G53 78 108 BB38
Kinarvie Rd G53 78 108 BB38
Kinarvie Ter G53 78 108 BB38
Kinbuck St G22 19 106 BT25
Kincaid Gdns (Camb.) G72 98 110 CC38
Kincardine Dr (Bishop.) G64 91 106 BX21
Kincardine Pl (Bishop.) G64 91 106 BY22
Kincardine Sq G33 94 107 CF27
Kincath Av (Ruther.) G73 103 110 BZ42
Kinclaven Av G15 88 105 BC18
Kincraig St G51 75 109 BF31
Kinellan Rd (Bears.) G61 89 105 BH20
Kinellar Dr G14 88 105 BC23
Kinfauns Dr G15 88 105 BB18
Kingarth La G42 82 109 BQ35
Kingarth St G42 82 109 BQ35
King Edward La G13 89 105 BG24
King Edward Rd G13 89 105 BH24
Kingfisher Dr G13 88 105 BB22
Kingfisher Gdns G13 88 105 BC22
King George Ct, Renf. PA4 72 105 BA28
King George V Br G1 54 109 BR31
King George V Br G5 54 109 BR31
King George V Dock G51 73 105 BD27
King George Gdns, Renf. PA4 72 105 BA27
King George Pk Av, Renf. PA4 72 105 BA28
King George Pl, Renf. PA4 72 105 BA28
King George Way, Renf. PA4 72 105 BA28
Kinghorn Dr G44 102 110 BS39
Kinglass Rd (Bears.) G61 88 105 BE19
Kingsacre Rd G44 83 110 BT38
Kingsacre Rd (Ruther.) G73 84 110 BU38
Kingsbarns Dr G44 83 109 BR38
Kingsborough Gdns G12 14 105 BK26
Kingsborough Gate G12 14 105 BK26
Kingsborough La G12 14 105 BK26
Kingsborough La E G12 14 105 BK26
Kingsbrae Av G44 83 110 BS38
King's Br G5 67 110 BT33
King's Br G40 67 110 BT33
Kingsbridge Cres G44 102 110 BT39
Kingsbridge Dr G44 102 110 BT39
Kingsbridge Dr (Ruther.) G73 102 110 BU39
Kingsburgh Dr, Pais. PA1 96 108 AX31
Kingsburn Dr (Ruther.) G73 102 110 BW39
Kingsburn Gro (Ruther.) G73 102 110 BW39
Kingscliffe Av G44 102 110 BS39
Kingscourt Av G44 83 110 BT38
Kings Cres (Camb.) G72 103 110 CD40
Kings Cross G31 45 106 BV30
Kingsdale Av G44 83 110 BS38
King's Dr G40 68 110 BU33
Kingsdyke Av G44 83 110 BS38
Kingsford Av G44 101 109 BN41
Kingsheath Av (Ruther.) G73 102 110 BU39
Kingshill Dr G44 102 110 BS39
Kingshouse Av G44 83 110 BS38
Kingshurst Av G44 83 110 BS38
Kings Inch Dr, Renf. PA4 73 105 BD28
Kings Inch Pl, Renf. PA4 72 105 BB27
Kings Inch Rd G51 72 105 BA25
Kings Inch Rd, Renf. PA4 72 105 BA25
Kingsknowe Dr (Ruther.) G73 102 110 BU39
Kingsland Cres G52 75 108 BD31
Kingsland Dr G52 75 108 BD31
Kingsland La G52 75 109 BE32
Kings La W, Renf. PA4 93 104 AZ25
Kingsley Av G42 83 109 BR36
Kingslynn Dr G44 102 109 BT39
Kingslynn La G44 102 110 BT39
Kingsmuir Dr (Ruther.) G73 102 110 BU39
King's Pk Av G44 102 110 BS39
King's Pk Av (Ruther.) G73 102 110 BU39
Kings Pk Rd G44 83 109 BR38
Kings Pl G22 90 106 BR22
Kingston Br G3 53 109 BQ31
Kingston Br G5 53 109 BQ31
Kingston Ind Est G5 52 109 BP32
Kingston Pl, Clyde. G81 86 104 AT17
Kingston St G5 53 109 BQ31
King St G1 55 110 BS31
King St (Ruther.) G73 85 110 BX37
King St, Clyde. G81 87 104 AZ21
King St, Pais. PA1 96 108 AS32
King's Vw (Ruther.) G73 85 110 BV38
Kingsway G14 88 105 BC24
Kingsway Ct G14 88 105 BD24
Kingswood Dr G44 102 110 BS39
Kingussie Dr G44 102 110 BS39
Kiniver Dr G15 88 105 BC20
Kinloch Av (Camb.) G72 103 110 CD41
Kinloch Rd, Renf. PA4 93 104 AX29
Kinloch St G40 70 110 BY33
Kinmount Av G44 83 109 BR38
Kinnaird Cres (Bears.) G61 89 105 BK17
Kinnaird Pl (Bishop.) G64 91 106 BX21
Kinnear Rd G40 70 110 BX34

Kinnell Av G52 77 109 BE34
Kinnell Cres G52 77 109 BE34
Kinnell Path G52 77 109 BE34
Kinnell Pl G52 77 109 BF34
Kinnell Sq G52 77 109 BE34
Kinning Pk Ind Est G5 52 109 BP32
Kinning St G5 53 109 BQ32
Kinnoul La G12 15 105 BL26
Kinpurnie Rd, Pais. PA1 97 108 AZ32
Kinross Av G52 77 108 BD33
Kinsail Dr G52 74 108 BB31
Kinstone Av G14 88 105 BC24
Kintessack Pl (Bishop.) G64 91 106 BZ19
Kintillo Dr G13 88 105 BD23
Kintore Rd G43 101 109 BP39
Kintra St G51 38 105 BK30
Kintyre St G21 33 106 BW28
Kippen St G22 90 106 BT23
Kippford St G32 98 111 CE33
Kirkaig Av, Renf. PA4 72 105 BB27
Kirkbean Av (Ruther.) G73 102 110 BW41
Kirkburn Av (Camb.) G72 103 110 CC41
Kirkcaldy Rd G41 81 109 BM35
Kirkconnel Av G13 88 105 BB22
Kirkconnel Dr (Ruther.) G73 102 110 BV40
Kirkdale Dr G52 60 109 BG33
Kirkhill Av (Camb.) G72 103 110 CC42
Kirkhill Dr G20 90 106 BN24
Kirkhill Gdns (Camb.) G72 103 110 CC42
Kirkhill Gro (Camb.) G72 103 110 CC42
Kirkhill Pl G20 89 105 BM24
Kirkhill Ter (Camb.) G72 103 110 CC42
Kirkhope Dr G15 88 105 BD19
Kirkinner Rd G32 98 111 CF34
Kirkintilloch Rd (Bishop.) G64 91 106 BV21
Kirklandneuk Cres, Renf. PA4 93 104 AW25
Kirklandneuk Rd, Renf. PA4 93 104 AX25
Kirkland St G20 17 106 BP26
Kirk La G43 81 109 BL38
Kirklee Circ G12 15 105 BL25
Kirklee Gdns G12 89 105 BL24
Kirklee Gdns La G12 15 105 BM25
Kirklee Pl G12 15 105 BM25
Kirklee Quad G12 15 105 BM25
Kirklee Quad La G12 15 105 BM25
Kirklee Rd G12 15 105 BL25
Kirklee Ter G12 15 105 BL25
Kirklee Ter La G12 15 105 BL25
Kirkliston St G32 98 110 CB31
Kirk Ms (Camb.) G72 103 110 CC40
Kirkmichael Av G11 13 105 BJ26
Kirkmichael Gdns G11 13 105 BJ26
Kirkmuir Dr (Ruther.) G73 102 110 BX42
Kirknewton St G32 98 110 CC31
Kirkoswald Dr, Clyde. G81 87 104 AY18
Kirkoswald Rd G43 101 109 BM39
Kirkpatrick St G40 57 110 BW32
Kirkriggs Av (Ruther.) G73 102 110 BX40
Kirkriggs Gdns (Ruther.) G73 102 110 BX40
Kirkriggs Vw (Ruther.) G73 102 110 BX40
Kirkriggs Way (Ruther.) G73 102 110 BX40
Kirk Rd (Carm.) G76 102 110 BT46
Kirkstall Gdns (Bishop.) G64 91 106 BX17
Kirkton, Ersk. PA8 86 104 AQ18
Kirkton Av G13 88 105 BC23
Kirkton Cres G13 88 105 BC23
Kirkton Rd (Camb.) G72 103 110 CD40
Kirkville Pl G15 88 105 BD20
Kirkwell Rd G44 101 109 BR40
Kirkwood Av G33 95 107 CH24
Kirkwood Av, Clyde. G81 87 104 AZ20
Kirkwood Quad, Clyde. G81 87 104 AZ20
Kirkwood St G51 50 109 BL32
Kirkwood St (Ruther.) G73 84 110 BW37
Kirn St G20 89 105 BL21
Kirriemuir Av G52 77 109 BE34
Kirriemuir Gdns (Bishop.) G64 91 106 BY19
Kirriemuir Pl G52 77 109 BE33
Kirriemuir Rd (Bishop.) G64 91 106 BY20
Kirtle Dr, Renf. PA4 72 105 BA27
Kishorn Pl G33 94 107 CE28
Knapdale St G22 90 106 BQ22
Knightsbridge St G13 88 105 BF22
Knightscliffe Av G13 88 105 BF21
Knightswood Ct G13 88 105 BF23
Knightswood Cross G13 88 105 BF22
Knightswood Rd G13 88 105 BE20
Knockhall St G33 94 107 CF27
Knockhill Dr G44 83 109 BR38
Knockhill Rd, Renf. PA4 93 104 AW28
Knockside Av, Pais. PA2 96 108 AT38
Knock Way, Pais. PA3 93 104 AW30
Knollpark Dr (Clark.) G76 101 109 BM46
Knowehead Gdns G41 64 109 BN34
Knowehead Ter G41 64 109 BN34
Knowe Rd, Pais. PA3 93 104 AX30
Knowetap St G20 90 106 BN22
Kyleakin Rd (Thornlie.) G46 100 109 BF42
Kyleakin Ter (Thornlie.) G46 100 109 BF42
Kyle Ct (Camb.) G72 103 110 CC39
Kyle Dr (Giff.) G46 101 109 BN42
Kylepark Cres (Udd.) G71 99 111 CM38
Kylepark Dr (Udd.) G71 99 111 CM38
Kylerhea Rd (Thornlie.) G46 100 109 BF42
Kyle Sq (Ruther.) G73 102 110 BV40
Kyle St G4 31 106 BS28

La Belle Allee G3 28 106 BN28
La Belle Pl G3 28 106 BN28
Laburnum Rd G41 63 109 BL33
Lachlan Cres, Ersk. PA8 86 104 AN20
La Crosse Ter G12 16 106 BN26
Lacy St, Pais. PA1 96 108 AW32
Lade Ter G52 76 108 BC33
Ladhope Pl G13 88 105 BA21
Ladyacres (Inch.), Renf. PA4 92 104 AT23
Ladyacres Way (Inch.),
Renf. PA4 92 104 AT23
Lady Anne St G14 88 105 BB23
Ladybank Dr G52 60 109 BG33
Ladyburn St, Pais. PA1 96 108 AW33
Ladyhill Dr (Baill.) G69 99 111 CJ33
Ladykirk Cres G52 75 108 BD31
Ladykirk Cres, Pais. PA2 96 108 AV34
Ladykirk Dr G52 75 108 BD31
Lady La, Pais. PA1 96 108 AT33
Ladyloan Av G15 88 105 BA17
Ladyloan Ct G15 88 105 BB17
Ladyloan Gdns G15 88 105 BB17
Ladyloan Pl G15 88 105 BA17
Ladymuir Circle, Ersk. PA8 86 104 AP20
Ladymuir Cres G53 77 109 BE35
Ladywell St G4 44 106 BU30
Laggan Rd G43 101 109 BN40
Laggan Rd (Bishop.) G64 91 106 BX20
Laggan Rd (Newt. M.) G77 100 109 BF46
Laggan Ter, Renf. PA4 93 104 AX25
Laidlaw St G5 53 109 BQ32
Laighpark Harbour, Pais. PA3 93 104 AU30
Laighpark Vw, Pais. PA3 93 104 AU30
Lainshaw Dr G45 101 109 BQ43
Laird Pl G40 68 110 BV33
Lamberton Dr G52 75 108 BD31
Lambhill Quad G41 52 109 BN32
Lambhill St G41 51 109 BM32
Lamb St G22 90 106 BR23
Lamington Rd G52 77 108 BD33
Lamlash Cres G33 94 107 CD29
Lamlash Pl G33 94 107 CD29
Lamlash Sq G33 94 107 CE29
Lammermoor Av G52 77 109 BE33
Lammermuir Ct, Pais. PA2 96 108 AU37
Lammermuir Dr, Pais. PA2 96 108 AT37
Lamont Rd G21 91 106 BX23
Lanark St G1 55 110 BT31
Lancaster Cres G12 14 105 BL25
Lancaster Cres La G12 14 105 BL25
Lancaster Rd (Bishop.) G64 91 106 BX17
Lancaster Ter G12 14 105 BL25
Lancaster Ter La G12 14/5 105 BL25
Lancaster Way, Renf. PA4 93 104 AY28
Lancefield Quay G3 40 106 BN30
Lancefield St G3 40 106 BP30
Landemer Dr (Ruther.) G73 102 110 BV39
Landressy Pl G40 68 110 BU33
Landressy St G40 68 110 BV33
Lane Gdns G11 14 105 BK26
Lanfine Rd, Pais. PA1 96 108 AX32
Langa St G20 90 106 BN22
Lang Av, Renf. PA4 93 104 AY28
Langbank St G5 54 109 BR32
Langbar Cres G33 95 107 CG30
Langbar Path G33 94 107 CF30
Langcroft Pl G51 75 108 BE30
Langcroft Rd G51 75 105 BF30
Langcroft Ter G51 75 105 BF30
Langdale Av G33 94 107 CA26
Langdale St G33 94 107 CA26
Langhaul Rd G53 76 108 BB36
Langlands Av G51 75 105 BF29
Langlands Ct G51 36/7 105 BH29
Langlands Dr G51 75 105 BF30
Langlands Rd G51 75 105 BF30
Langlea Av (Camb.) G72 103 110 BZ41
Langlea Ct (Camb.) G72 103 110 CA41
Langlea Dr (Camb.) G72 103 110 CA40
Langlea Gdns (Camb.) G72 103 110 CA40
Langlea Gro (Camb.) G72 103 110 CA41
Langlea Rd (Camb.) G72 103 110 CA41
Langlea Way (Camb.) G72 103 110 CA40
Langley Av G13 88 105 BD21
Langness Rd G33 94 107 CD29
Langrig Rd G21 21 106 BW25
Langshot St G51 51 109 BM32
Langside Av G41 82 109 BN36
Langside Dr G43 101 109 BN40
Langside Gdns G42 82 109 BQ38
Langside La G42 82 109 BQ36
Langside Pl G41 82 109 BP37
Langside Rd G42 82 109 BQ36
Langstile Pl G52 74 108 BB32
Langstile Rd G52 74 108 BB32
Lang St, Pais. PA1 96 108 AW33
Langton Cres G53 77 109 BE36
Langton Gdns (Baill.) G69 99 111 CH33
Langton Rd G53 79 109 BE37
Langtree Av (Giff.) G46 100 109 BJ44
Lansbury Gdns, Pais. PA3 92 104 AT30
Lansdowne Cres G20 28 106 BP27
Lansdowne Cres La G20 28 106 BP27
Lanton Dr G52 74 108 BD32
Lanton Rd G43 101 109 BN40
Lappin St, Clyde. G81 87 104 AZ21
Larbert St G4 30 106 BR28
Larch Av (Bishop.) G64 91 106 BX21
Larchfield Av G14 73 105 BD25
Larchfield Dr (Ruther.) G73 103 110 BY41
Larchfield Pl G14 73 105 BD25
Larchfield Rd (Bears.) G61 89 105 BH20
Larchgrove Av G32 98 111 CE31
Larchgrove Pl G32 94 107 CE30
Larchgrove Rd G32 94 107 CE30
Larch Rd G41 50 109 BK32
Largie Rd G43 101 109 BP40
Largo Pl G51 36 105 BG30
Largs St G31 46 106 BX30
Larkin Gdns, Pais. PA3 92 104 AT30
Lasswade St G14 88 105 BA23
Latherton Dr G20 89 105 BM24
Latherton Pl G20 89 105 BM24
Latimer Gdns G52 76 108 BC33
Latimer Path G52 76 108 BC33
Laudedale La G12 14 105 BK26
Lauderdale Gdns G12 14 105 BK26
Lauder Dr (Ruther.) G73 103 110 BZ39
Laundry La G33 94 107 CE24
Laurel Av, Clyde. G81 86 104 AT17
Laurel Pk Gdns G13 88 105 BE24
Laurel Pl G11 13 105 BJ26
Laurel St G11 25 105 BJ27
Laurel Wk (Ruther.) G73 103 110 BY42
Laurieston Rd G5 66 109 BR33
Laurieston Way (Ruther.) G73 102 110 BW41
Laverockhall St G21 20 106 BV26
Lawers Rd G43 100 109 BK40
Lawers Rd, Renf. PA4 93 104 AX28
Lawhill Av G44 102 110 BT41
Lawmoor Av G5 67 110 BS34
Lawmoor Pl G5 83 110 BS35
Lawmoor Rd G5 67 110 BS34
Lawmoor St G5 67 110 BS34
Lawn St, Pais. PA1 96 108 AV32
Lawrence Av (Giff.) G46 101 109 BL44
Lawrence St G11 26 105 BL27
Lawrie St G11 26 105 BK27
Law St G40 57 110 BW32
Laxford Av G44 101 109 BQ41
Laxford Rd, Ersk. PA8 86 104 AN20
Leabank Av, Pais. PA2 96 108 AU37
Leadburn Rd G21 22 106 BY25
Leadburn St G32 94 107 CA30
Leader St G33 35 106 BZ28
Leander Cres, Renf. PA4 72 105 BA27
Leathen Pl, Ersk. PA8 86 104 AN20
Leckie St G43 81 109 BL37
Ledaig Pl G31 47 106 BY30
Ledaig St G31 47 106 BY30
Ledard Rd G42 82 109 BP37
Ledcameroch Cres
(Bears.) G61 88 105 BF17
Ledcameroch Pk (Bears.) G61 88 105 BF17
Ledcameroch Rd (Bears.) G61 88 105 BF17
Ledgowan Pl G20 89 105 BM21
Ledi Rd G43 101 109 BL40
Ledmore Dr G15 88 105 BB17
Lednock Rd (Stepps) G33 94 107 CE24
Lednock Rd G52 74 108 BC32
Lee Av G33 94 107 CA28
Leebank Dr G44 101 109 BP44
Lee Cres (Bishop.) G64 91 106 BW21
Leefield Dr G44 101 109 BP43
Leehill Rd G21 91 106 BU22
Leeside Rd G21 91 106 BU22
Leewood Dr G44 101 109 BQ43
Leggatston Rd G53 100 109 BE43
Leglen Wd Cres G21 91 106 BZ23
Leglen Wd Dr G21 91 106 BZ23
Leglen Wd Pl G21 91 106 BZ23
Leglen Wd Rd G21 91 106 BZ23
Leicester Av G12 89 105 BK24
Leighton St G20 90 106 BN23
Leithland Av G53 77 108 BD36
Leithland Rd G53 77 108 BD36
Leith St G33 47 106 BZ29
Lembert Dr (Clark.) G76 101 109 BM45
Lendale La (Bishop.) G64 91 106 BW18
Lendel Pl G51 51 109 BM32
Lenihall Dr G45 102 110 BU43
Lenihall Ter G45 102 110 BU43
Lennox Av G14 73 105 BE26
Lennox Cres (Bishop.) G64 91 106 BV21
Lennox Gdns G14 73 105 BF25
Lennox La E G14 73 105 BF26
Lennox La W G14 73 105 BF25
Lennox Pl G14 73 105 BE26
Lennox Pl, Clyde. G81 87 104 AU18
Lennox St G20 89 105 BL22
Lennox Ter, Pais. PA3 93 104 AW29
Lennox Vw, Clyde. G81 87 104 AX18
Lentran St G34 95 107 CM30
Leny St G20 17 106 BP25
Lenzie Pl G21 91 106 BV23
Lenzie Rd (Stepps) G33 94 107 CF23
Lenzie St G21 91 106 BV24
Lenzie Ter G21 91 106 BV24
Lenzie Way G21 91 106 BV23
Leslie Av (Newt. M.) G77 100 109 BG46
Leslie Rd G41 64 109 BN34
Leslie St G41 64 109 BP34
Lesmuir Dr G14 88 105 BB24
Lesmuir Pl G14 88 105 BB24
Letham Ct G43 101 109 BN40
Letham Dr G43 101 109 BN40
Letham Dr (Bishop.) G64 91 106 BY21
Lethamhill Cres G33 94 107 CB28
Lethamhill Pl G33 94 107 CA28
Lethamhill Rd G33 94 107 CA28
Letham Oval (Bishop.) G64 91 106 BZ21
Letherby Dr G42 83 109 BR38
Letherby Dr G44 83 109 BR38
Lethington Av G41 82 109 BN37
Lethington Pl G41 82 109 BN37
Lethington Rd (Giff.) G46 100 109 BJ46
Letterfearn Dr G23 90 106 BN20
Lettoch St G51 37 105 BJ30
Leven Av (Bishop.) G64 91 106 BX20
Leven Dr (Bears.) G61 89 105 BH17
Leven Pl, Ersk. PA8 86 104 AN20
Leven Sq, Renf. PA4 93 104 AX25
Leven St G41 64 109 BP34
Leven Vw, Clyde. G81 87 104 AX18
Leverndale Ind Cen G53 78 108 BB37
Leverndale Rd G53 76 108 BB36
Levernside Av G53 79 109 BE37
Levernside Cres G53 77 108 BD36
Levernside Rd G53 77 109 BE36
Lewis Av, Renf. PA4 93 104 AZ28
Lewis Cres (Old Kil.) G60 86 104 AR16
Lewis Dr (Old Kil.) G60 86 104 AR16
Lewis Gdns (Old Kil.) G60 86 104 AS16
Lewis Gro (Old Kil.) G60 86 104 AS16
Lewis Pl (Old Kil.) G60 86 104 AS16
Lewiston Dr G23 89 105 BM20
Lewiston Pl G23 89 105 BM20
Lewiston Rd G23 89 105 BM20
Leyden Ct G20 90 106 BN24
Leyden Gdns G20 90 106 BN24
Leyden St G20 90 106 BN24
Leys, The (Bishop.) G64 91 106 BW20
Liberton St G33 47 106 BZ29
Libo Av G53 77 109 BF36
Libo Pl, Ersk. PA8 86 104 AN19
Library Gdns (Camb.) G72 103 110 CB39
Liddells Ct (Bishop.) G64 91 106 BW21
Liddell St G32 98 111 CE36
Liddesdale Pl G22 91 106 BU21
Liddesdale Rd G22 90 106 BS22
Liddesdale Sq G22 91 106 BU22
Liddesdale Ter G22 91 106 BU22
Liddoch Way (Ruther.) G73 84 110 BV37
Liff Gdns (Bishop.) G64 91 106 BZ21
Liff Pl G34 95 107 CL28
Lightburn Pl G32 94 107 CD30
Lightburn Rd G31 59 110 BY31
Lilac Av, Clyde. G81 86 104 AT16
Lilac Gdns (Bishop.) G64 91 106 BX21
Lilybank Gdns G12 27 105 BM27
Lilybank Gdns La G12 27 105 BM27
Lilybank La G12 27 105 BM27
Lilybank Ter G12 27 105 BM27
Lily St G40 70 110 BX34
Limecraigs Av, Pais. PA2 96 108 AS38
Limecraigs Cres, Pais. PA2 96 108 AS38
Lime La G14 73 105 BF26
Limeside Av (Ruther.) G73 85 110 BX38
Limeside Gdns (Ruther.) G73 85 110 BY38
Lime St G14 73 105 BF26
Limetree Dr, Clyde. G81 87 104 AW17
Linacre Dr G32 98 111 CE32
Linacre Gdns G32 98 111 CF32
Linburn Pl G52 74 108 BC31
Linburn Rd G52 74 105 BA30
Linburn Rd, Ersk. PA8 86 104 AN20
Lincluden Path G41 64 109 BP33
Lincoln Av G13 88 105 BE23
Lincuan Av (Giff.) G46 101 109 BL44
Linden Ct, Clyde. G81 87 104 AW15
Linden Dr, Clyde. G81 87 104 AW15
Linden Pl G13 89 105 BH22
Linden St G13 89 105 BH22
Linden Way G13 89 105 BH22
Lindores Av (Ruther.) G73 85 110 BX38
Lindores St G42 83 109 BR38
Lindrick Dr G23 90 106 BN20
Lindsay Dr G12 89 105 BK23
Lindsay Pl G12 89 105 BK23
Linfern Rd G12 14 105 BL26
Links Rd G32 98 111 CF34
Links Rd G44 102 110 BS41
Linkwood Av G15 88 105 BB18
Linkwood Cres G15 88 105 BC18
Linkwood Dr G15 88 105 BC18
Linkwood Gdns G15 88 105 BD18
Linkwood Pl G15 88 105 BB18
Linlithgow Gdns G32 98 111 CF32
Linn Cres, Pais. PA2 96 108 AS38
Linn Dr G44 101 109 BP42
Linnet Pl G13 88 105 BB22
Linnhead Dr G53 79 108 BD39
Linnhead Pl G14 73 105 BD25
Linnhe Av G44 101 109 BQ41
Linnhe Av (Bishop.) G64 91 106 BX20
Linnhe Pl, Ersk. PA8 86 104 AN20
Linn Pk G44 101 109 BR42
Linnpark Av G44 101 109 BP43
Linnpark Ct G44 101 109 BP43
Linn Pk Ind Est G45 101 109 BR43
Linn Valley Vw G45 102 110 BT42
Linnwell Cres, Pais. PA2 96 108 AT37
Linnwood Ct G44 101 109 BQ40
Linside Av, Pais. PA1 96 108 AW33
Linthaugh Rd G53 76 108 BC35
Linthaugh Ter G53 77 109 BF36
Linthouse Bldgs G51 36 105 BG29
Linthouse Rd G51 24 105 BG28
Lintlaw Dr G52 75 108 BD31
Linton St G33 94 107 CA29
Linwood Av (Clark.) G76 101 109 BP46
Lismore Av, Renf. PA4 93 104 AZ28
Lismore Dr, Pais. PA2 96 108 AT38
Lismore Rd G12 89 105 BK24
Lister Pl G52 74 105 BC30
Lister Rd G52 74 105 BC30
Lister St G4 31 106 BT28
Lithgow Cres, Pais. PA2 96 108 AW35
Little Dovehill G1 55 110 BT31
Littleholm Pl, Clyde. G81 87 104 AU17
Littlemill Cres G53 78 108 BC37
Littlemill Dr G53 78 108 BC37
Littlemill Gdns G53 78 108 BC37
Littleston Gdns, Ersk. PA8 86 104 AP20
Little St G3 41 106 BP30
Littleton Dr G23 89 105 BL20
Littleton St G23 89 105 BM20
Livingstone Av G52 74 105 BC29
Livingstone St, Clyde. G81 87 104 AY20
Lloyd Av G32 98 110 CC35
Lloyd St G31 45 106 BW29
Lloyd St (Ruther.) G73 85 110 BX36
Loanbank Quad G51 37 105 BJ30
Loancroft Av (Baill.) G69 99 111 CL34
Loancroft Pl (Baill.) G69 99 111 CK34
Loanfoot Av G13 88 105 BC22
Loanhead Av, Renf. PA4 93 104 AZ26
Loanhead St G32 94 107 CB30
Loaning, The (Giff.) G46 100 109 BJ45
Lobnitz Av, Renf. PA4 93 104 AZ26
Lochaber Dr (Ruther.) G73 103 110 BZ41
Lochaber Rd (Bears.) G61 89 105 BJ19
Loch Achray Gdns G32 98 111 CE33
Loch Achray St G32 98 111 CE33
Lochaline Dr G44 101 109 BQ41
Lochar Cres G53 77 109 BF35
Lochay St G32 98 111 CE33
Lochbrae Dr (Ruther.) G73 103 110 BZ41
Lochbridge Rd G34 95 107 CJ30
Lochburn Cres G20 90 106 BN22
Lochburn Gro G20 90 106 BN22
Lochburn Pas G20 90 106 BN22
Lochburn Rd G20 89 105 BM23
Lochdochart Path G34 95 107 CL30
Lochdochart Rd G34 95 107 CL30
Lochearnhead Rd G33 94 107 CD24
Lochend Cres (Bears.) G61 88 105 BF18
Lochend Dr (Bears.) G61 88 105 BF18
Lochend Rd G34 95 107 CK28
Lochend Rd (Bears.) G61 89 105 BG18
Lochfauld Rd G23 90 106 BQ19
Lochfield Cres, Pais. PA2 96 108 AV36
Lochfield Dr, Pais. PA2 96 108 AW36
Lochfield Gdns G34 95 107 CL28
Lochfield Rd, Pais. PA2 96 108 AV36
Lochgilp St G20 89 105 BL22
Lochgoin Av G15 88 105 BA17
Lochgreen St G33 23 106 BZ26
Lochiel La (Ruther.) G73 103 110 BZ41
Lochiel Rd (Thornlie.) G46 100 109 BH41
Lochinver Dr G44 101 109 BQ41
Lochinver Gro (Camb.) G72 103 110 CD40
Loch Katrine St G32 98 111 CE33
Loch Laidon St G32 98 111 CF33
Lochlea Av, Clyde. G81 87 104 AY18
Lochlea Rd G43 101 109 BM39
Lochlea Rd (Ruther.) G73 102 110 BV40
Lochleven La G42 82 109 BQ38
Lochleven Rd G42 82 109 BQ38
Lochlibo Av G13 88 105 BB23
Lochmaben Rd G52 76 108 BB33
Lochmaddy Av G44 101 109 BQ40
Lochore Av, Pais. PA3 93 104 AV30
Loch Rd (Stepps) G33 94 107 CF24
Lochside (Bears.) G61 89 105 BH18
Lochside St G41 82 109 BN36
Lochview Cres G33 94 107 CB26
Lochview Dr G33 94 107 CB26
Lochview Gdns G33 94 107 CB26
Lochview Pl G33 94 107 CB26
Lochview Rd (Bears.) G61 89 105 BG18
Loch Voil St G32 98 111 CF33
Lochwood St G33 94 107 CA27
Lochy Av, Renf. PA4 72 105 BB28
Lochy Gdns (Bishop.) G64 91 106 BX20
Lochy Pl, Ersk. PA8 86 104 AN20
Lockerbie Av G43 101 109 BP39
Lockhart St G21 34 106 BX27
Locksley Av G13 88 105 BE21
Logan Dr, Pais. PA3 96 108 AS31
Logan St G5 67 110 BT34
Loganswell Dr (Thornlie.) G46 100 109 BG43
Loganswell Gdns
(Thornlie.) G46 100 109 BG43
Loganswell Pl (Thornlie.) G46 100 109 BG43
Loganswell Rd (Thornlie.) G46 100 109 BG43
Lomax St G33 47 106 BZ29
Lomond Av, Renf. PA4 93 104 AX28
Lomond Cres, Pais. PA2 96 108 AT37
Lomond Dr (Bishop.) G64 91 106 BV18
Lomond Dr (Newt. M.) G77 100 109 BF46
Lomond Pl (Stepps) G33 95 107 CG25
Lomond Pl, Ersk. PA8 86 104 AN20
Lomond Rd (Bears.) G61 89 105 BG19
Lomondside Av (Clark.) G76 101 109 BL45
Lomond St G22 90 106 BR24
Lomond Vw, Clyde. G81 87 104 AX18
London Arc G1 55 110 BT31
London La G1 55 110 BT31
London Rd G1 55 110 BT31
London Rd G31 70 110 BX33
London Rd G32 98 110 CA35
London Rd G40 56 110 BU32
London St, Renf. PA4 93 104 AZ24
Lonend, Pais. PA1 96 108 AV33
Longay Pl G22 90 106 BS21
Longay St G22 90 106 BS21
Longcroft Dr, Renf. PA4 93 104 AY25
Longden St, Clyde. G81 87 104 AZ21
Longford St G33 47 106 BZ29
Longlee (Baill.) G69 99 111 CK33
Long Row (Baill.) G69 99 111 CL31
Longstone Pl G33 94 107 CD29
Longstone Rd G33 94 107 CD29
Lonmay Rd G33 94 107 CF29
Lonsdale Av (Giff.) G46 101 109 BL42
Lora Dr G52 60 109 BG33
Loretto Pl G33 94 107 CB29
Loretto St G33 94 107 CB29
Lorne Cres (Bishop.) G64 91 106 BZ19
Lorne Rd G52 74 105 BB29
Lorne St G51 51 109 BM31
Lorne Ter (Camb.) G72 103 110 CB42
Lorraine Gdns G12 14/5 105 BL25
Lorraine Gdns La G12 14/5 105 BL25
Lorraine Rd G12 14 105 BL25
Loskin Dr G22 90 106 BS22
Lossie Cres, Renf. PA4 72 105 BB27
Lossie St G33 35 106 BZ28
Lothian Cres, Pais. PA2 96 108 AT36
Lothian Dr (Clark.) G76 101 109 BM45
Lothian Gdns G20 16 106 BN26
Lothian St G52 74 105 BA29
Louden Hill Dr G33 94 107 CA23
Louden Hill Gdns G33 94 107 CA23
Louden Hill Pl G33 94 107 CA23
Louden Hill Rd G33 94 107 CA23
Louden Hill Way G33 91 106 BZ23

Loudon Rd G33 94 107 CD24
Loudon Ter G12 15 105 BM26
Lounsdale Pl G14 73 105 BD25
Lourdes Av G52 77 109 BF33
Lourdes Ct G52 77 109 BF33
Lovat Pl G52 74 105 BA30
Lovat Pl (Ruther.) G73 103 110 BZ41
Lovat St G4 30/1 106 BS27
Love St, Pais. PA3 93 104 AU30
Low Cres, Clyde. G81 87 104 AZ21
Lower Bourtree Dr (Ruther.) G73 103 110 BY41
Low Moss Ind Est (Bishop.) G64 91 106 BX17
Low Parksail, Ersk. PA8 86 104 AS21
Low Rd (Castlehead), Pais. PA2 96 108 AS34
Lowther Ter G12 14/5 105 BL25
Loyal Av, Ersk. PA8 86 104 AP20
Loyal Pl, Ersk. PA8 86 104 AP20
Loyne Dr, Renf. PA4 72 105 BB27
Luath St G51 37 105 BJ29
Lubas Av G42 83 110 BT38
Lubas Pl G42 83 110 BT38
Lubnaig Dr, Ersk. PA8 86 104 AP20
Lubnaig Rd G43 101 109 BN39
Luckingsford Av (Inch.), Renf. PA4 86 104 AT22
Luckingsford Dr (Inch.), Renf. PA4 86 104 AS22
Luckingsford Rd (Inch.), Renf. PA4 86 104 AS22
Luffness Gdns G32 98 110 CD35
Lugar Dr G52 60 109 BG33
Lugar Pl G44 102 110 BU40
Luing Rd G52 48 109 BG32
Luma Gdns G51 75 105 BE30
Lumloch St G21 21 106 BW25
Lumsden St G3 39 105 BM29
Lunan Dr (Bishop.) G64 91 106 BY21
Lunan Pl G51 36 105 BG30
Luncarty Pl G32 98 110 CC34
Luncarty St G32 98 110 CC34
Lunderston Dr G53 78 108 BC38
Lundie Gdns (Bishop.) G64 91 106 BZ21
Lundie St G32 98 110 CA34
Lusset Glen (Old Kil.) G60 86 104 AR15
Lusset Rd (Old Kil.) G60 86 104 AR15
Lusset Vw, Clyde. G81 87 104 AX18
Lusshill Ter (Udd.) G71 99 111 CK35
Luss Rd G51 36 105 BH30
Lybster Cres (Ruther.) G73 103 110 BZ42
Lyle Pl, Pais. PA2 96 108 AV35
Lylesland Ct, Pais. PA2 96 108 AU35
Lymburn St G3 27 105 BM28
Lyndale Pl G20 89 105 BM21
Lyndale Rd G20 89 105 BM21
Lyndhurst Gdns G20 16 106 BP26
Lyndhurst Gdns La G20 16 106 BN25
Lyne Cft (Bishop.) G64 91 106 BW17
Lynedoch Cres G3 28 106 BP28
Lynedoch Cres La G3 28 106 BP28
Lynedoch Pl G3 28 106 BP28
Lynedoch St G3 28 106 BP28
Lynedoch Ter G3 29 106 BP28
Lyne Dr G23 90 106 BN20
Lynton Av (Giff.) G46 100 109 BJ44
Lyoncross Rd G53 77 108 BD35
Lyon Rd, Ersk. PA8 86 104 AN20
Lysander Way, Renf. PA4 93 104 AZ28
Lytham Dr G23 90 106 BN20

McAlpine St G2 41 106 BQ30
McArthur St G43 81 109 BL38
McAslin Ct G4 43 106 BT29
McAslin St G4 44 106 BU29
Macbeth Pl G31 71 110 BZ33
Macbeth St G31 71 110 BZ33
McCallum Av (Ruther.) G73 85 110 BX38
McClue Av, Renf. PA4 93 104 AX25
McClue Rd, Renf. PA4 93 104 AY25
McCracken Av, Renf. PA4 93 104 AX27
McCreery St, Clyde. G81 87 104 AZ21
McCulloch St G41 64 109 BP33
McDonald Cres, Clyde. G81 87 104 AZ21
Macdonald St (Ruther.) G73 84 110 BW38
Macdougall St G43 81 109 BL38
Macdowall St, Pais. PA3 96 108 AT31
Macduff, Ersk. PA8 86 104 AQ19
Macduff Pl G31 71 110 BZ33
Macduff St G31 71 110 BZ33
Mace Rd G13 88 105 BE20
Macfarlane Rd (Bears.) G61 89 105 BH18
McFarlane St G4 56 110 BU31
McFarlane St, Pais. PA3 92 104 AS30
McGhee St, Clyde. G81 87 104 AX17
McGown St, Pais. PA3 96 108 AT31
McGregor Av, Renf. PA4 93 104 AX27
McGregor St G51 48 109 BH31
McGregor St, Clyde. G81 87 104 AZ21
Machrie Dr G45 102 110 BV41
Machrie Rd G45 102 110 BV41
Machrie St G45 102 110 BV41
McIntosh Ct G31 45 106 BV30
McIntosh St G31 44 106 BV30
McIntyre Pl, Pais. PA2 96 108 AU35
McIntyre St G3 41 106 BP30
McIntyre Ter (Camb.) G72 103 110 CC39
Mackean St, Pais. PA3 96 108 AS31
McKechnie St G51 37 105 BJ29
Mackeith St G40 68 110 BV33
McKenzie Av, Clyde. G81 87 104 AX17
McKenzie St, Pais. PA3 96 108 AS32
McKerrell St, Pais. PA1 96 108 AW32
Mackie St G4 30/1 106 BS27
Mackinlay St G5 66 109 BR33
McLaren Av, Renf. PA4 93 104 AY28
McLaren Ct (Giff.) G46 100 109 BK44
McLaren Cres G20 90 106 BN22
McLaren Gdns G20 90 106 BN22
Maclaren Pl G44 101 109 BP43
McLean Pl, Pais. PA3 92 104 AT30
Maclean Sq G51 51 109 BM31
Maclean St G51 51 109 BM31
Maclean St, Clyde. G81 88 105 BA21
Maclellan St G41 51 109 BL32
McLennan St G42 83 109 BR37
Macleod St G4 44 106 BU29
McNair St G32 98 110 CC32
McNeil Gdns G5 67 110 BT33
McNeill Av, Clyde. G81 88 105 BA20
McNeil St G5 67 110 BT33
McPhail St G40 68 110 BU33
McPhater St G4 30 106 BR28
Madison Av G44 101 109 BR40
Madras Pl G40 68 110 BV34
Madras St G40 68 110 BV34
Mafeking St G51 50 109 BK31
Magnus Cres G44 101 109 BR41
Maidland Rd G53 79 109 BE37
Mailing Av (Bishop.) G64 91 106 BY19
Mainhill Av (Baill.) G69 99 111 CM32
Mainhill Dr (Baill.) G69 99 111 CL32
Mainhill Pl (Baill.) G69 99 111 CL32
Main Rd (Castlehead), Pais. PA2 96 108 AT33
Mains Av (Giff.) G46 100 109 BK44
Mainscroft, Ersk. PA8 86 104 AS20
Mains Dr, Ersk. PA8 86 104 AS20
Mains Hill, Ersk. PA8 86 104 AR20
Mainshill Av, Ersk. PA8 86 104 AR20
Mainshill Gdns, Ersk. PA8 86 104 AR20
Mains River, Ersk. PA8 86 104 AS20
Main St G40 68 110 BV34
Main St (Thornlie.) G46 100 109 BH42
Main St (Baill.) G69 99 111 CL33
Main St (Camb.) G72 103 110 CC39
Main St (Ruther.) G73 84 110 BW37
Mains Wd, Ersk. PA8 86 104 AT20
Mair St G51 52 109 BN31
Maitland Pl, Renf. PA4 93 104 AX27
Maitland St G4 30 106 BR28
Malin Pl G33 94 107 CB29
Mallaig Path G51 75 105 BF30
Mallaig Pl G51 75 105 BF30
Mallaig Rd G51 75 105 BF30
Mallard Rd, Clyde. G81 87 104 AX16
Malloch St G20 90 106 BN24
Maltbarns St G20 17 106 BQ26
Malvern Ct G31 57 110 BW31
Malvern Way, Pais. PA3 92 104 AT29
Mambeg Dr G51 36 105 BG29
Mamore Pl G43 101 109 BL39
Mamore St G43 101 109 BL39
Manchester Dr G12 89 105 BJ23
Mannering Ct G41 81 109 BL37
Mannering Rd G41 81 109 BL37
Mannofield (Bears.) G61 88 105 BE17
Manor Rd G14 12 105 BG25
Manor Rd G15 88 105 BB20
Manor Way (Ruther.) G73 103 110 BY41
Manresa Pl G4 30 106 BR27
Manse Brae G44 101 109 BR39
Mansefield Av (Camb.) G72 103 110 CC41
Manse Gdns G32 98 111 CF33
Mansel St G21 91 106 BV24
Manse Rd G32 98 111 CF33
Manse Rd (Clark.) G76 102 110 BT46
Manse St, Renf. PA4 93 104 AZ25
Mansewood Rd G43 100 109 BK39
Mansfield Rd G52 74 105 BB30
Mansfield St G11 26 105 BL27
Mansion Ct (Camb.) G72 103 110 CC39
Mansionhouse Av G32 98 111 CE37
Mansionhouse Dr G32 98 111 CE31
Mansionhouse Gdns G41 82 109 BN38
Mansionhouse Gro G32 99 111 CG34
Mansionhouse Rd G32 99 111 CG33
Mansionhouse Rd G41 82 109 BN38
Mansionhouse Rd, Pais. PA1 96 108 AW32
Mansion St G22 90 106 BS24
Mansion St (Camb.) G72 103 110 CC39
Maple Dr, Clyde. G81 87 104 AV16
Maple Rd G41 62 109 BK33
Marchbank Gdns, Pais. PA1 97 108 AZ33
Marchfield (Bishop.) G64 91 106 BU18
Marchfield Av, Pais. PA3 92 104 AT29
Marchglen Pl G51 75 105 BF30
March La G41 82 109 BP35
Marchmont Gdns (Bishop.) G64 91 106 BV18
Marchmont Ter G12 14/5 105 BL26
March St G41 82 109 BP35
Maree Dr G52 60 109 BG33
Maree Gdns (Bishop.) G64 91 106 BX20
Marfield St G32 94 107 CA30
Mar Gdns (Ruther.) G73 103 110 BZ41
Margaretta Bldgs G44 101 109 BQ39
Marine Cres G51 52 109 BN31
Marine Gdns G51 52/3 109 BP31
Mariscat Rd G41 82 109 BN35
Marjory Dr, Pais. PA3 93 104 AW30
Marjory Rd, Renf. PA4 93 104 AW28
Markdow Av G53 76 108 BC36
Marlach Pl G53 76 108 BC36
Marlborough Av G11 13 105 BH26
Marlborough La N G11 12 105 BH26
Marlborough La S G11 13 105 BH26
Marldon La G11 12 105 BH26
Marlow St G41 64 109 BN33
Marne St G31 46 106 BX30
Marnock Ter, Pais. PA2 96 108 AW34
Marshall's La, Pais. PA1 96 108 AU33
Martha St G1 43 106 BS29
Martin Cres (Baill.) G69 99 111 CL32
Martin St G40 69 110 BV34
Mart St G1 54/5 110 BS31
Martyrs Pl (Bishop.) G64 91 106 BW21
Marwick St G31 46 106 BX30
Maryhill Rd G20 17 106 BP26
Maryhill Rd (Bears.) G61 89 105 BJ19
Maryhill Shop Cen G20 90 106 BN24
Maryland Dr G52 60 109 BG33
Maryland Gdns G52 48 109 BG32
Maryston Pl G33 35 106 BZ27
Maryston St G33 35 106 BZ27
Mary St G4 30 106 BR27
Mary St, Pais. PA2 96 108 AU35
Maryville Av (Giff.) G46 101 109 BL43
Maryville Gdns (Giff.) G46 101 109 BL43
Maryville Vw (Udd.) G71 99 111 CM36
Marywood Sq G41 82 109 BP35
Masterton St G21 19 106 BS26
Mathieson Rd (Ruther.) G73 85 110 BY36
Mathieson St G5 67 110 BT33
Mathieson St, Pais. PA1 96 108 AX32
Matilda Rd G41 64 109 BN34
Mauchline St G5 65 109 BQ33
Maukinfauld Ct G32 71 110 BZ34
Maukinfauld Gdns G32 98 110 CA33
Maukinfauld Rd G32 98 110 CA34
Mauldslie St G40 70 110 BX33
Maule Dr G11 25 105 BJ27
Mavis Bk (Bishop.) G64 91 106 BV21
Mavisbank Gdns G51 52 109 BN31
Mavisbank Ter, Pais. PA1 96 108 AV34
Maxton Ter (Camb.) G72 103 110 CB42
Maxwell Av G41 64 109 BN33
Maxwell Av (Bears.) G61 89 105 BG18
Maxwell Av (Baill.) G69 99 111 CJ33
Maxwell Ct G41 64 109 BN33
Maxwell Dr G41 62 109 BL33
Maxwell Dr (Baill.) G69 99 111 CJ32
Maxwell Dr, Ersk. PA8 86 104 AP18
Maxwell Gdns G41 63 109 BM33
Maxwell Gro G41 63 109 BM33
Maxwell La G41 64 109 BN33
Maxwell Oval G41 65 109 BP33
Maxwell Pl G41 65 109 BQ34
Maxwell Rd G41 65 109 BP33
Maxwell St G1 54 110 BS31
Maxwell St (Baill.) G69 99 111 CK33
Maxwell St, Clyde. G81 87 104 AV17
Maxwell St, Pais. PA3 96 108 AU32
Maxwell Ter G41 64 109 BN33
Maxwellton Ct, Pais. PA1 96 108 AS33
Maxwellton St, Pais. PA1 96 108 AS34
Maxwelton Rd G33 35 106 BZ27
Maybank La G42 82 109 BQ36
Maybank St G42 82 109 BQ36
Mayberry Cres G32 98 111 CF32
Mayberry Gdns G32 98 111 CF32
Mayberry Gro G32 98 111 CF32
Maybole St G53 78 108 BB39
Mayfield Av (Clark.) G76 101 109 BN46
Mayfield St G20 90 106 BP23
May Rd, Pais. PA2 96 108 AU38
May Ter G42 83 109 BR37
May Ter (Giff.) G46 101 109 BL42
Meadowburn (Bishop.) G64 91 106 BV17
Meadow La, Renf. PA4 93 104 AZ24
Meadowpark St G31 46 106 BX30
Meadow Rd G11 25 105 BJ27
Meadows Dr, Ersk. PA8 86 104 AS20
Meadowside Ind Est, Renf. PA4 93 104 AZ23
Meadowside Quay G11 24 105 BG28
Meadowside St G11 25 105 BJ28
Meadowside St, Renf. PA4 93 104 AZ24
Meadowwell St G32 98 110 CD32
Mearns Rd (Clark.) G76 101 109 BL46
Mearns Way (Bishop.) G64 91 106 BZ19
Medwyn St G14 73 105 BF26
Meek Pl (Camb.) G72 103 110 CD40
Meetinghouse La, Pais. PA1 96 108 AU32
Megan Gate G40 68 110 BV33
Megan St G40 69 110 BV33
Meikle Av, Renf. PA4 93 104 AY27
Meiklerig Cres G53 77 109 BE35
Meikle Rd G53 79 109 BE37
Meiklewood Rd G51 75 109 BF31
Melbourne Av, Clyde. G81 86 104 AT16
Melbourne Ct (Giff.) G46 101 109 BM42
Melbourne St G31 56 110 BV31
Meldon Pl G51 36 105 BG30
Meldrum Gdns G41 81 109 BM35
Meldrum St, Clyde. G81 87 104 AZ21
Melford Av (Giff.) G46 101 109 BM43
Melford Way, Pais. PA3 93 104 AW30
Melfort Av G41 62 109 BK33
Melfort Av, Clyde. G81 87 104 AX18
Melfort Ct, Clyde. G81 87 104 AY19
Mellerstain Dr G14 88 105 BA23
Melness Pl G51 75 105 BF30
Melrose Av (Ruther.) G73 85 110 BX38
Melrose Ct (Ruther.) G73 85 110 BX38
Melrose Gdns G20 16 106 BP26
Melrose St G4 29 106 BP27
Melvaig Pl G20 89 105 BM24
Melvick Pl G51 75 105 BF30
Melville Ct G1 55 110 BT31
Melville Gdns (Bishop.) G64 91 106 BW19
Melville St G41 64 109 BP34
Memel St G21 91 106 BU24
Memus Av G52 77 109 BE33
Mennock Dr (Bishop.) G64 91 106 BW17
Menock Rd G44 101 109 BR39
Menteith Av (Bishop.) G64 91 106 BX20
Menteith Dr (Ruther.) G73 103 110 BZ43
Menteith Pl (Ruther.) G73 103 110 BZ43
Menzies Dr G21 91 106 BW24
Menzies Pl G21 91 106 BW24
Menzies Rd G21 91 106 BW24
Merchant La G1 55 110 BS31
Merchiston St G32 94 107 CA30
Merkland Ct G11 26 105 BK28
Merkland St G11 26 105 BK27
Merksworth Way, Pais. PA3 93 104 AU30
Merlinford Av, Renf. PA4 72 105 BA26
Merlinford Cres, Renf. PA4 72 105 BA26
Merlinford Dr, Renf. PA4 72 105 BA26
Merlinford Way, Renf. PA4 72 105 BA26
Merlin Way, Pais. PA3 93 104 AX30
Merrick Gdns G51 50 109 BK32
Merrick Path G51 50 109 BK32
Merrick Way (Ruther.) G73 102 110 BX42
Merryburn Av (Giff.) G46 101 109 BM40
Merrycrest Av (Giff.) G46 101 109 BM41
Merrycroft Av (Giff.) G46 101 109 BM41
Merryland Pl G51 38 105 BK30
Merryland St G51 38 105 BK30
Merrylee Cres (Giff.) G46 101 109 BL40
Merrylee Pk Av (Giff.) G46 101 109 BM41
Merrylee Pk La (Giff.) G46 101 109 BL41
Merrylee Pk Ms (Giff.) G46 101 109 BM40
Merrylee Rd G43 101 109 BM40
Merrylee Rd G44 101 109 BN40
Merryton Av G15 88 105 BD18
Merryton Av (Giff.) G46 101 109 BL41
Merryton Pl G15 88 105 BD18
Merryvale Av (Giff.) G46 101 109 BM41
Merryvale Pl (Giff.) G46 101 109 BL40
Merton Dr G52 74 108 BC32
Meryon Gdns G32 98 111 CF35
Meryon Rd G32 98 111 CF34
Methil St G14 73 105 BE26
Methuen Rd, Pais. PA3 93 104 AV28
Methven St G31 71 110 BZ34
Methven St, Clyde. G81 87 104 AV17
Metropole La G1 54/5 110 BS31
Mews La, Pais. PA3 93 104 AV30
Micklehouse Oval (Baill.) G69 99 111 CK31
Micklehouse Pl (Baill.) G69 99 111 CK31
Micklehouse Rd (Baill.) G69 99 111 CK31
Micklehouse Wynd (Baill.) G69 99 111 CK31
Mid Cotts (Gart.) G69 95 107 CL26
Midcroft (Bishop.) G64 91 106 BU18
Midcroft Av G44 102 110 BT40
Middle Pk, Pais. PA2 96 108 AT35
Middlesex Gdns G41 52 109 BN31
Middlesex St G41 52 109 BN32
Middleton St G51 50 109 BL31
Midfaulds Av, Renf. PA4 72 105 BA27
Midland St G1 42 106 BR30
Midlem Dr G52 75 109 BE32
Midlem Oval G52 75 109 BE32
Midlock St G51 50 109 BL32
Midlothian Dr G41 81 109 BM36
Midton St G21 20 106 BV26
Midwharf St G4 30 106 BS27
Migvie Pl G20 89 105 BM24
Milan St G41 65 109 BQ34
Milford St G33 94 107 CC29
Millarbank St G21 20 106 BU25
Millar St, Pais. PA1 96 108 AV32
Millar Ter (Ruther.) G73 85 110 BX36
Millbeg Cres G33 99 111 CH31
Millbeg Pl G33 99 111 CG32
Millbrae Ct G42 82 109 BP38
Millbrae Cres G42 82 109 BN38
Millbrae Cres, Clyde. G81 87 104 AZ22
Millbrae Gdns G42 82 109 BP38
Millbrae Rd G42 82 109 BN38
Millbrix Av G14 88 105 BC24
Millburn Av (Ruther.) G73 102 110 BW39
Millburn Av, Clyde. G81 88 105 BA21
Millburn Av, Renf. PA4 93 104 AZ26
Millburn Dr, Renf. PA4 72 105 BA26
Millburn Rd, Renf. PA4 93 104 AZ26
Millburn St G21 33 106 BW28
Millburn Way, Renf. PA4 72 105 BA26
Mill Ct (Ruther.) G73 84 110 BW37
Mill Cres G40 68 110 BV34
Millcroft Rd (Ruther.) G73 84 110 BV35
Millennium Gdns G34 95 107 CL30
Millerfield Pl G40 70 110 BX34
Millerfield Rd G40 70 110 BX34
Miller La, Clyde. G81 87 104 AX20
Millersneuk Cres G33 94 107 CC27
Millerston St G31 56 110 BW31
Miller St G1 42 106 BS30
Miller St (Baill.) G69 99 111 CK33
Miller St, Clyde. G81 87 104 AX20
Millfield Av, Ersk. PA8 86 104 AP20
Millfield Cres, Ersk. PA8 86 104 AQ20
Millfield Dr, Ersk. PA8 86 104 AQ21
Millfield Gdns, Ersk. PA8 86 104 AQ20
Millfield Hill, Ersk. PA8 86 104 AP20
Millfield La, Ersk. PA8 86 104 AP20
Millfield Meadows, Ersk. PA8 86 104 AP20
Millfield Pl, Ersk. PA8 86 104 AP20
Millfield Vw, Ersk. PA8 86 104 AP20
Millfield Wk, Ersk. PA8 86 104 AQ21
Millfield Wynd, Ersk. PA8 86 104 AP20
Millholm Rd G44 101 109 BR41
Millhouse Cres G20 89 105 BL22
Millhouse Dr G20 89 105 BK22
Millport Av G44 83 110 BS38
Mill Rd, Clyde. G81 87 104 AZ22
Millroad Dr G40 56 110 BU31
Millroad Gdns G40 56 110 BV31
Millroad St G40 56 110 BU31
Millstream Ct, Pais. PA1 96 108 AV33
Mill St G40 68 110 BW34
Mill St (Ruther.) G73 102 110 BW39
Mill St, Pais. PA1 96 108 AV33
Millwood St G41 82 109 BN37
Milnbank St G31 45 106 BW29
Milncroft Pl G33 94 107 CC28
Milncroft Rd G33 94 107 CC28
Milner La G13 89 105 BG24
Milner Rd G13 89 105 BG24
Milngavie Rd (Bears.) G61 89 105 BH18
Milnpark Gdns G41 51 109 BM32
Milnpark St G41 52 109 BN32
Milovaig Av G23 89 105 BM20
Milovaig St G23 89 105 BM20
Milrig Rd (Ruther.) G73 84 110 BV38
Milton Av (Camb.) G72 103 110 CA40
Milton Douglas Rd, Clyde. G81 87 104 AW15
Milton Dr (Bishop.) G64 91 106 BU22
Milton Mains Rd, Clyde. G81 87 104 AW16
Milton St G4 30 106 BS28
Milverton Rd (Giff.) G46 100 109 BJ44
Minard Rd G41 82 109 BN36
Minerva St G3 40 106 BN29
Minerva Way G3 40 106 BN29
Mingarry La G20 16 106 BN25
Mingarry St G20 16 106 BN25
Mingulay Cres G22 90 106 BT21
Mingulay Pl G22 91 106 BU21
Mingulay St G22 90 106 BT21
Minmoir Rd G53 78 108 BB38
Minstrel Rd G13 88 105 BF20
Minto Av (Ruther.) G73 103 110 BZ41
Minto Cres G52 49 109 BH32
Minto St G52 48 109 BH32
Mireton St G22 90 106 BR24
Mirrlees Dr G12 15 105 BL25
Mirrlees La G12 15 105 BL25
Mitchell Arc (Ruther.) G73 85 110 BX37
Mitchell Av, Renf. PA4 93 104 AX27
Mitchell Dr (Ruther.) G73 102 110 BX39
Mitchellhill Rd G45 102 110 BV43
Mitchell La G1 42 106 BR30
Mitchell St G1 42 106 BR30
Mitre Ct G11 12 105 BH25
Mitre La G14 73 105 BF25
Mitre La W G14 73 105 BF25
Mitre Rd G11 12 105 BH25
Mitre Rd G14 12 105 BG25
Moat Av G13 88 105 BE22
Mochrum Rd G43 101 109 BN39
Moffat St G5 67 110 BT33
Moidart Av, Renf. PA4 93 104 AX25
Moidart Cres G52 48 109 BG32
Moidart Pl G52 48 109 BG32
Moidart Rd G52 48 109 BG32
Moir St G1 55 110 BT31
Molendinar St G1 55 110 BT31
Mollinsburn St G21 20 106 BU26
Monach Rd G33 94 107 CE29
Monar Dr G22 18 106 BR26
Monar Pl G22 18 106 BR26
Monar St G22 18 106 BR26
Monart Pl G20 90 106 BP24
Moncrieff St, Pais. PA3 96 108 AU32
Moncur St G40 56 110 BU31
Moness Dr G52 60 109 BG33
Monifieth Av G52 77 109 BF34
Monikie Gdns (Bishop.) G64 91 106 BZ20
Monkcastle Dr (Camb.) G72 103 110 CC39
Monksbridge Av G13 88 105 BE20
Monkscroft Av G11 13 105 BJ26
Monkscroft Ct G11 25 105 BJ27
Monkscroft Gdns G11 13 105 BJ26
Monkton Dr G15 88 105 BD19
Monmouth Av G12 89 105 BJ23
Monreith Av (Bears.) G61 89 105 BG19
Monreith Rd G43 101 109 BN39
Monreith Rd E G44 101 109 BQ40
Montague La G12 14 105 BK25
Montague St G4 28 106 BP27
Monteith Dr (Clark.) G76 101 109 BP45
Monteith Gdns (Clark.) G76 101 109 BP45
Monteith Pl G40 56 110 BU32
Monteith Row G40 56 110 BU32
Monteith Row La G40 56 110 BU32
Montford Av G44 83 110 BT38
Montford Av (Ruther.) G73 84 110 BU38
Montgomery Av, Pais. PA3 93 104 AX29
Montgomery Dr (Giff.) G46 101 109 BL44
Montgomery Rd, Pais. PA3 93 104 AW29
Montgomery St G40 69 110 BW33
Montraive St (Ruther.) G73 85 110 BY36
Montrave Path G52 77 109 BF33
Montrave St G52 77 109 BF33
Montreal Ho, Clyde. G81 86 104 AT15
Montrose Av G32 98 111 CE36
Montrose Av G52 74 105 BB29
Montrose St G1 43 106 BT29
Montrose St G4 43 106 BT29
Montrose St, Clyde. G81 87 104 AX19
Montrose Ter (Bishop.) G64 91 106 BY22
Monument Dr G33 94 107 CA24
Monymusk Gdns (Bishop.) G64 91 106 BZ19
Moodiesburn St G33 35 106 BZ27
Moorburn Av (Giff.) G46 100 109 BK42
Moore Dr (Bears.) G61 89 105 BH18
Moore St G31 56 110 BV31
Moorfoot (Bishop.) G64 91 106 BY19
Moorfoot Av (Thornlie.) G46 100 109 BJ42
Moorfoot Av, Pais. PA2 96 108 AT36
Moorfoot Path, Pais. PA2 96 108 AT37
Moorfoot St G32 98 110 CA31
Moorhouse Av G13 88 105 BB23
Moorpark Av G52 74 108 BB31
Moorpark Dr G52 74 108 BC31
Moorpark Pl G52 74 108 BB31
Moorpark Sq, Renf. PA4 93 104 AX27
Moraine Av G15 88 105 BD20
Moraine Circ G15 88 105 BC20
Moraine Dr G15 88 105 BC20
Moraine Dr (Clark.) G76 101 109 BM45

Moraine Pl G15 88 105 BD20
Morar Av, Clyde. G81 87 104 AX17
Morar Ct, Clyde. G81 87 104 AX17
Morar Cres (Bishop.) G64 91 106 BV19
Morar Cres, Clyde. G81 87 104 AX17
Morar Dr (Bears.) G61 89 105 BK18
Morar Dr (Ruther.) G73 102 110 BX42
Morar Dr, Clyde. G81 87 104 AX17
Morar Pl (Newt. M.) G77 100 109 BF46
Morar Pl, Clyde. G81 87 104 AX17
Morar Pl, Renf. PA4 93 104 AX25
Morar Rd G52 48 109 BG32
Morar Rd, Clyde. G81 87 104 AX17
Morar Ter (Ruther.) G73 103 110 BZ42
Moray Ct (Ruther.) G73 84 110 BW37
Moray Dr (Clark.) G76 101 109 BP46
Moray Gdns (Clark.) G76 101 109 BP45
Moray Pl G41 82 109 BN35
Moray Pl (Bishop.) G64 91 106 BY20
Mordaunt St G40 69 110 BW34
Moredun Cres G32 94 107 CE30
Moredun St G32 94 107 CE30
Morefield Rd G51 75 105 BF30
Morgan Ms G42 66 109 BR34
Morina Gdns G53 100 109 BE43
Morion Rd G13 88 105 BF21
Morley St G42 82 109 BQ38
Morna Pl G14 24 105 BG27
Morningside St G33 47 106 BZ29
Morrin Path G21 20 106 BU25
Morrin Sq G4 44 106 BU29
Morrin St G21 20 106 BU25
Morrison Quad, Clyde. G81 88 105 BA19
Morrison St G5 53 109 BQ31
Morrison St, Clyde. G81 87 104 AV15
Morriston Cres, Renf. PA4 72 105 BB28
Morriston Pk Dr (Camb.) G72 103 110 CC39
Morriston St (Camb.) G72 103 110 CC39
Morton Gdns G41 81 109 BL36
Morven Av (Bishop.) G64 91 106 BY20
Morven Av, Pais. PA2 96 108 AT37
Morven Dr (Clark.) G76 101 109 BM45
Morven Gait, Ersk. PA8 87 104 AU21
Morven Rd (Camb.) G72 103 110 CB42
Morven St G52 48 109 BG32
Mosesfield St G21 91 106 BV24
Mosque Av G5 54 110 BS32
Mossbank Av G33 94 107 CB25
Mossbank Dr G33 94 107 CB25
Mosscastle Rd G33 94 107 CE27
Moss Dr, Ersk. PA8 86 104 AR22
Mossend La G33 94 107 CF29
Mossend St G33 94 107 CF30
Mossgiel Av (Ruther.) G73 102 110 BW40
Mossgiel Dr, Clyde. G81 87 104 AY18
Mossgiel Pl (Ruther.) G73 102 110 BW40
Mossgiel Rd G43 81 109 BM38
Moss Hts Av G52 75 109 BF32
Mossland Rd G52 75 105 BA29
Mosslands Rd, Pais. PA3 92 104 AT29
Mossneuk Dr, Pais. PA2 96 108 AS37
Mosspark Av G52 60 109 BH34
Mosspark Boul G52 60 109 BG33
Mosspark Dr G52 77 109 BE33
Mosspark La G52 60 109 BG34
Mosspark Oval G52 60 109 BG34
Mosspark Sq G52 60 109 BG34
Moss Path (Baill.) G69 99 111 CH34
Moss Rd G51 75 109 BE31
Moss-Side Rd G41 81 109 BM36
Moss St, Pais. PA1 96 108 AU32
Mossvale La, Pais. PA3 96 108 AT31
Mossvale Path G33 94 107 CE26
Mossvale Rd G33 94 107 CD26
Mossvale Sq G33 94 107 CD26
Mossvale Sq, Pais. PA3 96 108 AT31
Mossvale St, Pais. PA3 92 104 AT30
Mossvale Wk G33 94 107 CE27
Mossvale Way G33 94 107 CE26
Mossview Quad G52 75 109 BE32
Mossview Rd G33 95 107 CG24
Mote Hill Rd, Pais. PA3 96 108 AW31
Moulin Circ G52 76 108 BC33
Moulin Pl G52 76 108 BC33
Moulin Rd G52 76 108 BC33
Moulin Ter G52 76 108 BC33
Mountainblue St G31 57 110 BW32
Mount Annan Dr G44 83 109 BR38
Mountblow Ho, Clyde. G81 86 104 AT16
Mountblow Rd, Clyde. G81 87 104 AU15
Mountgarrie Path G51 75 105 BF30
Mountgarrie Rd G51 75 105 BF30
Mount Harriet Av (Stepps) G33 95 107 CG23
Mount Harriet Dr (Stepps) G33 94 107 CF23
Mount Lockhart (Udd.) G71 99 111 CK35
Mount Lockhart Gdns (Udd.) G71 99 111 CK35
Mount Pleasant Pl (Old Kil.) G60 86 104 AR15
Mount St G20 17 106 BP26
Mount Stuart St G41 82 109 BN37
Mount Vernon Av G32 99 111 CG34
Moyne Rd G53 76 108 BC35
Moy St G11 26/7 105 BL27
Muirbank Av (Ruther.) G73 84 110 BV38
Muirbank Gdns (Ruther.) G73 84 110 BV38
Muirbrae Rd (Ruther.) G73 102 110 BX41
Muirbrae Way (Ruther.) G73 102 110 BX41
Muirburn Av G44 101 109 BN41
Muir Ct G44 101 109 BP43
Muirdrum Av G52 77 109 BF34
Muirdykes Av G52 74 108 BC32
Muirdykes Rd G52 74 108 BC32
Muiredge Ter (Baill.) G69 99 111 CK33
Muirend Av G44 101 109 BP40
Muirend Rd G44 101 109 BN41
Muirfield Ct G44 101 109 BN41
Muirfield Cres G23 90 106 BN20
Muirhead Ct (Baill.) G69 99 111 CL33
Muirhead Gdns (Baill.) G69 99 111 CL33
Muirhead Gro (Baill.) G69 99 111 CL33
Muirhead Rd (Baill.) G69 99 111 CK34
Muirhead St G11 26 105 BK27
Muirhead Way (Bishop.) G64 91 106 BZ20
Muirhill Av G44 101 109 BN41
Muirhill Cres G13 88 105 BC22
Muirkirk Dr G13 89 105 BH22
Muirpark Av, Renf. PA4 93 104 AY27
Muirpark Dr (Bishop.) G64 91 106 BW21
Muirpark St G11 26 105 BK27
Muir Pk Ter (Bishop.) G64 91 106 BV21
Muirshiel Av G53 79 109 BE39
Muirshiel Cres G53 79 109 BE39
Muirside Av G32 99 111 CG34
Muirside Rd (Baill.) G69 99 111 CK33
Muirside Rd, Pais. PA3 92 104 AR30
Muirside St (Baill.) G69 99 111 CK33
Muirskeith Cres G43 101 109 BP39
Muirskeith Pl G43 101 109 BP39
Muirskeith Rd G43 101 109 BP39
Muir St (Bishop.) G64 91 106 BW20
Muir St, Renf. PA4 93 104 AZ25
Muir Ter, Pais. PA3 93 104 AW30
Muirton Dr (Bishop.) G64 91 106 BV18
Muiryfauld Dr G31 98 110 CA33
Mulben Cres G53 78 108 BB38
Mulben Pl G53 78 108 BB38
Mulben Ter G53 78 108 BB38
Mulberry Rd G43 101 109 BM40
Mullardoch St G23 89 105 BM20
Mull Av, Pais. PA2 96 108 AT38
Mull Av, Renf. PA4 93 104 AY28
Mull St G21 34 106 BX27
Munlochy Rd G51 75 105 BF30
Munro Ct, Clyde. G81 87 104 AV15
Munro La G13 89 105 BG24
Munro La E G13 89 105 BG24
Munro Pl G13 89 105 BG22
Munro Rd G13 89 105 BG24
Murano St G20 16 106 BP25
Murchison G12 89 105 BH23
Murdoch St G21 91 106 BV24
Murray Business Area, Pais. PA3 96 108 AT31
Murrayfield (Bishop.) G64 91 106 BW18
Murrayfield Dr (Bears.) G61 89 105 BG20
Murrayfield St G32 94 107 CA30
Murray St, Pais. PA3 96 108 AS31
Murray St, Renf. PA4 93 104 AY26
Murrin Av (Bishop.) G64 91 106 BZ20
Murroes Rd G51 75 105 BF30
Muslin St G40 68 110 BV33
Mybster Pl G51 75 105 BF30
Mybster Rd G51 75 105 BF30
Myreside Pl G32 59 110 BZ31
Myreside St G32 59 110 BZ31
Myres Rd G53 79 109 BF37
Myrie Gdns (Bishop.) G64 91 106 BX19
Myroch Pl G34 95 107 CL28
Myrtle Hill La G42 83 110 BS37
Myrtle Pk G42 83 109 BR36
Myrtle Pl G42 83 110 BS36
Myrtle Rd, Clyde. G81 86 104 AT17
Myrtle Sq (Bishop.) G64 91 106 BW21
Myrtle Vw Rd G42 83 110 BS37
Myrtle Wk (Camb.) G72 103 110 CB39

Naburn Gate G5 66 110 BS33
Nairn Pl, Clyde. G81 87 104 AV18
Nairnside Rd G21 91 106 BY22
Nairn St G3 27 105 BM28
Nairn St, Clyde. G81 87 104 AV18
Naismith St G32 98 111 CE36
Nansen St G20 17 106 BQ26
Napier Ct (Old Kil.) G60 86 104 AS16
Napier Dr G51 38 105 BK29
Napier Pl G51 38 105 BK29
Napier Pl (Old Kil.) G60 86 104 AS16
Napier Rd G51 38 105 BK29
Napier Rd G52 72 105 BB28
Napiershall La G20 29 106 BP27
Napiershall Pl G20 28/9 106 BP27
Napiershall St G20 29 106 BP27
Napier St G51 38 105 BK29
Napier St, Clyde. G81 87 104 AY22
Napier Ter G51 38 105 BK29
Naseby Av G11 13 105 BH26
Naseby La G11 13 105 BH26
Nasmyth Pl G52 74 105 BC30
Nasmyth Rd G52 74 105 BC30
Nasmyth Rd N G52 74 105 BC30
Nasmyth Rd S G52 74 105 BC30
Navar Pl, Pais. PA2 96 108 AW35
Naver St G33 94 107 CA28
Neidpath (Baill.) G69 99 111 CJ33
Neidpath Rd W (Giff.) G46 100 109 BJ46
Neilsland Oval G53 79 109 BF37
Neilsland Sq G53 77 109 BF36
Neilston Av G53 79 109 BE40
Neilston Rd, Pais. PA2 96 108 AU34
Neil St, Pais. PA1 96 108 AS33
Neil St, Renf. PA4 93 104 AZ24
Neilvaig Dr (Ruther.) G73 103 110 BY42
Neistpoint Dr G33 94 107 CC29
Nelson Mandela Pl G2 42 106 BS29
Nelson Pl (Baill.) G69 99 111 CK33
Nelson St G5 53 109 BQ31
Nelson St (Baill.) G69 99 111 CK33
Neptune St G51 38 105 BK30
Ness Gdns (Bishop.) G64 91 106 BX20
Ness Rd, Renf. PA4 93 104 AX25
Ness St G33 94 107 CA28
Nethan St G51 37 105 BJ29
Nether Auldhouse Rd G43 81 109 BK38
Netherburn Av G44 101 109 BP43
Netherby Dr G41 63 109 BM33
Nethercairn Rd G43 101 109 BL41
Nethercliffe Av G44 101 109 BP43
Nethercommon Harbour, Pais. PA3 93 104 AU30
Nethercraigs Dr, Pais. PA2 96 108 AS37
Netherdale Dr, Pais. PA1 76 108 BB34
Netherfield St G31 58 110 BY31
Nethergreen Cres, Renf. PA4 93 104 AX26
Nethergreen Rd, Renf. PA4 93 104 AX26
Nethergreen Wynd, Renf. PA4 93 104 AX26
Netherhill Av G44 101 109 BP44
Netherhill Cotts, Pais. PA3 93 104 AX30
Netherhill Cres, Pais. PA3 96 108 AW31
Netherhill Rd, Pais. PA3 96 108 AV31
Netherhill Way, Pais. PA3 93 104 AX30
Netherhouse Rd (Baill.) G69 95 107 CM30
Netherlee Pl G44 101 109 BQ41
Netherlee Rd G44 101 109 BP42
Netherpark Av G44 101 109 BP44
Netherplace Cres G53 79 108 BD37
Netherplace Rd G53 79 108 BD37
Netherton Ct G45 102 110 BV43
Netherton Ct (Newt. M.) G77 100 109 BJ46
Netherton Rd G13 89 105 BG21
Netherton St G13 89 105 BH22
Nethervale Av G44 101 109 BP44
Netherview Rd G44 101 109 BQ44
Netherway G44 101 109 BP44
Nethy Way, Renf. PA4 72 105 BB28
Neuk Way G32 98 111 CE37
Nevis Rd G43 100 109 BK40
Nevis Rd, Renf. PA4 93 104 AX28
Nevis Way (Abbots.), Pais. PA3 93 104 AU28
Newark Dr G41 63 109 BM34
Newark Dr, Pais. PA2 96 108 AS37
Newbank Ct G32 98 110 CA33
Newbank Gdns G32 71 110 BZ33
Newbank Rd G32 98 110 CA33
Newbattle Ct G32 98 110 CD35
Newbattle Gdns G32 98 110 CD35
Newbattle Pl G32 98 110 CD35
Newbattle Rd G32 98 110 CC36
Newbold Av G21 91 106 BU22
Newburgh, Ersk. PA8 86 104 AQ18
Newburgh St G43 81 109 BM38
Newcastleton Dr G23 90 106 BN20
New City Rd G4 30 106 BR28
Newcraigs Dr (Clark.) G76 102 110 BT46
Newcroft Dr G44 102 110 BT40
Newfield Pl (Thornlie.) G46 100 109 BH43
Newfield Pl (Ruther.) G73 84 110 BU38
Newfield Sq G53 78 108 BC39
Newgrove Gdns (Camb.) G72 103 110 CC39
Newhall St G40 68 110 BU34
Newhaven Rd G33 94 107 CD29
Newhaven St G32 94 107 CC30
Newhills Rd G33 95 107 CG30
New Inchinnan Rd, Pais. PA3 93 104 AU30
Newington St G32 98 110 CB31
Newlandsfield Rd G43 81 109 BM38
Newlands Rd G43 101 109 BN39
Newlands Rd G44 101 109 BQ39
New Luce Dr G32 98 111 CF34
Newmains Av (Inch.), Renf. PA4 92 104 AQ24
Newmains Rd, Renf. PA4 93 104 AX27
Newmill Rd G21 91 106 BY24
Newnham Rd, Pais. PA1 97 108 AZ33
Newpark Cres (Camb.) G72 98 110 CC38
Newshot Ct, Clyde. G81 87 104 AZ22
Newshot Dr, Ersk. PA8 86 104 AS22
New Sneddon St, Pais. PA3 96 108 AU32
Newstead Gdns G23 90 106 BN20
New St, Clyde. G81 87 104 AW15
New St, Pais. PA1 96 108 AU33
Newton Fm Rd (Camb.) G72 99 111 CH38
Newtongrange Av G32 98 110 CD34
Newtongrange Gdns G32 98 110 CD35
Newton Pl G3 28 106 BP28
Newton St G3 41 106 BQ29
Newton St, Pais. PA1 96 108 AS33
Newton Ter G3 40 106 BP29
Newton Ter La G3 40 106 BP29
Newton Way, Pais. PA3 93 104 AX30
Newtyle Dr G53 76 108 BB36
Newtyle Pl G53 76 108 BB36
Newtyle Pl (Bishop.) G64 91 106 BZ20
Newtyle Rd, Pais. PA1 96 108 AX33
New Wynd G1 55 110 BS31
Nicholas St G1 43 106 BT30
Nicholson La G5 54 109 BR31
Nicholson St G5 54 109 BR31
Nicolson Ct (Stepps) G33 95 107 CG24
Niddrie Rd G42 82 109 BP35
Niddrie Sq G42 82 109 BP35
Niddry St, Pais. PA3 96 108 AV32
Nigel Gdns G41 81 109 BM36
Nigg Pl G34 95 107 CJ29
Nimmo Dr G51 36 105 BG30
Nisbet St G31 59 110 BZ32
Nith Dr, Renf. PA4 72 105 BA27
Nithsdale Dr G41 82 109 BP35
Nithsdale Pl G41 64 109 BP34
Nithsdale Rd G41 82 109 BP35
Nithsdale St G41 82 109 BP35
Nith St G33 35 106 BZ28
Nitshill Rd (Thornlie.) G46 100 109 BF42
Nitshill Rd G53 78 108 BB39
Niven St G20 89 105 BL23
Noldrum Av G32 98 111 CE37
Noldrum Gdns G32 98 111 CE37
Norbreck Dr (Giff.) G46 101 109 BL41
Norby Rd G11 12 105 BH26
Norfield Dr G44 83 109 BR38
Norfolk Ct G5 54 109 BR32
Norfolk Cres (Bishop.) G64 91 106 BU18
Norfolk La G5 54 109 BR32
Norfolk St G5 54 110 BS32
Norham St G41 82 109 BN36
Norman St G40 69 110 BV34
Norse La N G14 73 105 BE25
Norse La S G14 73 105 BE25
Norse Pl G14 73 105 BE25
Norse Rd G14 73 105 BE25
Northampton Dr G12 89 105 BK23
Northampton La G12 89 105 BK23
North Av (Camb.) G72 103 110 CB39
North Av, Clyde. G81 87 104 AW19
North Bk Pl, Clyde. G81 87 104 AY21
North Bk St, Clyde. G81 87 104 AY21
North Barr Av, Ersk. PA8 86 104 AQ19
North Brae Pl G13 88 105 BD22
North Calder Gro (Udd.) G71 99 111 CK35
North Calder Pl (Udd.) G71 99 111 CK35
North Canal Bk G4 31 106 BS27
North Canal Bk St G4 30 106 BS27
North Claremont St G3 28 106 BN28
North Corsebar Rd, Pais. PA2 96 108 AS35
North Ct G1 42 106 BS30
North Ct La G1 42 106 BS30
Northcroft Rd G21 20 106 BV25
North Cft St, Pais. PA3 96 108 AV32
North Douglas St, Clyde. G81 87 104 AY21
North Elgin Pl, Clyde. G81 87 104 AY22
North Elgin St, Clyde. G81 87 104 AY22
North Frederick St G1 43 106 BS30
North Gardner St G11 26 105 BK27
Northgate Quad G21 91 106 BY22
Northgate Rd G21 91 106 BY22
North Gower St G51 51 109 BL32
North Hanover Pl G4 42/3 106 BS29
North Hanover St G1 43 106 BS29
Northinch Ct G14 73 105 BF27
Northinch St G14 73 105 BF27
Northland Av G14 88 105 BE24
Northland Dr G14 88 105 BE24
Northland Gdns G14 88 105 BE24
Northland La G14 73 105 BE25
North Lo Rd, Renf. PA4 93 104 AY25
North Moraine La G15 88 105 BE19
Northmuir Rd G15 88 105 BD17
North Pk Av (Thornlie.) G46 100 109 BH41
Northpark St G20 17 106 BP25
North Pk Vil (Thornlie.) G46 100 109 BH41
North Pl G3 40/1 106 BP29
North Portland St G1 43 106 BT30
North St G3 41 106 BP29
North St, Pais. PA3 96 108 AU31
Northumberland St G20 16 106 BN25
North Vw (Bears.) G61 88 105 BF19
North Wallace St G4 31 106 BT28
North Woodside Rd G20 16 106 BP26
Norval St G11 25 105 BJ27
Norwich Dr G12 89 105 BK24
Norwood Dr (Giff.) G46 100 109 BJ44
Norwood Pk (Bears.) G61 89 105 BH18
Nottingham Av G12 89 105 BJ23
Nottingham La G12 89 105 BK23
Novar Dr G12 13 105 BJ25
Novar Gdns (Bishop.) G64 91 106 BU19
Nuneaton St G40 69 110 BW34
Nuneaton St Ind Est G40 69 110 BW34
Nurseries Rd (Baill.) G69 99 111 CH31
Nursery Av (Erskine Hosp.), Bish. PA7 86 104 AN17
Nursery La G41 82 109 BP35
Nursery St G41 65 109 BQ34
Nutberry Ct G42 83 109 BR36

Oakbank Ind Est G20 18 106 BR26
Oak Cres (Baill.) G69 99 111 CJ33
Oakfield Av G12 28 106 BN27
Oakfield La G12 28 106 BN27
Oakhill Av (Baill.) G69 99 111 CH34
Oakley Dr G44 101 109 BP42
Oakley Ter G31 45 106 BV30
Oak Pk (Bishop.) G64 91 106 BX20
Oak Rd, Clyde. G81 87 104 AV16
Oak Rd, Pais. PA2 96 108 AW36
Oakshaw Brae, Pais. PA1 96 108 AT32
Oakshawhead, Pais. PA1 96 108 AT32
Oakshaw St E, Pais. PA1 96 108 AT32
Oakshaw St W, Pais. PA1 96 108 AT32
Oak St G2 41 106 BQ30
Oaktree Gdns G45 102 110 BV41
Oakwood Cres G34 95 107 CM28
Oakwood Dr G34 95 107 CM29
Oatfield St G21 22 106 BX25
Oban Ct G20 16 106 BN25
Oban Dr G20 16 106 BN25
Oban La G20 16 106 BN25
Observatory La G12 15 105 BM26
Observatory Rd G12 15 105 BL26
Ochil Dr, Pais. PA2 96 108 AU37
Ochil Pl G32 98 110 CC33
Ochil Rd (Bishop.) G64 91 106 BY20
Ochil Rd, Renf. PA4 93 104 AX28
Ochil St G32 98 110 CC33
Ochiltree Av G13 89 105 BH22
Ogilvie Pl G31 71 110 BZ33
Ogilvie St G31 71 110 BZ33
Old Castle Rd G44 101 109 BR39
Old Cotts, Pais. PA2 97 108 AY37
Old Dalmarnock Rd G40 69 110 BV33
Old Dalnottar Rd (Old Kil.) G60 86 104 AR16
Old Dumbarton Rd G3 27 105 BL28
Old Fm Rd, Pais. PA2 97 108 AZ36
Old Glasgow Rd (Udd.) G71 99 111 CM37
Old Govan Rd, Renf. PA4 72 105 BB26
Old Greenock Rd, Ersk. PA8 86 104 AN20
Old Greenock Rd (Inch.), Renf. PA4 86 104 AT22
Oldhall Rd, Pais. PA1 97 108 AY32
Old Manse Rd G32 98 111 CF33
Old Mill Ct (Dunt.), Clyde. G81 87 104 AW16
Old Mill Rd, Clyde. G81 87 104 AW15
Old Playfield Rd (Carm.) G76 102 110 BT45
Old Rutherglen Rd G5 67 110 BS33
Old Shettleston Rd G32 98 110 CC32
Old Sneddon St, Pais. PA3 96 108 AU32
Old St, Clyde. G81 87 104 AV15
Old Wd Rd (Baill.) G69 99 111 CJ34
Old Wynd G1 55 110 BS31
Olive St G33 23 106 BZ25
Olympia St G40 57 110 BV32
O'Neil Av (Bishop.) G64 91 106 BX21
Onslow Dr G31 45 106 BW30
Onslow Rd, Clyde. G81 87 104 AY19
Onslow Sq G31 45 106 BW30
Oran Gdns G20 90 106 BN24
Oran Gate G20 90 106 BN24
Oran Pl G20 16 106 BN25
Oran St G20 90 106 BN24
Orbiston Gdns G32 98 110 CC32
Orcades Dr G44 101 109 BR41
Orchard Ct G32 98 110 CD37
Orchard Ct (Thornlie.) G46 100 109 BJ42
Orchard Dr (Giff.) G46 100 109 BK42
Orchard Dr (Ruther.) G73 84 110 BV37
Orchard Gro (Giff.) G46 100 109 BK41
Orchard Pk (Giff.) G46 101 109 BL42
Orchard Pk Av (Giff.) G46 100 109 BJ41
Orchard St (Baill.) G69 99 111 CH34
Orchard St, Pais. PA1 96 108 AU33
Orchard St, Renf. PA4 93 104 AZ25
Orchy Av (Clark.) G76 101 109 BP44
Orchy Ct, Clyde. G81 87 104 AY16
Orchy Cres (Bears.) G61 88 105 BF19
Orchy Dr (Clark.) G76 101 109 BP44
Orchy Gdns (Clark.) G76 101 109 BP44
Orchy St G44 101 109 BQ39
Oregon Pl G5 67 110 BS33
Orion Way (Camb.) G72 103 110 CC39
Orkney Pl G51 37 105 BJ30
Orkney St G51 38 105 BK30
Orleans Av G14 12 105 BG26
Orleans La G14 12 105 BG26
Ormiston Av G14 73 105 BE25
Ormiston La G14 73 105 BE25
Ormiston La N G14 73 105 BE25
Ormiston La S G14 73 105 BE25
Ormonde Av G44 101 109 BP42
Ormonde Ct G44 101 109 BN42
Ormonde Cres G44 101 109 BP42
Ormonde Dr G44 101 109 BP42
Ornsay St G22 90 106 BT22
Oronsay Ct (Old Kil.) G60 86 104 AS15
Oronsay Cres (Old Kil.) G60 86 104 AS15
Oronsay Cres (Bears.) G61 89 105 BK18
Oronsay Gdns (Old Kil.) G60 86 104 AS15
Oronsay Pl (Old Kil.) G60 86 104 AS15
Oronsay Sq (Old Kil.) G60 86 104 AS15
Orr Pl G40 57 110 BV31
Orr Sq, Pais. PA1 96 108 AU32
Orr St G40 57 110 BV31
Orr St, Pais. PA1 96 108 AT32
Orr St, Pais. PA2 96 108 AU34
Osborne St G1 55 110 BS31
Osborne St, Clyde. G81 87 104 AW18
Osborne Vil G44 101 109 BQ40
Ossian Av, Pais. PA1 74 108 BB32
Ossian Rd G43 101 109 BN39
Oswald St G1 42 106 BR30
Otago La G12 28 106 BN27
Otago La N G12 28 106 BN27
Otago St G12 28 106 BN27
Ottawa Cres, Clyde. G81 86 104 AT17
Otterburn Dr (Giff.) G46 101 109 BL43
Otterswick Pl G33 94 107 CE27
Oval, The (Clark.) G76 101 109 BP44
Overdale Av G42 82 109 BP37
Overdale Gdns G42 82 109 BP37
Overdale St G42 82 109 BP37
Overdale Vil G42 82 109 BP37
Overlea Av (Ruther.) G73 103 110 BZ39
Overlee Rd (Clark.) G76 101 109 BN46
Overnewton Pl G3 39 105 BM29
Overnewton Sq G3 27 105 BM28
Overnewton St G3 27 105 BM28
Overtoun Ct, Clyde. G81 87 104 AU18
Overtoun Dr (Ruther.) G73 84 110 BW38
Overtoun Dr, Clyde. G81 87 104 AV17
Overtoun Rd, Clyde. G81 87 104 AU17
Overtown Av G53 78 108 BC39
Overtown St G31 57 110 BW32
Overwood Dr G44 102 110 BS39
Oxford La G5 54 109 BR32
Oxford La, Renf. PA4 93 104 AY26
Oxford Rd, Renf. PA4 93 104 AY26
Oxford St G5 54 109 BR31
Oxton Dr G52 75 108 BD32

Pacific Dr G51 50 109 BL31
Pacific Quay G51 39 105 BM30
Paisley Rd G5 53 109 BQ31
Paisley Rd, Renf. PA4 93 104 AX28
Paisley Rd W G51 51 109 BL32
Paisley Rd W G52 49 109 BJ32
Paladin Av G13 88 105 BD21
Palermo St G21 20 106 BU25
Palladium Pl G14 73 105 BF26
Palmer Av G13 88 105 BF20
Palmerston Pl G3 39 105 BM29
Panmure St G20 17 106 BQ25
Park Av G3 28 106 BP27
Park Av (Bishop.) G64 91 106 BW18
Park Av, Pais. PA2 96 108 AS36
Park Bk, Ersk. PA8 86 104 AR20

Park Brae, Ersk. PA8 86 104 AS21
Parkbrae Gdns G20 90 106 BQ23
Parkbrae Pl G20 90 106 BQ23
Park Circ G3 28 106 BN28
Park Circ La G3 28 106 BN28
Park Circ Pl G3 28 106 BP28
Park Ct (Giff.) G46 101 109 BL43
Park Ct (Bishop.) G64 91 106 BX18
Park Ct, Clyde. G81 87 104 AU17
Park Cres (Bishop.) G64 91 106 BW19
Park Cres (Inch.), Renf. PA4 86 104 AS22
Park Dr G3 28 106 BN27
Park Dr (Ruther.) G73 84 110 BW38
Park Dr, Ersk. PA8 86 104 AS21
Parker St G14 24 105 BG27
Park Gdns G3 28 106 BN28
Park Gdns La G3 28 106 BN28
Park Gate G3 28 106 BN28
Park Gate, Ersk. PA8 86 104 AR21
Park Glade, Ersk. PA8 86 104 AR21
Park Grn, Ersk. PA8 86 104 AR21
Park Gro, Ersk. PA8 86 104 AS21
Parkgrove Av (Giff.) G46 101 109 BM42
Parkgrove Ct (Giff.) G46 101 109 BM42
Parkgrove Ter G3 28 106 BN28
Parkgrove Ter La G3 28 106 BN28
Parkhall Rd, Clyde. G81 87 104 AV17
Parkhall Ter, Clyde. G81 87 104 AV16
Parkhead Cross G31 59 110 BZ32
Parkhill, Ersk. PA8 86 104 AR20
Parkhill Dr (Ruther.) G73 84 110 BW38
Parkhill Rd G43 81 109 BM37
Park Holdings, Ersk. PA8 86 104 AR22
Parkinch, Ersk. PA8 86 104 AS21
Parklands Rd G44 101 109 BP42
Parklea (Bishop.) G64 91 106 BU18
Parklee Dr (Carm.) G76 102 110 BU46
Park Moor, Ersk. PA8 86 104 AR21
Parkneuk Rd G43 101 109 BL41
Park Quad G3 28 106 BN28
Park Ridge, Ersk. PA8 86 104 AS20
Park Rd G4 28 106 BN27
Park Rd G32 98 111 CE37
Park Rd (Giff.) G46 101 109 BL43
Park Rd (Bishop.) G64 91 106 BW19
Park Rd, Clyde. G81 87 104 AV17
Park Rd, Pais. PA2 96 108 AT36
Park Rd (Inch.), Renf. PA4 86 104 AT22
Parksail, Ersk. PA8 86 104 AS22
Parksail Dr, Ersk. PA8 86 104 AS21
Parkside Gdns G20 90 106 BQ23
Parkside Pl G20 90 106 BQ23
Park St S G3 28 106 BN28
Park Ter G3 28 106 BN28
Park Ter (Giff.) G46 101 109 BL43
Park Ter E La G3 28 106 BN28
Park Ter La G3 28 106 BN28
Park Top, Ersk. PA8 86 104 AS20
Parkvale Av, Ersk. PA8 86 104 AT20
Parkvale Cres, Ersk. PA8 86 104 AT21
Parkvale Dr, Ersk. PA8 86 104 AT21
Parkvale Gdns, Ersk. PA8 86 104 AT20
Parkvale Pl, Ersk. PA8 86 104 AT20
Parkvale Way, Ersk. PA8 86 104 AT21
Park Vw, Pais. PA2 96 108 AT35
Parkview Dr (Stepps) G33 95 107 CG23
Park Way G32 98 111 CE37
Park Winding, Ersk. PA8 86 104 AS21
Park Wd, Ersk. PA8 86 104 AS20
Parnie St G1 55 110 BS31
Parsonage Row G1 43 106 BT30
Parsonage Sq G4 43 106 BT30
Parson St G4 44 106 BU29
Partick Br St G11 26 105 BL27
Partickhill Av G11 26 105 BK27
Partickhill Ct G11 14 105 BK26
Partickhill Rd G11 14 105 BK26
Paterson St G5 53 109 BQ32
Pathhead Gdns G33 94 107 CB23
Pathhead Rd (Carm.) G76 102 110 BT46
Patna St G40 70 110 BX34
Paton St G31 46 106 BX30
Patrick St, Pais. PA2 96 108 AV34
Pattison St, Clyde. G81 87 104 AU17
Payne St G4 30 106 BS27
Pearce La G51 37 105 BJ29
Pearce St G51 37 105 BJ29
Pearson Dr, Renf. PA4 93 104 AZ27
Peathill St G21 19 106 BS26
Peat Pl G53 78 108 BC40
Peat Rd G53 79 108 BD39
Pedmyre La (Carm.) G76 102 110 BS46
Peebles Dr (Ruther.) G73 85 110 BZ38
Peel Glen Rd G15 88 105 BC17
Peel La G11 26 105 BK27
Peel St G11 26 105 BK27
Peel Vw, Clyde. G81 87 104 AZ18
Pembroke St G3 40 106 BP29
Pencaitland Dr G32 98 110 CC34
Pencaitland Gro G32 98 110 CC35
Pencaitland Pl G23 90 106 BN20
Pendale Ri G45 102 110 BT42
Pendeen Cres G33 99 111 CG32
Pendeen Pl G33 99 111 CH31
Pendeen Rd G33 99 111 CG32
Pendicle Cres (Bears.) G61 88 105 BF18
Pendicle Rd (Bears.) G61 88 105 BF18
Penicuik St G32 59 110 BZ31
Penilee Rd G52 93 104 AZ29
Penilee Rd, Pais. PA1 74 108 BA32
Penilee Ter G52 74 108 BA31
Peninver Dr G51 75 105 BF29
Penman Av (Ruther.) G73 84 110 BV37
Pennan, Ersk. PA8 86 104 AQ19
Pennan Pl G14 88 105 BC24
Penneld Rd G52 74 108 BB32
Penrith Av (Giff.) G46 101 109 BL42
Penrith Dr G12 89 105 BJ23
Penryn Gdns G32 98 111 CF34
Penston Rd G33 94 107 CF29
Pentland Cres, Pais. PA2 96 108 AT37
Pentland Dr (Bishop.) G64 91 106 BZ19
Pentland Dr, Renf. PA4 93 104 AX29
Pentland Rd G43 101 109 BL40
Percy Dr (Giff.) G46 101 109 BL44
Percy Rd, Renf. PA4 93 104 AW29
Percy St G51 51 109 BM31
Perth Cres, Clyde. G81 86 104 AT16
Perth St G3 40/1 106 BP30
Petershill Ct G21 22 106 BY25
Petershill Dr G21 22 106 BX25
Petershill Pl G21 22 106 BX25
Petershill Rd G21 21 106 BV26
Peterson Dr G13 88 105 BA21
Peterson Gdns G13 88 105 BA21
Pettigrew St G32 98 110 CC32
Peveril Av G41 81 109 BM36
Peveril Av (Ruther.) G73 103 110 BY40
Peveril Ct (Ruther.) G73 103 110 BY40
Pharonhill St G31 98 110 CA32
Phoenix Ind Est, Pais. PA3 93 104 AU29
Phoenix Pk Ter G4 30 106 BR27
Phoenix Rd G4 29 106 BQ28
Piccadilly St G3 41 106 BP30
Picketlaw Dr (Carm.) G76 102 110 BT46
Picketlaw Fm Rd (Carm.) G76 102 110 BS46
Piershill St G32 94 107 CB30
Pikeman Rd G13 88 105 BE23
Pilmuir Av G44 101 109 BP41
Pilrig St G32 94 107 CA30
Pilton Rd G15 88 105 BC17
Pinelands (Bishop.) G64 91 106 BW17
Pine Pl G5 67 110 BS33
Pine Rd, Clyde. G81 86 104 AT17
Pine St, Pais. PA2 96 108 AW35
Pinewood Sq G15 88 105 BD17
Pinkerton Av (Ruther.) G73 84 110 BU37
Pinkerton La, Renf. PA4 93 104 AZ28
Pinkston Dr G21 32 106 BU27
Pinkston Rd G4 19 106 BT26
Pinkston Rd G21 19 106 BT26
Pinmore Path G53 78 108 BB40
Pinmore Pl G53 78 108 BB39
Pinmore St G53 78 108 BB39
Pinwherry Dr G33 94 107 CB23
Pitcairn St G31 98 110 CA33
Pitcaple Dr G43 100 109 BK39
Pitlochry Dr G52 77 108 BD33
Pitmedden Rd (Bishop.) G64 91 106 BZ19
Pitmilly Rd G15 88 105 BE17
Pitreavie Pl G33 94 107 CE27
Pitt St G2 41 106 BQ30
Pladda Rd, Renf. PA4 93 104 AZ28
Plaintrees Ct, Pais. PA2 96 108 AU35
Planetree Rd, Clyde. G81 87 104 AW17
Plantation Pk Gdns G51 51 109 BM32
Plantation Sq G51 52 109 BN31
Plant St G31 58 110 BY31
Playfair St G40 69 110 BW34
Plean St G14 88 105 BC24
Pleasance La G43 81 109 BL38
Pleasance St G43 81 109 BL37
Pointhouse Rd G3 40 106 BN30
Pollock Rd (Bears.) G61 89 105 BJ18
Pollok Av G43 81 109 BK37
Pollok Dr (Bishop.) G64 91 106 BU20
Pollokshaws Rd G41 82 109 BP36
Pollokshaws Rd G43 81 109 BK38
Pollokshields Sq G41 82 109 BP35
Pollok Shop Cen G53 79 109 BE38
Polmadie Av G5 83 110 BT35
Polmadie Ind Est G5 84 110 BU35
Polmadie Rd G5 68 110 BU34
Polmadie Rd G42 83 110 BS36
Polmadie St G42 83 110 BS36
Polnoon Av G13 88 105 BC23
Polquhap Ct G53 78 108 BC37
Polquhap Gdns G53 78 108 BC37
Polquhap Pl G53 78 108 BC37
Polquhap Rd G53 78 108 BC37
Polsons Cres, Pais. PA2 96 108 AT35
Polwarth La G12 14 105 BK25
Polwarth St G12 14 105 BK26
Poplar Av G11 12/3 105 BH25
Poplar Dr, Clyde. G81 87 104 AV16
Poplar Rd G41 50 109 BK32
Poplin St G40 69 110 BV34
Porchester St G33 94 107 CF27
Portal Rd G13 88 105 BE21
Port Dundas Ind Est G4 31 106 BS27
Port Dundas Pl G2 42 106 BS29
Port Dundas Rd G4 30 106 BR28
Port Dundas Trd Centres G4 31 106 BS27
Porterfield Rd, Renf. PA4 93 104 AX26
Porter St G51 50/1 109 BL32
Portessie, Ersk. PA8 86 104 AQ19
Portland St, Pais. PA2 96 108 AX34
Portlethen, Ersk. PA8 86 104 AQ19
Portman Pl G12 28 106 BN27
Portman St G41 52 109 BN32
Portmarnock Dr G23 90 106 BN21
Portsoy, Ersk. PA8 86 104 AQ19
Portsoy Av G13 88 105 BB21
Portsoy Pl G13 88 105 BA21
Port St G3 40 106 BP29
Portugal La G5 54 109 BR32
Portugal St G5 54 109 BR32
Possil Cross G22 18 106 BS26
Possil Rd G4 18 106 BR26
Potter Cl G32 98 110 CA34
Potter Gro G32 98 110 CA34
Potterhill Av, Pais. PA2 96 108 AU37
Potterhill Rd G53 77 108 BD35
Potter Path G32 98 110 CA34
Potter Pl G32 98 110 CA34
Potter St G32 98 110 CA34
Powburn Cres (Udd.) G71 99 111 CM38
Powfoot St G31 59 110 BZ32
Powrie St G33 94 107 CE26
Preston Pl G42 83 109 BR35
Preston St G42 83 109 BR35
Prestwick St G53 78 108 BC39
Priesthill Av G53 79 109 BE39
Priesthill Cres G53 79 109 BE39
Priesthill Rd G53 79 108 BD39
Primrose Ct G14 73 105 BE26
Primrose St G14 73 105 BE26
Prince Albert Rd G12 14 105 BK26
Prince Edward St G42 82 109 BQ35
Prince of Wales Gdns G20 89 105 BL21
Prince's Dock G51 39 105 BL30
Princes Gdns G12 14 105 BK26
Princes Gate (Ruther.) G73 84 110 BW37
Princes Pl G12 14 105 BL26
Princess Cres, Pais. PA1 96 108 AX32
Princess Pk (Erskine Hosp.), Bish. PA7 86 104 AN17
Princes Sq G1 42 106 BS30
Princes St (Ruther.) G73 84 110 BW37
Princes Ter G12 14 105 BL26
Priory Av, Pais. PA3 93 104 AW30
Priory Dr (Udd.) G71 99 111 CM38
Priory Pl G13 88 105 BF22
Priory Rd G13 88 105 BF22
Prosen St G32 98 110 CB34
Prospect Av (Camb.) G72 103 110 CB39
Prospecthill Circ G42 83 110 BT36
Prospecthill Cres G42 84 110 BU37
Prospecthill Dr G42 83 110 BS37
Prospecthill Pl G42 84 110 BU37
Prospecthill Rd G42 82 109 BQ37
Prospecthill Sq G42 83 110 BT37
Prospect Rd G43 81 109 BM37
Provand Hall Cres (Baill.) G69 99 111 CK34
Provanhill St G21 32 106 BV28
Provanmill Pl G33 23 106 BZ26
Provanmill Rd G33 23 106 BZ26
Provan Rd G33 35 106 BY28
Provost Driver Ct, Renf. PA4 93 104 AZ27
Purdon St G11 26 105 BK27

Quadrant Rd G43 101 109 BN40
Quadrant, The (Clark.) G76 101 109 BP45
Quarrybrae Av (Clark.) G76 101 109 BM46
Quarrybrae St G31 98 110 CA32
Quarryknowe (Ruther.) G73 84 110 BV38
Quarryknowe St G31 98 110 CA32
Quarry Pl (Camb.) G72 103 110 CA39
Quarry Rd, Pais. PA2 96 108 AV36
Quarrywood Av G21 23 106 BY25
Quarrywood Rd G21 23 106 BZ25
Quay Rd (Ruther.) G73 84 110 BW36
Quay Rd N (Ruther.) G73 84 110 BW36
Quebec Ho, Clyde. G81 86 104 AT15
Quebec Wynd G32 98 111 CE37
Queen Elizabeth Av G52 74 105 BA30
Queen Elizabeth Sq G5 67 110 BT33
Queen Margaret Ct G20 16 106 BN25
Queen Margaret Dr G12 15 105 BM26
Queen Margaret Dr G20 15 105 BM26
Queen Margaret Rd G20 16 106 BN25
Queen Mary Av G42 83 109 BR36
Queen Mary Av, Clyde. G81 87 104 AZ19
Queen Mary St G40 69 110 BV33
Queens Av (Camb.) G72 103 110 CD39
Queensberry Av (Clark.) G76 101 109 BN46
Queensborough Gdns G12 13 105 BJ25
Queensby Av (Baill.) G69 99 111 CK31
Queensby Dr (Baill.) G69 99 111 CK31
Queensby Pl (Baill.) G69 99 111 CL31
Queensby Rd (Baill.) G69 99 111 CK31
Queens Cres G4 29 106 BP27
Queens Dr G42 82 109 BP35
Queens Dr La G42 83 109 BR36
Queensferry St G5 84 110 BU35
Queens Gdns G12 14 105 BL26
Queens Gate (Clark.) G76 101 109 BN45
Queens Gate La G12 14/5 105 BL26
Queenside Cres, Ersk. PA8 86 104 AP20
Queensland Ct G52 75 109 BE31
Queensland Dr G52 75 109 BE31
Queensland Gdns G52 75 109 BE31
Queensland La E G52 75 109 BE31
Queensland La W G52 75 109 BE31
Queenslie Ind Est G33 94 107 CE29
Queenslie St G33 35 106 BZ27
Queens Pk Av G42 83 109 BR36
Queens Pl G12 14 105 BL26
Queen Sq G41 82 109 BP35
Queen St G1 42 106 BS30
Queen St (Ruther.) G73 84 110 BW37
Queen St, Pais. PA1 96 108 AS33
Queen St, Renf. PA4 93 104 AZ26
Queen Victoria Ct G14 73 105 BE25
Queen Victoria Dr G13 88 105 BE24
Queen Victoria Dr G14 73 105 BE25
Queen Victoria Gate G13 88 105 BE24
Quendale Dr G32 98 110 CB34
Quentin St G41 82 109 BN36
Quinton Gdns (Baill.) G69 99 111 CJ32

Raasay Dr, Pais. PA2 96 108 AT38
Raasay Pl G22 90 106 BS21
Raasay St G22 90 106 BS21
Radnor St G3 27 105 BM28
Radnor St, Clyde. G81 87 104 AW18
Raeberry St G20 16 106 BP26
Raeswood Dr G53 78 108 BB37
Raeswood Gdns G53 78 108 BB37
Raeswood Pl G53 78 108 BC37
Raeswood Rd G53 78 108 BB37
Rafford St G51 37 105 BJ30
Raglan St G4 29 106 BQ27
Raith Av G44 102 110 BT41
Raithburn Av G45 102 110 BS42
Raithburn Rd G45 102 110 BS42
Ralston Av G52 76 108 BB33
Ralston Av, Pais. PA1 76 108 BB34
Ralston Ct G52 76 108 BB33
Ralston Dr G52 76 108 BB33
Ralston Path G52 76 108 BB33
Ralston Pl G52 76 108 BB33
Ralston St, Pais. PA1 96 108 AW33
Rampart Av G13 88 105 BC21
Ramsay St, Clyde. G81 87 104 AV18
Ram St G32 98 110 CB32
Ranald Gdns (Ruther.) G73 103 110 BZ42
Randolph Av (Clark.) G76 101 109 BQ44
Randolph Dr (Clark.) G76 101 109 BP44
Randolph Gdns (Clark.) G76 101 109 BP44
Randolph La G11 13 105 BH26
Randolph Rd G11 12 105 BH25
Ranfurly Rd G52 74 108 BB32
Rankines La, Renf. PA4 93 104 AZ25
Rannoch Av (Bishop.) G64 91 106 BX20
Rannoch Av (Newt. M.) G77 100 109 BF46
Rannoch Dr (Bears.) G61 89 105 BJ19
Rannoch Dr, Renf. PA4 93 104 AY25
Rannoch Gdns (Bishop.) G64 91 106 BY19
Rannoch Pl, Pais. PA2 96 108 AW34
Rannoch St G44 101 109 BQ39
Raploch Av G14 73 105 BD25
Raploch La G14 73 105 BD25
Rashieburn, Ersk. PA8 86 104 AQ19
Rashieglen, Ersk. PA8 86 104 AQ19
Rashiehill, Ersk. PA8 86 104 AQ19
Rashielea Av, Ersk. PA8 86 104 AR19
Rashiewood, Ersk. PA8 86 104 AR19
Rathlin St G51 37 105 BJ29
Ratho Dr G21 91 106 BU24
Rattray, Ersk. PA8 86 104 AQ18
Rattray St G32 98 110 CA34
Ravel Row G31 59 110 BZ32
Ravelston Rd (Bears.) G61 89 105 BG19
Ravelston St G32 59 110 BZ31
Ravenscliffe Dr (Giff.) G46 100 109 BK42
Ravens Ct (Bishop.) G64 91 106 BV21
Ravenscraig Av, Pais. PA2 96 108 AS35
Ravenscraig Dr G53 79 108 BD39
Ravenscraig Ter G53 79 109 BE40
Ravenshall Rd G41 81 109 BL37
Ravenstone Dr (Giff.) G46 101 109 BL40
Ravenswood Dr G41 81 109 BM36
Ravenswood Rd (Baill.) G69 99 111 CL33
Rayne Pl G15 88 105 BD17
Redan St G40 57 110 BV32
Redburn Av (Giff.) G46 100 109 BK45
Redcastle Sq G33 94 107 CF28
Redford St G33 47 106 BZ29
Redgate Pl G14 73 105 BD25
Redlands La G12 15 105 BL25
Redlands Rd G12 15 105 BL25
Redlands Ter G12 14 105 BL25
Redlands Ter La G12 15 105 BL25
Redmoss St G22 90 106 BR24
Rednock St G22 19 106 BS25
Redpath Dr G52 75 109 BE32
Red Rd G21 22 106 BX25
Red Rd Ct G21 22 106 BX25
Redwood Dr G21 21 106 BW26
Reelick Av G13 88 105 BA21
Reelick Quad G13 88 105 BA21
Regent Dr (Ruther.) G73 84 110 BW37
Regent Moray St G3 27 105 BM28
Regent Pk Sq G41 82 109 BP35
Regent Pl, Clyde. G81 87 104 AU17
Regent St, Clyde. G81 87 104 AU17
Regent St, Pais. PA1 96 108 AX32
Regwood St G41 81 109 BM37
Reid Pl G40 69 110 BV33
Reid St G40 69 110 BV34
Reid St (Ruther.) G73 85 110 BX37
Reidvale St G31 57 110 BV31
Renfield La G2 42 106 BR30
Renfield St G2 42 106 BR29
Renfield St, Renf. PA4 93 104 AZ25
Renfrew Ct G2 42 106 BR29
Renfrew La G2 42 106 BR29
Renfrew Rd G51 75 105 BD29
Renfrew Rd, Pais. PA3 96 108 AV32
Renfrew Rd, Renf. PA4 72 105 BC28
Renfrew St G2 42 106 BR29
Renfrew St G3 29 106 BQ28
Rennies Rd (Inch.), Renf. PA4 86 104 AS22
Renshaw Dr G52 75 108 BD31
Renton St G4 30 106 BS28
Resipol Rd (Stepps) G33 95 107 CG24
Reston Dr G52 75 108 BD31
Reuther Av (Ruther.) G73 85 110 BX38
Revoch Dr G13 88 105 BC22
Rhannan Rd G44 101 109 BQ40
Rhannan Ter G44 101 109 BQ40
Rhindhouse Pl (Baill.) G69 99 111 CM32
Rhindhouse Rd (Baill.) G69 99 111 CM32
Rhindmuir Av (Baill.) G69 99 111 CL32
Rhindmuir Ct (Baill.) G69 99 111 CL31
Rhindmuir Cres (Baill.) G69 99 111 CM31
Rhindmuir Dr (Baill.) G69 99 111 CL31
Rhindmuir Gdns (Baill.) G69 99 111 CL31
Rhindmuir Gro (Baill.) G69 99 111 CM31
Rhindmuir Path (Baill.) G69 99 111 CM31
Rhindmuir Pl (Baill.) G69 99 111 CM31
Rhindmuir Rd (Baill.) G69 99 111 CL31
Rhindmuir Vw (Baill.) G69 99 111 CM31
Rhindmuir Wynd (Baill.) G69 99 111 CM31
Rhinsdale Cres (Baill.) G69 99 111 CL32
Rhymer St G21 32 106 BU28
Rhymie Rd G32 98 111 CF34
Rhynie Dr G51 50 109 BK32
Riccarton St G42 83 110 BS35
Riccartsbar Av, Pais. PA2 96 108 AS34
Richard St G2 41 106 BQ30
Richard St, Renf. PA4 93 104 AZ25
Richmond Av (Clark.) G76 101 109 BN46
Richmond Ct (Ruther.) G73 85 110 BY37
Richmond Dr (Bishop.) G64 91 106 BX17
Richmond Dr (Camb.) G72 103 110 CA40
Richmond Dr (Ruther.) G73 85 110 BY38
Richmond Gro (Ruther.) G73 85 110 BY38
Richmond Pl (Ruther.) G73 85 110 BY37
Richmond St G1 43 106 BT30
Richmond St, Clyde. G81 87 104 AY20
Riddell St, Clyde. G81 87 104 AY18
Riddon Av G13 88 105 BA21
Riddon Av, Clyde. G81 88 105 BA21
Riddon Pl G13 88 105 BA21
Riddrie Cres G33 94 107 CA29
Riddrie Knowes G33 94 107 CA29
Riddrievale Ct G33 94 107 CA28
Riddrievale St G33 94 107 CA28
Rigby St G32 98 110 CA31
Rigg Pl G33 95 107 CG30
Riggside Rd G33 94 107 CE27
Riglands Way, Renf. PA4 93 104 AY25
Riglaw Pl G13 88 105 BC22
Rigmuir Rd G51 75 105 BE30
Rimsdale St G40 57 110 BW32
Ringford St G21 20 106 BV26
Ripon Dr G12 89 105 BJ23
Risk St G40 56 110 BU32
Risk St, Clyde. G81 87 104 AV17
Ristol Rd G13 88 105 BD24
Ritchie St G5 65 109 BQ33
Riverbank St G43 81 109 BL38
River Cart Wk, Pais. PA1 96 108 AU33
River Dr (Inch.), Renf. PA4 92 104 AS24
Riverford Rd G43 81 109 BL38
Riverford Rd (Ruther.) G73 85 110 BY36
River Rd G32 98 111 CE37
River Rd G41 82 109 BP37
Riversdale La G14 72 105 BC25
Riverside Ct G44 101 109 BP43
Riverside Ind Est, Clyde. G81 87 104 AW20
Riverside Pk G44 101 109 BQ42
Riverside Rd G43 82 109 BN38
Riverview Dr G5 53 109 BQ31
Riverview Gdns G5 53 109 BQ31
Riverview Pl G5 53 109 BQ31
Robert Burns Av, Clyde. G81 87 104 AY18
Robert Dr G51 37 105 BJ29
Roberton Av G41 81 109 BL35
Robertson La G2 42 106 BR30
Robertson St G2 42 106 BR30
Robertson Ter (Baill.) G69 99 111 CL32
Roberts St, Clyde. G81 87 104 AU18
Robert St G51 37 105 BJ29
Robert Templeton Dr (Camb.) G72 103 110 CD40
Robin Way G32 98 111 CE37
Robroyston Av G33 94 107 CA26
Robroyston Dr G33 94 107 CA25
Robroyston Rd G33 94 107 CA23
Robslee Cres (Giff.) G46 100 109 BJ42
Robslee Dr (Giff.) G46 100 109 BK42
Robslee Rd (Thornlie.) G46 100 109 BJ43
Robson Gro G42 66 109 BR34
Rockall Dr G44 102 110 BS41
Rockbank Pl G40 57 110 BW32
Rockbank Pl, Clyde. G81 87 104 AY15
Rockbank St G40 57 110 BW32
Rockburn Dr (Clark.) G76 101 109 BL45
Rockcliffe St G40 69 110 BV34
Rockfield Pl G21 91 106 BY24
Rockfield Rd G21 91 106 BY24
Rockmount Av (Thornlie.) G46 100 109 BJ41
Rock St G4 18 106 BR26
Rockwell Av, Pais. PA2 96 108 AS37
Rodger Dr (Ruther.) G73 102 110 BW39
Rodger Pl (Ruther.) G73 102 110 BW39
Rodil Av G44 102 110 BS41
Rodney St G4 30 106 BR27
Roebank St G31 46 106 BX29
Roffey Pk Rd, Pais. PA1 97 108 AZ32
Rogart St G40 57 110 BV32
Rogerfield Rd (Baill.) G69 95 107 CL30
Roman Av G15 88 105 BC20
Roman Rd, Clyde. G81 87 104 AW15
Romney Av G44 102 110 BS40
Ronaldsay Dr (Bishop.) G64 91 106 BZ19
Ronaldsay Pas G22 90 106 BT22
Ronaldsay St G22 90 106 BS22
Rona St G21 34 106 BX27
Rona Ter (Camb.) G72 103 110 CB42
Ronay St G22 90 106 BT21
Rooksdell Av, Pais. PA2 96 108 AS36
Ropework La G1 54 110 BS31
Rosebank Gdns (Udd.) G71 99 111 CK35
Rosebank Pl (Udd.) G71 99 111 CK35
Roseberry St G5 68 110 BU34
Rosedale (Bishop.) G64 91 106 BX21
Rosedale Dr (Baill.) G69 99 111 CJ33
Rosedale Gdns G20 89 105 BL21
Rose Knowe Rd G42 83 110 BT36
Roseland Brae, Ersk. PA8 86 104 AT21
Roselea Gdns G13 89 105 BH22
Rosemount Cres G21 45 106 BV29
Rosemount St G21 33 106 BV28
Roseness Pl G33 94 107 CC29
Rose St G3 30 106 BR28
Rosevale Rd (Bears.) G61 89 105 BG17
Rosevale St G11 25 105 BJ27
Rosewood St G13 89 105 BG22
Roslea Dr G31 45 106 BW30
Roslin Twr (Camb.) G72 103 110 CA42
Rosneath St G51 37 105 BJ29

Ross Av, Renf. PA4 93 104 AW28
Rossendale Ct G43 81 109 BL37
Rossendale Rd G41 81 109 BL37
Rossendale Rd G43 81 109 BL37
Rosshall Av, Pais. PA1 97 108 AY33
Ross Hall Pl, Renf. PA4 93 104 AZ26
Rosshill Av G52 74 108 BB32
Rosshill Rd G52 74 108 BB32
Rossie Cres (Bishop.) G64 91 106 BY21
Rosslea Dr (Giff.) G46 101 109 BL43
Rosslyn Av (Ruther.) G73 85 110 BY38
Rosslyn Ter G12 15 105 BL25
Ross Pl (Ruther.) G73 103 110 BZ41
Ross St G40 55 110 BT31
Ross St, Pais. PA1 96 108 AV34
Rostan Rd G43 101 109 BL40
Rosyth Rd G5 84 110 BU35
Rosyth St G5 84 110 BU35
Rotherwick Dr, Pais. PA1 76 108 BA33
Rotherwood Av G13 88 105 BE20
Rotherwood La G13 88 105 BE19
Rotherwood Pl G13 89 105 BG21
Rothes Dr G23 89 105 BM20
Rothes Pl G23 89 105 BL20
Rottenrow G4 43 106 BT29
Rottenrow E G4 43 106 BT30
Roukenburn St (Thornlie.) G46 100 109 BG41
Rouken Glen Pk (Thornlie.) G46 100 109 BH44
Rouken Glen Rd (Thornlie.) G46 100 109 BH43
Roundknowe Rd (Udd.) G71 99 111 CL36
Rowallan Gdns G11 13 105 BJ26
Rowallan La G11 13 105 BH26
Rowallan La (Clark.) G76 101 109 BN46
Rowallan La E G11 13 105 BJ26
Rowallan Rd (Thornlie.) G46 100 109 BH43
Rowallan Ter G33 94 107 CD25
Rowan Av, Renf. PA4 93 104 AY25
Rowan Ct, Pais. PA2 96 108 AU35
Rowandale Av (Baill.) G69 99 111 CJ33
Rowand Av (Giff.) G46 101 109 BL43
Rowan Dr, Clyde. G81 87 104 AV17
Rowan Gdns G41 62 109 BK33
Rowan Gate, Pais. PA2 96 108 AV35
Rowanlea Dr (Giff.) G46 101 109 BM41
Rowan Rd G41 62 109 BK33
Rowans, The (Bishop.) G64 91 106 BV19
Rowan St, Pais. PA2 96 108 AU35
Rowantree Av (Ruther.) G73 102 110 BX40
Rowantree Gdns (Ruther.) G73 102 110 BX40
Rowchester St G40 57 110 BW32
Rowena Av G13 88 105 BF20
Roxburgh La G12 15 105 BM26
Roxburgh St G12 15 105 BM26
Royal Bk Pl G1 42/3 106 BS30
Royal Cres G3 40 106 BN29
Royal Cres G42 82 109 BQ36
Royal Ex Bldgs G1 42/3 106 BS30
Royal Ex Sq G1 42 106 BS30
Royal Inch Cres, Renf. PA4 93 104 AZ24
Royal Ter G3 28 106 BN28
Royal Ter La G3 28 106 BN28
Roystonhill G21 32 106 BV28
Royston Rd G21 32 106 BU28
Royston Rd G33 94 107 CA26
Royston Sq G21 32 106 BU28
Roy St G21 19 106 BT26
Rozelle Av G15 88 105 BD18
Rubislaw Dr (Bears.) G61 89 105 BG17
Ruby St G40 69 110 BW33
Ruchazie Pl G33 94 107 CB29
Ruchazie Rd G32 94 107 CB30
Ruchazie Rd G33 94 107 CB30
Ruchill Pl G20 90 106 BP24
Ruchill St G20 90 106 BN24
Ruel St G44 82 109 BQ38
Rugby Av G13 88 105 BD21
Rullion Pl G33 94 107 CB29
Rumford St G40 68 110 BV34
Rupert St G4 29 106 BP27
Rushyhill St G21 21 106 BW25
Ruskin La G12 16 106 BN26
Ruskin Pl G12 16 106 BN26
Ruskin Sq (Bishop.) G64 91 106 BW20
Ruskin Ter G12 16 106 BN26
Ruskin Ter (Ruther.) G73 85 110 BX37
Russell Cres (Baill.) G69 99 111 CM33
Russell St G11 26 105 BK27
Russell St, Pais. PA3 92 104 AT30
Rutherglen Br G40 68 110 BV34
Rutherglen Br G42 68 110 BV34
Rutherglen Ind Est G73 84 110 BW36
Rutherglen Rd G5 67 110 BT34
Rutherglen Rd (Ruther.) G73 67 110 BT34
Ruthven Av (Giff.) G46 101 109 BM44
Ruthven La G12 15 105 BM26
Ruthven Pl (Bishop.) G64 91 106 BY21
Ruthven St G12 15 105 BM26
Rutland Ct G51 52 109 BN31
Rutland Cres G51 52 109 BN31
Rutland Pl G51 52 109 BN31
Ryan Rd (Bishop.) G64 91 106 BX20
Ryan Way (Ruther.) G73 103 110 BY42
Ryat Linn, Ersk. PA8 86 104 AP20
Ryebank Rd G21 91 106 BY24
Rye Cres G21 91 106 BX24
Ryecroft Dr (Baill.) G69 99 111 CK32
Ryedale Pl G15 88 105 BC17
Ryefield Rd G21 91 106 BX24
Ryehill Pl G21 91 106 BY24
Ryehill Rd G21 91 106 BY24
Ryemount Rd G21 91 106 BY24
Rye Rd G21 91 106 BX24
Ryeside Rd G21 91 106 BX24
Rylands Dr G32 99 111 CG33
Rylands Gdns G32 99 111 CG33
Rylees Cres G52 74 108 BA31
Rylees Pl G52 74 108 BA31
Rylees Rd G52 74 108 BA31
Ryvra Rd G13 88 105 BF23

Sackville Av G13 89 105 BH24
Sackville La G13 89 105 BH23
Saddell Rd G15 88 105 BD17
St. Andrews Av (Bishop.) G64 91 106 BU19
St. Andrews Cres G41 64 109 BN33
St. Andrews Cres, Pais. PA3 92 104 AS28
St. Andrews Cross G41 65 109 BQ34
St. Andrews Dr G41 63 109 BM34
St. Andrews Dr (Abbots.), Pais. PA3 92 104 AT29
St. Andrews Dr W (Abbots.), Pais. PA3 92 104 AS28
St. Andrews La G1 55 110 BT31
St. Andrews Rd G41 64 109 BP33
St. Andrews Rd, Renf. PA4 93 104 AY26
St. Andrews Sq G1 55 110 BT31
St. Andrews St G1 55 110 BT31
St. Annes Av, Ersk. PA8 86 104 AT21
St. Annes Wynd, Ersk. PA8 86 104 AS21
St. Anns Dr (Giff.) G46 101 109 BL43
St. Blanes Dr (Ruther.) G73 102 110 BU39
St. Brides Rd G43 101 109 BM39
St. Catherines Rd (Giff.) G46 101 109 BL43
St. Clair Av (Giff.) G46 101 109 BL42
St. Clair St G20 29 106 BP27
St. Cyrus Gdns (Bishop.) G64 91 106 BY20
St. Cyrus Rd (Bishop.) G64 91 106 BY20
St. Enoch Pl G1 54 109 BR31
St. Enoch Shop Cen G1 54 110 BS31
St. Enoch Sq G1 54 109 BR31
St. Fillans Rd G33 94 107 CE24
St. Georges Pl G20 29 106 BQ28
St. Georges Rd G3 29 106 BQ27
St. Germains (Bears.) G61 89 105 BG17
St. Helena Cres, Clyde. G81 87 104 AY15
St. James Av, Pais. PA3 92 104 AR30
St. James Rd G4 43 106 BT29
St. James St, Pais. PA3 96 108 AU32
St. John's Ct G41 64 109 BN33
St. John's Quad G41 64 109 BN33
St. John's Rd G41 64 109 BN34
St. Joseph's Ct G21 33 106 BV28
St. Joseph's Pl G21 33 106 BV28
St. Joseph's Vw G21 33 106 BV28
St. Kenneth Dr G51 75 105 BF29
St. Kilda Dr G14 12 105 BG25
St. Leonards Dr (Giff.) G46 101 109 BL42
St. Margarets Pl G1 54/5 110 BS31
St. Mark Gdns G32 98 110 CB32
St. Mark St G32 98 110 CA32
St. Marnock St G40 57 110 BW32
St. Marys La G2 42 106 BR30
St. Marys Rd (Bishop.) G64 91 106 BU19
St. Michael's Ct G31 59 110 BY32
St. Michael's La G31 59 110 BY32
St. Mirren St, Pais. PA1 96 108 AU32
St. Monance St G21 91 106 BV24
St. Mungo Av G4 43 106 BS29
St. Mungo Pl G4 43 106 BT29
St. Mungo St (Bishop.) G64 91 106 BV21
St. Ninians Cres, Pais. PA2 96 108 AV35
St. Ninians Rd, Pais. PA2 96 108 AV35
St. Ninian Ter G5 54/5 110 BS32
St. Peters La G2 41 106 BQ30
St. Peter's Path G4 29 106 BQ27
St. Peters St G4 29 106 BQ27
St. Rollox Brae G21 32 106 BU27
St. Ronans Dr G41 81 109 BM36
St. Ronans Dr (Ruther.) G73 103 110 BY39
St. Stephens Av (Ruther.) G73 103 110 BZ42
St. Stephens Cres (Ruther.) G73 103 110 CA42
St. Vincent Cres G3 39 105 BM29
St. Vincent Cres La G3 39 105 BM29
St. Vincent La G2 41 106 BQ29
St. Vincent Pl G1 42 106 BS30
St. Vincent St G2 41 106 BQ29
St. Vincent St G3 40 106 BP29
St. Vincent Ter G3 40 106 BP29
Salamanca St G31 98 110 BZ32
Salasaig Ct G33 94 107 CC30
Salen St G52 49 109 BH32
Salisbury Pl, Clyde. G81 86 104 AT16
Salisbury St G5 66 109 BR33
Salkeld St G5 66 109 BR33
Salmona St G22 18 106 BR25
Salterland Rd G53 78 108 BA40
Salterland Rd (Barr.) G78 78 108 BA40
Saltmarket G1 55 110 BS31
Saltmarket Pl G1 55 110 BS31
Saltoun Gdns G12 15 105 BM26
Saltoun La G12 15 105 BM26
Saltoun St G12 15 105 BL26
Salvia St (Camb.) G72 103 110 CB39
Sandaig Rd G33 99 111 CG31
Sanda St G20 16 106 BN25
Sandbank Av G20 89 105 BM22
Sandbank Cres G20 89 105 BM23
Sandbank Dr G20 89 105 BM22
Sandbank St G20 89 105 BM23
Sandbank Ter G20 89 105 BM22
Sandend, Ersk. PA8 86 104 AQ18
Sandend Rd G53 78 108 BC38
Sanderling Rd, Pais. PA3 92 104 AT29
Sandfield St G20 90 106 BN24
Sandford Gdns (Baill.) G69 99 111 CK32
Sandgate Av G32 98 111 CF34
Sandhaven Pl G53 78 108 BC38
Sandhaven Rd G53 78 108 BC38
Sandholes St, Pais. PA1 96 108 AS33
Sandholm Pl G14 88 105 BB24
Sandholm Ter G14 88 105 BB24
Sandiefield Rd G5 66 110 BS33
Sandielands Av, Ersk. PA8 86 104 AT22
Sandilands St G32 98 110 CD32
Sandmill St G21 33 106 BW28
Sandra Rd (Bishop.) G64 91 106 BY19
Sandringham La G12 15 105 BM26
Sandwood Cres G52 74 108 BC32
Sandwood Path G52 74 108 BC32
Sandwood Rd G52 76 108 BC33
Sandyfaulds Sq G5 67 110 BS33
Sandyfaulds St G5 67 110 BT33
Sandyford Pl G3 40 106 BP29
Sandyford Pl La G3 40 106 BN29
Sandyford Rd, Pais. PA3 93 104 AV29
Sandyford St G3 39 105 BL29
Sandyhills Cres G32 98 110 CD34
Sandyhills Dr G32 98 110 CD34
Sandyhills Gro G32 98 111 CE35
Sandyhills Pl G32 98 110 CD34
Sandyhills Rd G32 98 110 CD34
Sandy La G11 25 105 BJ27
Sandy Rd G11 25 105 BJ28
Sandy Rd, Renf. PA4 93 104 AY28
Sannox Gdns G31 46 106 BX29
Sanquhar Dr G53 78 108 BC37
Sanquhar Gdns G53 78 108 BC37
Sanquhar Pl G53 78 108 BC37
Sanquhar Rd G53 78 108 BC37
Saracen Head La G1 56 110 BU31
Saracen St G22 18 106 BS26
Sardinia La G12 15 105 BM26
Sardinia Ter G12 15 105 BM26
Saucelhill Ter, Pais. PA2 96 108 AV34
Saucel St, Pais. PA1 96 108 AU33
Sauchiehall La G2 41 106 BQ29
Sauchiehall St G2 41 106 BQ29
Sauchiehall St G3 27 105 BM28
Saughs Av G33 94 107 CB23
Saughs Dr G33 94 107 CB23
Saughs Gate G33 94 107 CB23
Saughs Pl G33 94 107 CB23
Saughs Rd G33 94 107 CA24
Saughton St G32 98 110 CA30
Savoy St G40 68 110 BV33
Sawmillfield St G4 30 106 BR27
Sawmill Rd G11 25 105 BH27
Saxon Rd G13 88 105 BF22
Scalpay Pas G22 90 106 BT22
Scalpay Pl G22 90 106 BT22
Scalpay St G22 90 106 BS22
Scapa St G23 90 106 BN21
Scaraway Dr G22 90 106 BT21
Scaraway Pl G22 90 106 BT21
Scaraway St G22 90 106 BS21
Scaraway Ter G22 90 106 BT21
Scarba Dr G43 100 109 BK40
Scarrel Dr G45 102 110 BW41
Scarrel Gdns G45 102 110 BW41
Scarrel Rd G45 102 110 BW41
Scarrel Ter G45 102 110 BW41
Schaw Rd, Pais. PA3 96 108 AW31
Schipka Pas G1 55 110 BT31
School Av (Camb.) G72 103 110 CD40
School Rd (Stepps) G33 95 107 CG23
School Rd, Pais. PA1 74 108 BA32
School Wynd, Pais. PA1 96 108 AU32
Scioncroft Av (Ruther.) G73 85 110 BY38
Scone St G21 19 106 BS26
Scone Wk (Baill.) G69 99 111 CJ34
Sconser St G23 90 106 BN20
Scorton Gdns (Baill.) G69 99 111 CG33
Scotland St G5 52 109 BP32
Scotland St W G41 52 109 BN32
Scotsburn Rd G21 22 106 BY25
Scotstoun Mill Rd G11 26/7 105 BL28
Scotstoun Pl G14 73 105 BE26
Scotstoun St G14 73 105 BE26
Scott Rd G52 74 105 BB29
Scotts Rd, Pais. PA2 97 108 AY34
Scott St G3 41 106 BQ29
Scott St (Baill.) G69 99 111 CK33
Scott St, Clyde. G81 87 104 AU17
Seafield Dr (Ruther.) G73 103 110 BZ42
Seaforth Rd G52 74 105 BC30
Seaforth Rd, Clyde. G81 87 104 AX20
Seaforth Rd N G52 74 105 BC30
Seaforth Rd S G52 74 105 BC30
Seagrove St G32 59 110 BZ31
Seamill Path G53 78 108 BB40
Seamill Pl G53 78 108 BB40
Seamill St G53 78 108 BB40
Seamore St G20 29 106 BP27
Seath Rd (Ruther.) G73 84 110 BW36
Seath St G42 83 110 BS35
Seaward La G41 52 109 BN31
Seaward Pl G41 64 109 BN33
Seaward St G41 52 109 BP32
Second Av (Stepps) G33 94 107 CD24
Second Av G44 101 109 BR39
Second Av (Bears.) G61 89 105 BJ18
Second Av, Clyde. G81 87 104 AV18
Second Av, Renf. PA4 93 104 AY27
Second Gdns G41 61 109 BJ33
Seedhill, Pais. PA1 96 108 AV33
Seedhill Rd, Pais. PA1 96 108 AV33
Seggielea La G13 88 105 BF24
Seggielea Rd G13 88 105 BF23
Seil Dr G44 101 109 BR41
Selborne Pl G13 89 105 BG24
Selborne Pl La G13 89 105 BG24
Selborne Rd G13 89 105 BG24
Selby Gdns G32 98 111 CF32
Selkirk Av G52 77 109 BE33
Selkirk Dr (Ruther.) G73 85 110 BY38
Sella Rd (Bishop.) G64 91 106 BZ19
Selvieland Rd G52 74 108 BB32
Sempill Av, Ersk. PA8 86 104 AP19
Seres Rd (Clark.) G76 101 109 BM45
Seton Ter G31 45 106 BV30
Settle Gdns (Baill.) G69 99 111 CH33
Seyton Av (Giff.) G46 101 109 BL44
Shaftesbury St G3 41 106 BP29
Shaftesbury St, Clyde. G81 87 104 AV19
Shafton Pl G13 89 105 BG21
Shafton Rd G13 89 105 BG21
Shakespeare Av, Clyde. G81 87 104 AV17
Shakespeare St G20 90 106 BN24
Shamrock St G4 29 106 BQ28
Shandwick Sq Shop Cen G34 95 107 CJ28
Shandwick St G34 95 107 CJ29
Shanks St G20 90 106 BN24
Shannon St G20 90 106 BP24
Shapinsay St G22 90 106 BT21
Shawbridge Arc G43 81 109 BL37
Shawbridge St G43 81 109 BK38
Shaw Ct, Ersk. PA8 86 104 AP18
Shawfield Dr G5 84 110 BU35
Shawfield Ind Est G73 84 110 BV35
Shawfield Rd G5 84 110 BV34
Shawhill Rd G41 81 109 BL37
Shawhill Rd G43 81 109 BL37
Shawholm Cres G43 81 109 BK38
Shawlands Arc G41 82 109 BN37
Shawlands Sq G41 81 109 BM37
Shawmoss Rd G41 81 109 BL36
Shawpark St G20 90 106 BN23
Shaw St G51 37 105 BJ29
Shearers La, Renf. PA4 93 104 AZ26
Shearer St G5 52/3 109 BP31
Sheddens Pl G32 98 110 CB32
Sheila St G33 94 107 CA25
Shelley Ct G12 89 105 BJ24
Shelley Dr, Clyde. G81 87 104 AW17
Shelley Rd G12 89 105 BH24
Sheppard St G21 20 106 BU25
Sherbrooke Av G41 62 109 BL34
Sherbrooke Dr G41 62 109 BL33
Sherbrooke Gdns G41 62 109 BL34
Sherburn Gdns (Baill.) G69 99 111 CH33
Sheriff Pk Av (Ruther.) G73 84 110 BW38
Sherry Hts (Camb.) G72 103 110 CC39
Sherwood Av, Pais. PA1 96 108 AW31
Sherwood Dr (Thornlie.) G46 100 109 BJ42
Sherwood Pl G15 88 105 BD18
Shetland Dr G44 101 109 BR41
Shettleston Rd G31 59 110 BZ31
Shettleston Rd G32 98 110 CD32
Shettleston Sheddings G31 98 110 CA32
Shielbridge Gdns G23 90 106 BN19
Shieldaig Dr (Ruther.) G73 102 110 BX41
Shieldaig Rd G22 90 106 BR21
Shieldburn Rd G51 75 105 BE30
Shieldhall Gdns G51 75 105 BE30
Shieldhall Rd G51 75 105 BD29
Shields Rd G41 52 109 BP32
Shiel Rd (Bishop.) G64 91 106 BX20
Shilford Av G13 88 105 BC22
Shillay St G22 91 106 BU21
Shilton Dr G53 79 109 BE40
Shilton La, Bish. PA7 86 104 AN17
Shinwell Av, Clyde. G81 87 104 AZ20
Shipbank La G1 55 110 BS31
Shiskine Dr G20 89 105 BL22
Shiskine Pl G20 89 105 BL21
Shiskine St G20 89 105 BL21
Shore St G40 84 110 BV35
Shortridge St G20 90 106 BN24
Shortroods Av, Pais. PA3 92 104 AT30
Shortroods Cres, Pais. PA3 92 104 AT30
Shortroods Rd, Pais. PA3 92 104 AT30
Shotts St G33 94 107 CF29
Shuna Pl G20 90 106 BN24
Shuna St G20 90 106 BN23
Shuttle La G1 43 106 BT30
Shuttle St G1 43 106 BT30
Shuttle St, Pais. PA1 96 108 AU33
Sidland Rd G21 91 106 BY24
Sielga Pl G34 95 107 CJ29
Siemens Pl G21 34 106 BX27
Siemens St G21 34 106 BX27
Sievewright St (Ruther.) G73 85 110 BY36
Silkin Av, Clyde. G81 87 104 AZ20
Silk St, Pais. PA1 96 108 AV32
Silverburn St G33 94 107 CA29
Silverdale St G31 71 110 BY33
Silverfir Ct G5 67 110 BT34
Silverfir Pl G5 67 110 BT34
Silverfir St G5 67 110 BT34
Silvergrove St G40 56 110 BU32
Simons Cres, Renf. PA4 93 104 AZ24
Simpson Ct, Clyde. G81 87 104 AW19
Simpson St G20 17 106 BP26
Simshill Rd G44 101 109 BR42
Sinclair Dr G42 82 109 BP38
Sinclair Gdns (Bishop.) G64 91 106 BW21
Sinclair St, Clyde. G81 87 104 AZ21
Singer Rd, Clyde. G81 87 104 AV18
Singer St, Clyde. G81 87 104 AX18
Sir Michael Pl, Pais. PA1 96 108 AT33
Sixth Av, Renf. PA4 93 104 AY28
Skaethorn Rd G20 89 105 BK22
Skaterigg Dr G13 89 105 BH24
Skaterigg Gdns G13 89 105 BH24
Skaterig La G13 89 105 BG24
Skelbo Path G34 95 107 CM28
Skelbo Pl G34 95 107 CM28
Skene Rd G51 50 109 BK32
Skerray Quad G22 90 106 BS21
Skerray St G22 90 106 BS21
Skerryvore Pl G33 94 107 CD29
Skerryvore Rd G33 94 107 CD29
Skibo Dr (Thornlie.) G46 100 109 BG42
Skibo La (Thornlie.) G46 100 109 BG42
Skipness Dr G51 36 105 BG29
Skirsa Ct G23 90 106 BQ21
Skirsa Pl G23 90 106 BP22
Skirsa Sq G23 90 106 BQ22
Skirsa St G23 90 106 BP21
Skirving St G41 82 109 BN37
Skye Av, Renf. PA4 93 104 AY28
Skye Cres (Old Kil.) G60 86 104 AS16
Skye Cres, Pais. PA2 96 108 AT38
Skye Dr (Old Kil.) G60 86 104 AS16
Skye Rd (Ruther.) G73 103 110 BZ42
Slatefield Ct G31 57 110 BW31
Slatefield St G31 57 110 BW31
Slenavon Av (Ruther.) G73 103 110 BZ42
Sloy St G22 19 106 BT25
Smeaton Dr (Bishop.) G64 91 106 BW17
Smeaton St G20 90 106 BP23
Smith Cres, Clyde. G81 87 104 AX16
Smithhills St, Pais. PA1 96 108 AU32
Smiths La, Pais. PA3 96 108 AU31
Smith St G14 24 105 BG27
Smith Ter (Ruther.) G73 85 110 BX36
Smithycroft Rd G33 94 107 CA28
Snaefell Av (Ruther.) G73 103 110 BY41
Snaefell Cres (Ruther.) G73 103 110 BY40
Snowdon Pl G5 67 110 BT33
Snowdon St G5 67 110 BT33
Snuff Mill Rd G44 101 109 BR40
Society St G31 58 110 BX32
Soho St G40 57 110 BW32
Sollas Pl G13 88 105 BA21
Solway Rd (Bishop.) G64 91 106 BZ19
Solway St G40 84 110 BV35
Somerford Rd (Bears.) G61 89 105 BH20
Somerled Av, Pais. PA3 93 104 AV28
Somerset Pl G3 28 106 BP28
Somerset Pl Ms G3 28 106 BP28
Somervell St (Camb.) G72 103 110 CB39
Somerville Dr G42 83 109 BR37
Sorby St G31 59 110 BZ32
Sorley St G11 25 105 BH27
Sorn St G40 70 110 BX34
Southampton Dr G12 89 105 BK23
Southampton La G12 89 105 BK23
South Annandale St G42 83 109 BR35
South Av, Clyde. G81 87 104 AW19
South Av, Pais. PA2 96 108 AV37
South Av, Renf. PA4 93 104 AZ26
Southbank St G31 59 110 BZ32
South Bk St, Clyde. G81 87 104 AY22
Southbar Av G13 88 105 BC22
Southbar Rd, Ersk. PA8 92 104 AQ23
Southbar Rd, Renf. PA4 92 104 AQ23
Southbrae Dr G13 88 105 BE24
Southbrae La G13 89 105 BG24
South Campbell St, Pais. PA2 96 108 AU34
South Chester St G32 98 110 CC32
Southcroft Rd (Ruther.) G73 84 110 BU36
Southcroft St G51 38 105 BK30
South Cft St, Pais. PA1 96 108 AV32
South Crosshill Rd (Bishop.) G64 91 106 BW20
Southdeen Av G15 88 105 BD18
Southdeen Rd G15 88 105 BC18
South Douglas St, Clyde. G81 87 104 AY21
South Elgin Pl, Clyde. G81 87 104 AY22
South Elgin St, Clyde. G81 87 104 AY22
Southend Rd, Clyde. G81 87 104 AX16
Southern Av (Ruther.) G73 102 110 BX40
Southesk Av (Bishop.) G64 91 106 BV18
Southesk Gdns (Bishop.) G64 91 106 BV18
Southfield Av, Pais. PA2 96 108 AU37
Southfield Cres G53 79 109 BE37
South Frederick St G1 43 106 BS30
Southhill Av (Ruther.) G73 103 110 BY40
Southinch Av G14 88 105 BA23
Southinch La G14 88 105 BA23
Southlea Av (Thornlie.) G46 100 109 BJ42
Southloch Gdns G21 21 106 BV26
Southloch St G21 21 106 BV26
South Moraine La G15 88 105 BE19
Southmuir Pl G20 89 105 BM24
Southpark Av G12 27 105 BM27
South Pk Dr, Pais. PA2 96 108 AU35
Southpark La G12 28 106 BN27
Southpark Ter G12 28 106 BN27
South Portland St G5 54 109 BR32
South Scott St (Baill.) G69 99 111 CK33
South St G11 73 105 BF27
South St G14 73 105 BF27
South St (Inch.), Renf. PA4 92 104 AR25
South Vesalius St G32 98 110 CC32
South Vw, Clyde. G81 87 104 AV18
Southview Ct (Bishop.) G64 91 106 BV22
Southview Ter (Bishop.) G64 91 106 BV22
Southwold Rd, Pais. PA1 74 108 BA32
Southwood Dr G44 102 110 BS40
South Woodside Rd G4 28 106 BN27
South Woodside Rd G20 16 106 BP26
Soutra Pl G33 94 107 CD29
Spean St G44 101 109 BQ39
Speirsfield Ct, Pais. PA2 96 108 AT34
Speirsfield Gdns, Pais. PA2 96 108 AU34
Speirshall Cl G14 88 105 BB23
Speirshall Ter G14 88 105 BA23
Speirs Rd (Bears.) G61 89 105 BJ18
Spencer St G13 89 105 BH22
Spencer St, Clyde. G81 87 104 AW18
Spence St G20 89 105 BL21
Spey Dr, Renf. PA4 72 105 BA27
Spey Rd (Bears.) G61 88 105 BE19
Spey St G33 94 107 CB29
Spiersbridge Av (Thornlie.) G46 100 109 BH42
Spiersbridge La (Thornlie.) G46 100 109 BG42
Spiersbridge Rd (Thornlie.) G46 100 109 BH42

Spiersbridge Ter (Thornlie.) G46 100 109 BG42
Spiers Gro (Thornlie.) G46 100 109 BH42
Spiers Wf G4 30 106 BR27
Spittal Rd (Ruther.) G73 102 110 BV41
Spoolers Rd, Pais. PA1 96 108 AS34
Spoutmouth G1 55 110 BT31
Springbank Rd, Pais. PA3 92 104 AT30
Springbank St G20 17 106 BP25
Springbank Ter, Pais. PA3 92 104 AT30
Springboig Av G32 98 111 CE31
Springboig Rd G32 94 107 CE30
Springburn Rd G21 32 106 BU27
Springburn Rd (Bishop.) G64 91 106 BU23
Springburn Shop Cen G21 21 106 BV25
Springburn Way G21 20 106 BU25
Springcroft Av (Baill.) G69 99 111 CK31
Springcroft Cres (Baill.) G69 99 111 CK31
Rhindhouse Dr (Baill.) G69 99 111 CJ31
Springcroft Gdns (Baill.) G69 99 111 CL31
Springcroft Gro (Baill.) G69 99 111 CK31
Springcroft Rd (Baill.) G69 99 111 CK31
Springcroft Wynd (Baill.) G69 99 111 CK31
Springfield Av (Bishop.) G64 91 106 BW21
Springfield Av, Pais. PA1 96 108 AX33
Springfield Ct G1 42 106 BS30
Springfield Cres (Bishop.) G64 91 106 BW21
Springfield Pk Rd (Ruther.) G73 103 110 BY39
Springfield Quay G5 53 109 BP31
Springfield Rd G31 71 110 BY33
Springfield Rd G40 70 110 BX34
Springfield Rd (Bishop.) G64 91 106 BW20
Springfield Sq (Bishop.) G64 91 106 BW21
Springhall Ct (Ruther.) G73 103 110 BZ42
Springhill Dr N (Baill.) G69 95 107 CJ30
Springhill Dr S (Baill.) G69 95 107 CJ30
Springhill Fm Pl (Baill.) G69 99 111 CJ31
Springhill Fm Rd (Baill.) G69 99 111 CJ31
Springhill Fm Way (Baill.) G69 99 111 CJ31
Springhill Gdns G41 82 109 BN36
Springhill Rd (Baill.) G69 99 111 CH32
Springhill Rd (Clark.) G76 101 109 BP46
Springkell Av G41 62 109 BL34
Springkell Dr G41 81 109 BK35
Springkell Gdns G41 81 109 BL35
Springkell Gate G41 81 109 BM35
Spring La G5 66/7 110 BS34
Springside Pl G15 88 105 BC17
Springvale Ter G21 20 106 BU25
Spruce St G22 90 106 BT24
Spynie Pl (Bishop.) G64 91 106 BZ19
Squire St G14 73 105 BF27
Staffa Av, Renf. PA4 93 104 AY28
Staffa Dr, Pais. PA2 96 108 AU38
Staffa Rd (Camb.) G72 103 110 CB42
Staffa St G31 46 106 BX29
Staffa Ter (Camb.) G72 103 110 CB42
Staffin Dr G23 89 105 BM20
Staffin Path G23 90 106 BN20
Staffin St G23 90 106 BN20
Stafford St G4 31 106 BT28
Stag St G51 38 105 BK30
Stair St G20 16 106 BP25
Stamford St G31 58 110 BX32
Stamford St G40 58 110 BX32
Stamperland Av (Clark.) G76 101 109 BP45
Stamperland Cres (Clark.) G76 101 109 BN45
Stamperland Dr (Clark.) G76 101 109 BP45
Stamperland Gdns (Clark.) G76 101 109 BP44
Stamperland Hill (Clark.) G76 101 109 BN45
Stanalane St (Thornlie.) G46 100 109 BH41
Standburn Rd G21 91 106 BZ22
Stanely Dr, Pais. PA2 96 108 AS36
Stanely Rd, Pais. PA2 96 108 AS36
Stanford St, Clyde. G81 87 104 AY20
Stanhope Dr (Ruther.) G73 103 110 BZ40
Stanley Dr (Bishop.) G64 91 106 BX19
Stanley St G41 52 109 BN32
Stanley St La G41 52 109 BN32
Stanmore Rd G42 83 109 BR37
Stark Av, Clyde. G81 87 104 AU15
Startpoint St G33 94 107 CC29
Station Cres, Renf. PA4 93 104 AZ25
Station Rd G20 89 105 BL21
Station Rd (Millerston) G33 94 107 CC24
Station Rd (Stepps) G33 94 107 CF24
Station Rd (Giff.) G46 101 109 BL42
Station Rd (Old Kil.) G60 86 104 AR15
Station Rd (Bears.) G61 88 105 BE18
Station Rd (Baill.) G69 99 111 CL33
Station Rd (Muir.) G69 95 107 CL23
Station Rd, Renf. PA4 93 104 AZ25
Steel St G1 55 110 BT31
Stenton St G32 94 107 CA30
Stepford Pl G33 95 107 CH30
Stepford Rd G33 95 107 CH30
Stephen Cres (Baill.) G69 99 111 CH32
Stephenson St G52 74 105 BA29
Steppshill Ter G33 94 107 CE24
Stepps Rd G33 94 107 CE28
Stevenson St G40 56 110 BU31
Stevenson St, Clyde. G81 87 104 AV17
Stevenston St, Pais. PA2 96 108 AU34
Stewart Av, Renf. PA4 93 104 AX28
Stewart Ct (Ruther.) G73 85 110 BY38
Stewart Dr (Clark.) G76 101 109 BM45
Stewart Dr, Clyde. G81 87 104 AX15
Stewarton Dr (Camb.) G72 103 110 CA40
Stewarton Rd (Thornlie.) G46 100 109 BG43
Stewarton Rd (Newt. M.) G77 100 109 BE46
Stewart Rd, Pais. PA2 96 108 AU38
Stewart St G4 30 106 BR28
Stewart St, Clyde. G81 87 104 AU18
Stewartville St G11 26 105 BK27
Stirling Av (Bears.) G61 89 105 BG19
Stirling Dr (Bishop.) G64 91 106 BU18
Stirling Dr (Ruther.) G73 102 110 BX40
Stirlingfauld Pl G5 54 109 BR32
Stirling Gdns (Bishop.) G64 91 106 BU18
Stirling Rd G4 43 106 BT29
Stirling Way (Baill.) G69 99 111 CJ33
Stirling Way, Renf. PA4 93 104 AZ28
Stirrat St G20 89 105 BL23
Stirrat St, Pais. PA3 92 104 AR30
Stobcross Rd G3 39 105 BM29
Stobcross St G3 40 106 BP30
Stobcross Wynd G3 39 105 BL29
Stobhill Cotts G21 91 106 BV24
Stobhill Rd G21 91 106 BV22
Stobs Pl G34 95 107 CL28
Stock Av, Pais. PA2 96 108 AU34
Stockholm Cres, Pais. PA2 96 108 AU34
Stock St, Pais. PA2 96 108 AU34
Stockwell Pl G1 54 110 BS31
Stockwell St G1 54 110 BS31
Stonebank Gro G45 102 110 BT42
Stonedyke Gro G15 88 105 BD19
Stonefield Av G12 89 105 BK23
Stonefield Av, Pais. PA2 96 108 AV36
Stonefield Cres (Clark.) G76 100 109 BK45
Stonefield Cres, Pais. PA2 96 108 AV36
Stonefield Dr, Pais. PA2 96 108 AV36
Stonefield Gdns, Pais. PA2 96 108 AV36
Stonefield Grn, Pais. PA2 96 108 AU36
Stonefield Gro, Pais. PA2 96 108 AU36
Stonefield Pk, Pais. PA2 96 108 AU37
Stonelaw Dr (Ruther.) G73 85 110 BX38
Stonelaw Rd (Ruther.) G73 85 110 BX38
Stonelaw Twrs (Ruther.) G73 103 110 BY39
Stoneside Dr G43 100 109 BJ39
Stoneside Sq G43 100 109 BJ39
Stoney Brae, Pais. PA1 96 108 AU32
Stoney Brae, Pais. PA2 96 108 AU37
Stonyhurst St G22 18 106 BR25
Storie St, Pais. PA1 96 108 AU33
Stornoway St G22 90 106 BS21
Stow Brae, Pais. PA1 96 108 AU33
Stow St, Pais. PA1 96 108 AU33
Strachur St G22 90 106 BQ22
Straiton St G32 94 107 CA30
Stranka Av, Pais. PA2 96 108 AS34
Stranraer Dr G15 88 105 BE19
Stratford St G20 89 105 BM24
Strathallon Pl (Ruther.) G73 103 110 BZ42
Strathbran St G31 71 110 BZ33
Strathcarron Cres, Pais. PA2 96 108 AX36
Strathcarron Dr, Pais. PA2 96 108 AX36
Strathcarron Pl G20 90 106 BN23
Strathcarron Pl, Pais. PA2 96 108 AX36
Strathcarron Rd, Pais. PA2 96 108 AX37
Strathcarron Way, Pais. PA2 96 108 AX36
Strathclyde Dr (Ruther.) G73 84 110 BW38
Strathclyde St G40 84 110 BW35
Strathcona Dr G13 89 105 BH22
Strathcona Gdns G13 89 105 BJ22
Strathcona Pl (Ruther.) G73 103 110 BZ41
Strathcona St G13 89 105 BH22
Strathdee Av, Clyde. G81 87 104 AX16
Strathdee Rd G44 101 109 BN43
Strathdon Av G44 101 109 BP43
Strathdon Av, Pais. PA2 96 108 AS35
Strathdon Dr G44 101 109 BP43
Strathendrick Dr G44 101 109 BN41
Strathkelvin Av (Bishop.) G64 91 106 BV22
Strathmore Av, Pais. PA1 97 108 AZ33
Strathmore Gdns (Ruther.) G73 103 110 BZ41
Strathmore Rd G22 90 106 BR22
Strathord St G32 98 110 CC34
Strathtay Av G44 101 109 BP43
Strathview Gdns (Bears.) G61 88 105 BF17
Strathview Gro G44 101 109 BN43
Strathview Pk G44 101 109 BP43
Strathy Pl G20 89 105 BM24
Strathyre St G41 82 109 BN37
Stratton Dr (Giff.) G46 100 109 BK43
Strauss Av, Clyde. G81 88 105 BA20
Stravanan Av G45 102 110 BU43
Stravanan Ct G45 102 110 BU43
Stravanan Rd G45 102 110 BT43
Stravanan St G45 102 110 BT43
Stravanan Ter G45 102 110 BT43
Strawhill Rd (Clark.) G76 101 109 BN46
Streamfield Gdns G33 91 106 BZ22
Streamfield Gate G33 91 106 BZ22
Streamfield Pl G33 91 106 BZ22
Strenabey Av (Ruther.) G73 103 110 BZ41
Striven Gdns G20 16 106 BP26
Stroma St G21 34 106 BX27
Stromness St G5 65 109 BQ33
Stronend St G22 90 106 BR24
Strone Rd G33 94 107 CD30
Stronsay Pl (Bishop.) G64 91 106 BZ19
Stronsay St G21 34 106 BX27
Stronvar Dr G14 73 105 BD25
Stronvar La G14 73 105 BD25
Strowan Cres G32 98 110 CD33
Strowan St G32 98 110 CD33
Struan Av (Giff.) G46 100 109 BK42
Struan Gdns G44 101 109 BQ40
Struan Rd G44 101 109 BQ40
Struie St G34 95 107 CJ29
Struma Dr (Clark.) G76 101 109 BL45
Stuart Av (Old Kil.) G60 86 104 AR16
Stuart Av (Ruther.) G73 102 110 BX40
Stuart Dr (Bishop.) G64 91 106 BU21
Stuart Rd (Carm.) G76 102 110 BT45
Stuart St (Old Kil.) G60 86 104 AR16
Succoth St G13 89 105 BH22
Suffolk St G40 56 110 BU31
Sugworth Av (Baill.) G69 99 111 CK32
Sumburgh St G33 94 107 CB29
Summerfield Cotts G14 24 105 BG27
Summerfield St G40 85 110 BX35
Summerhill Dr G15 88 105 BD17
Summerhill Gdns G15 88 105 BD17
Summerhill Pl G15 88 105 BD17
Summerhill Rd G15 88 105 BC17
Summerhill Rd (Clark.) G76 101 109 BP46
Summerlea Rd (Thornlie.) G46 100 109 BH41
Summerlee St G33 94 107 CE29
Summer St G40 57 110 BV32
Summertown Rd G51 38 105 BK30
Sunart Av, Renf. PA4 93 104 AX25
Sunart Gdns (Bishop.) G64 91 106 BY20
Sunart Rd G52 48 109 BG32
Sunart Rd (Bishop.) G64 91 106 BY20
Sunbury Av (Clark.) G76 101 109 BL46
Sundale Av (Clark.) G76 101 109 BM46
Sunningdale Rd G23 89 105 BM21
Sunnybank St G40 70 110 BX34
Sunnylaw St G22 18 106 BR25
Sunnyside Dr G15 88 105 BC20
Sunnyside Dr (Clark.) G76 101 109 BM45
Sunnyside Oval, Pais. PA2 96 108 AU36
Sunnyside Pl G15 88 105 BC20
Sunnyside Rd, Pais. PA2 96 108 AT35
Surrey St G5 66 109 BR33
Sussex St G41 52 109 BN32
Sutcliffe Ct G13 89 105 BG22
Sutcliffe Rd G13 89 105 BG22
Sutherland Av G41 62 109 BK34
Sutherland Dr (Giff.) G46 101 109 BM44
Sutherland La G12 27 105 BL27
Sutherland Rd, Clyde. G81 87 104 AX19
Sutherland St, Pais. PA1 96 108 AT32
Sutherness Dr G33 94 107 CC30
Swallow Gdns G13 88 105 BB22
Swanston St G40 84 110 BW35
Swan St G4 31 106 BS28
Swan St, Clyde. G81 87 104 AV18
Sween Av G44 101 109 BQ41
Swift Cres G13 88 105 BB22
Swindon St, Clyde. G81 87 104 AU18
Swinton Av (Baill.) G69 99 111 CL32
Swinton Cres (Baill.) G69 99 111 CL32
Swinton Dr G52 75 108 BD32
Swinton Gdns (Baill.) G69 99 111 CM32
Swinton Path (Baill.) G69 99 111 CM32
Swinton Pl G52 75 108 BD32
Swinton Rd (Baill.) G69 99 111 CL32
Swinton Vw (Baill.) G69 99 111 CL32
Switchback Rd (Bears.) G61 89 105 BH19
Swordale Path G34 95 107 CJ29
Swordale Pl G34 95 107 CJ29
Sword St G31 57 110 BV31
Sycamore Dr, Clyde. G81 87 104 AV17
Sycamore Way (Carm.) G76 102 110 BU46
Sydenham La G12 14 105 BK26
Sydenham Rd G12 14 105 BL26
Sydney St G31 56 110 BU31
Sydney St, Clyde. G81 86 104 AT17
Sylvania Way, Clyde. G81 87 104 AX19
Sylvania Way S, Clyde. G81 87 104 AX20
Symington Dr, Clyde. G81 87 104 AW19
Syriam Pl G21 20/1 106 BV25
Syriam St G21 21 106 BV25

Tabard Pl G13 88 105 BE21
Tabard Pl N G13 88 105 BE21
Tabard Pl S G13 88 105 BE21
Tabard Rd G13 88 105 BE21
Tabernacle La (Camb.) G72 103 110 CC40
Tabernacle St (Camb.) G72 103 110 CC40
Tain Pl G34 95 107 CM29
Talbot Ct G13 88 105 BD24
Talbot Dr G13 88 105 BD24
Talbot Pl G13 88 105 BD24
Talbot Ter G13 88 105 BD24
Talisman, Clyde. G81 87 104 AZ19
Talisman Rd G13 89 105 BE23
Tallant Rd G15 88 105 BD18
Tallant Ter G15 88 105 BE18
Talla Rd G52 75 108 BD32
Tambowie St G13 89 105 BG22
Tamshill St G20 90 106 BP23
Tamworth St G40 57 110 BW32
Tanar Av, Renf. PA4 72 105 BB28
Tanar Way, Renf. PA4 72 105 BA28
Tanera Av G44 102 110 BS40
Tanfield Pl G32 94 107 CE30
Tanfield St G32 94 107 CE30
Tankerland Rd G44 101 109 BQ39
Tannadice Av G52 77 109 BE34
Tannadice Path G52 77 109 BE33
Tanna Dr G52 61 109 BH34
Tannahill Rd G43 101 109 BP39
Tannock St G22 18 106 BR25
Tantallon Rd G41 82 109 BN37
Tantallon Rd (Baill.) G69 99 111 CJ34
Tanzieknowe Av (Camb.) G72 103 110 CD41
Tanzieknowe Dr (Camb.) G72 103 110 CD42
Tanzieknowe Pl (Camb.) G72 103 110 CD42
Tanzieknowe Rd (Camb.) G72 103 110 CD42
Taransay Ct G22 90 106 BT22
Taransay St G51 37 105 BJ29
Tarbolton Dr, Clyde. G81 87 104 AY18
Tarbolton Rd G43 101 109 BM39
Tarbolton Sq, Clyde. G81 87 104 AY18
Tarfside Av G52 77 109 BE33
Tarfside Gdns G52 77 109 BF33
Tarfside Oval G52 77 109 BF33
Tarland St G51 49 109 BH31
Tarn Gro G33 91 106 BZ22
Tarras Dr, Renf. PA4 72 105 BA28
Tassie St G41 81 109 BM37
Tattershall Rd G33 94 107 CE27
Tavistock Dr G43 101 109 BM40
Tay Av, Renf. PA4 72 105 BA26
Tay Cres G33 94 107 CA28
Tay Cres (Bishop.) G64 91 106 BX20
Taylor Pl G4 43 106 BT29
Taylor St G4 43 106 BT30
Taylor St, Clyde. G81 87 104 AY21
Taymouth St G32 98 110 CD34
Taynish Dr G44 101 109 BR41
Tay Rd (Bears.) G61 88 105 BF19
Tay Rd (Bishop.) G64 91 106 BX20
Teal Dr G13 88 105 BC22
Tealing Av G52 77 109 BE33
Tealing Cres G52 77 109 BE33
Teith Av, Renf. PA4 72 105 BB27
Teith Dr (Bears.) G61 88 105 BF18
Teith St G33 94 107 CA28
Telephone La G12 15 105 BL26
Telford Ct, Clyde. G81 87 104 AW19
Templar Av G13 88 105 BF21
Temple Gdns G13 89 105 BH22
Templeland Av G53 77 109 BE35
Templeland Rd G53 77 109 BE35
Temple Locks Ct G13 89 105 BJ22
Temple Locks Pl G13 89 105 BH22
Temple Rd G13 89 105 BJ22
Templetons Business Cen G40 56 110 BU32
Templeton St G40 56 110 BU32
Tennant St, Renf. PA4 93 104 AZ25
Tennyson Dr G31 98 110 CA33
Terregles Av G41 81 109 BL35
Terregles Cres G41 81 109 BK35
Terregles Dr G41 81 109 BL35
Teviot Av (Bishop.) G64 91 106 BW18
Teviot Cres (Bears.) G61 88 105 BF19
Teviot St G3 39 105 BL29
Teviot Ter G20 16 106 BN25
Thane Rd G13 88 105 BE23
Tharsis St G21 33 106 BV28
Third Av (Millerston) G33 94 107 CD24
Third Av G44 83 109 BR38
Third Av, Renf. PA4 93 104 AY27
Third Gdns G41 61 109 BJ33
Thirdpart Cres G13 88 105 BA22
Thistle St, Pais. PA2 96 108 AS35
Thistle Ter G5 66 110 BS33
Thomas Muir Av (Bishop.) G64 91 106 BW21
Thompson Pl, Clyde. G81 87 104 AY15
Thomson Gro (Camb.) G72 98 110 CC38
Thomson St G31 57 110 BW31
Thomson St, Renf. PA4 93 104 AY27
Thornbank St G3 27 105 BL28
Thornbridge Av G12 89 105 BL24
Thornbridge Av (Baill.) G69 99 111 CJ31
Thornbridge Gdns (Baill.) G69 99 111 CJ32
Thornbridge Rd (Baill.) G69 99 111 CJ32
Thorncliffe Gdns G41 82 109 BN35
Thorncliffe La G41 82 109 BN35
Thorncroft Dr G44 102 110 BT41
Thornden La G14 72 105 BC25
Thorn Dr (Ruther.) G73 103 110 BY41
Thornhill Path G31 71 110 BZ33
Thornlea Dr (Giff.) G46 101 109 BM41
Thornley Av G13 88 105 BD23
Thornliebank Ind Est (Thornlie.) G46 100 109 BG42
Thornliebank Rd G43 100 109 BJ40
Thornliebank Rd (Deac.) G46 100 109 BF45
Thornliebank Rd (Thornlie.) G46 100 109 BJ41
Thornly Pk Av, Pais. PA2 96 108 AV37
Thornly Pk Dr, Pais. PA2 96 108 AV37
Thornly Pk Gdns, Pais. PA2 96 108 AU36
Thornly Pk Rd, Pais. PA2 96 108 AU36
Thornton La G20 90 106 BN22
Thornton St G20 90 106 BN22
Thornwood Av G11 25 105 BJ27
Thornwood Cres G11 13 105 BH26
Thornwood Dr G11 25 105 BH27
Thornwood Gdns G11 25 105 BJ27
Thornwood Pl G11 13 105 BH26
Thornwood Quad G11 12/3 105 BH26
Thornwood Rd G11 25 105 BH27
Thornwood Ter G11 25 105 BH27
Thornyburn Dr (Baill.) G69 99 111 CM33
Thornyburn Pl (Baill.) G69 99 111 CL33
Threestonehill Av G32 98 110 CD31
Thrums Av (Bishop.) G64 91 106 BY20
Thrums Gdns (Bishop.) G64 91 106 BY20
Thrushcraig Cres, Pais. PA2 96 108 AV35
Thurso St G11 26/7 105 BL28
Thurston Rd G52 74 108 BC32
Tibbermore Rd G11 13 105 BJ26
Tillet Oval, Pais. PA3 92 104 AT30
Tillie St G20 16 106 BP26
Tillycairn Av G33 94 107 CF27
Tillycairn Dr G33 94 107 CF27
Tillycairn Pl G33 95 107 CG27
Tillycairn Rd G33 95 107 CG27
Tillycairn St G33 95 107 CG27
Tilt St G33 94 107 CA27
Tinto Rd G43 101 109 BL40
Tinto Rd (Bishop.) G64 91 106 BY20
Tinto Sq, Renf. PA4 93 104 AX28
Tinwald Path G52 74 108 BC32
Tiree Av, Pais. PA2 96 108 AT38
Tiree Av, Renf. PA4 93 104 AY29
Tiree Gdns (Old Kil.) G60 86 104 AS15
Tiree Pl (Old Kil.) G60 86 104 AS15
Tiree St G21 34 106 BY27
Tirry Av, Renf. PA4 72 105 BB27
Tirry Way, Renf. PA4 72 105 BB27
Titwood Rd G41 82 109 BN36
Tiverton Av G32 98 111 CF34
Tobago Pl G40 56 110 BV32
Tobago St G40 56 110 BU32
Tobermory Rd (Ruther.) G73 103 110 BZ43
Todburn Dr, Pais. PA2 96 108 AV37
Todd St G31 47 106 BY30
Todholm Cres, Pais. PA2 96 108 AX35
Todholm Rd, Pais. PA2 96 108 AX35
Todholm Ter, Pais. PA2 96 108 AW35
Tofthill Av (Bishop.) G64 91 106 BV19
Tofthill Gdns (Bishop.) G64 91 106 BU19
Tollcross Pk Gdns G32 98 110 CA34
Tollcross Pk Gro G32 98 110 CB34
Tollcross Pk Vw G32 98 110 CA34
Tollcross Rd G31 59 110 BZ32
Tollcross Rd G32 98 110 CA33
Tolsta St G23 90 106 BN20
Tontine La G1 55 110 BT31
Tontine Pl (Ruther.) G73 103 110 CA41
Torbreck St G52 48 109 BH32
Torburn Av (Giff.) G46 100 109 BK41
Torgyle St G23 89 105 BM20
Tormore St G51 75 109 BF31
Tormusk Dr G45 102 110 BW41
Tormusk Gdns G45 102 110 BW41
Tormusk Gro G45 102 110 BW41
Tormusk Rd G45 102 110 BW41
Torness St G11 27 105 BL27
Torogay Pl G22 91 106 BU21
Torogay St G22 90 106 BS22
Torogay Ter G22 90 106 BS21
Toronto Wk G32 98 111 CE37
Torphin Cres G32 94 107 CC30
Torphin Wk G32 98 110 CD31
Torrance St G21 20 106 BV25
Torran Dr, Ersk. PA8 87 104 AU22
Torran Rd G33 95 107 CH30
Torridon Av G41 62 109 BK34
Torridon Path G41 61 109 BJ34
Torrington Av (Giff.) G46 100 109 BJ45
Torrington Cres G32 98 111 CF34
Torrin Rd G23 89 105 BM20
Torrisdale St G42 82 109 BP35
Torr Rd (Bishop.) G64 91 106 BZ20
Torr St G22 19 106 BT25
Torryburn Rd G21 22 106 BY25
Toryglen Rd (Ruther.) G73 84 110 BU37
Toryglen St G5 83 110 BT35
Toward Rd G33 94 107 CE30
Tower Cres, Renf. PA4 93 104 AX27
Tower Dr, Renf. PA4 93 104 AX27
Towerhill Rd G13 88 105 BE20
Towerside Cres G53 76 108 BC35
Towerside Rd G53 76 108 BC35
Tower St G41 52 109 BN32
Tower Ter, Pais. PA1 96 108 AT33
Towie Pl G20 89 105 BM23
Townhead Ter, Pais. PA1 96 108 AT33
Townmill Rd G31 45 106 BV29
Townsend St G4 30 106 BS28
Tradeston St G5 53 109 BQ32
Trafalgar St G40 68 110 BV34
Trafalgar St, Clyde. G81 87 104 AV18
Trainard Av G32 98 110 CB33
Tranent Pl G33 94 107 CA29
Traquair Dr G52 77 108 BD33
Treeburn Av (Giff.) G46 100 109 BK42
Treemain Rd (Giff.) G46 100 109 BJ45
Trefoil Av G41 81 109 BM37
Tresta Rd G23 90 106 BP21
Trident Way, Renf. PA4 93 104 AY28
Trinity Av G52 77 109 BE33
Trinley Brae G13 88 105 BE20
Trinley Rd G13 88 105 BF20
Trondra Path G34 95 107 CH29
Trondra Pl G34 95 107 CH30
Trondra Rd G34 95 107 CH29
Trongate G1 55 110 BS31
Troon St G40 70 110 BX34
Trossachs Ct G20 17 106 BQ26
Trossachs Rd (Ruther.) G73 103 110 BZ43
Trossachs St G20 17 106 BQ26
Truce Rd G13 88 105 BD21
Tudor Rd G14 12 105 BG26
Tudor St (Baill.) G69 99 111 CH34
Tullis Ct G40 68 110 BU33
Tullis St G40 68 110 BU33
Tulloch-Ard Pl (Ruther.) G73 103 110 BZ41
Tulloch St G44 101 109 BQ39
Tummel St G33 94 107 CA27
Tunnel St G3 40 106 BN30
Turnberry Av G11 14 105 BK26
Turnberry Dr (Ruther.) G73 102 110 BV41
Turnberry Pl (Ruther.) G73 102 110 BV41
Turnberry Rd G11 13 105 BJ26
Turnbull St G1 55 110 BT31
Turner Rd G21 33 106 BV27
Turner Rd, Pais. PA3 93 104 AV29
Turnhill Av, Ersk. PA8 86 104 AQ22
Turnhill Cres, Ersk. PA8 86 104 AR22
Turnhill Dr, Ersk. PA8 86 104 AR22
Turnhill Gdns, Ersk. PA8 86 104 AR22
Turnlaw Rd (Camb.) G72 103 110 CC43
Turnlaw St G5 67 110 BT33
Turnyland Meadows, Ersk. PA8 86 104 AR22
Turnyland Way, Ersk. PA8 86 104 AR22
Turret Cres G13 88 105 BE21
Turret Rd G13 88 105 BE21
Turriff St G5 66 109 BR33
Tweed Cres G33 35 106 BZ28
Tweed Cres, Renf. PA4 72 105 BA26
Tweed Dr (Bears.) G61 88 105 BF18
Tweedsmuir (Bishop.) G64 91 106 BY19
Tweedsmuir Rd G52 77 108 BD33
Tweedvale Av G14 88 105 BA23
Tweedvale Pl G14 88 105 BA23
Twinlaw St G34 95 107 CM28
Tylney Rd, Pais. PA1 97 108 AZ32
Tyndrum St G4 30 106 BS28
Tynecastle Cres G32 94 107 CD30
Tynecastle Path G32 94 107 CD30
Tynecastle Pl G32 94 107 CD30
Tynecastle St G32 94 107 CD30